P9-CKY-059

DATE DUE

DEMCO 38-296

A Bed Called Home

A Bed Called Home

LIFE IN THE MIGRANT LABOUR HOSTELS OF CAPE TOWN

Mamphela Ramphele

photographs by Roger Meintjes

DAVID PHILIP *Cape Town*
OHIO UNIVERSITY PRESS *Athens*
EDINBURGH UNIVERSITY PRESS *Edinburgh*
in association with The International African Institute

Riverside Community College
Library
NOV '94 4800 Magnolia Avenue
Riverside, California 92506

To my sons,
Hlumelo and Malusi

First published 1993 in southern Africa by David Philip Publishers (Pty) Ltd, 208 Werdmuller Centre, Claremont 7700, South Africa

Published 1993 in the United States of America by Ohio University Press, Scott Quadrangle, Athens, Ohio 45701

Published 1993 in the United Kingdom by Edinburgh University Press Ltd, 22 George Square, Edinburgh EH8 9LF, in association with the International African Institute

ISBN 0-86486-227-X (David Philip)
ISBN 0-8214-1063-6 (Ohio University Press)
ISBN 0-7486-0448-0 (Edinburgh University Press)

© 1993 text Mamphela Ramphele; photographs Roger Meintjes

All rights reserved

Printed by Clyson Printers, 11th Avenue, Maitland, Cape

A CIP record of this book is available from the British Library

Library of Congress Cataloging-in-Publication Data:

Ramphele, Mamphela
A bed called home: life in the migrant labour hostels of Cape Town/ Mamphela Ramphele.
p. cm.
Includes bibliographical references and index.
ISBN 0-8214-1063-6
1. Lodging-houses—South Africa—Cape Town. 2. Migrant labor—South Africa—Cape Town—Social conditions. 3. Migrant labor—Housing—South Africa—Cape Town. I. Title.
HD7288.S6R36 1993
305.5'62—dc 20 93-19117
CIP

Contents

Illustrations by Roger Meintjes

'I came to know the people of Khikhi, the Guguletu hostels, from socialising in their shebeens. It was they who initiated this project by inviting me to their rooms to see how they lived, and later asking to be photographed for their families in the Transkei.' *Roger Meintjes*

Acknowledgements

I am indebted to residents of the hostels of Langa, Nyanga and Guguletu for their generosity in sharing their limited space and time with me. Their trust and confidence in me was an essential ingredient of our relationship. I can never thank them enough.

I am deeply grateful to Martin West, the supervisor of the thesis on which this book is based. His support, encouragement and constructive criticism have enriched this study.

Pieter Le Roux, Professor of Development Studies at the University of the Western Cape, played an important part in encouraging me to define and expand the concept of space in relation to that of power. Pamela Reynolds pointed me to relevant literature on the issues I was exploring, thus sharpening my arguments. I am grateful to both of them.

My colleagues in the Department of Social Anthropology at the University of Cape Town played an important support role, both academically and emotionally. They have also generously assisted in survey work in the hostels. I am particularly grateful to Emile Boonzaier and Martin West, who helped me photograph conditions of life in the hostels.

My research assistants, Julia Segar and Marion Heap, went beyond the call of duty in their work with me. Julia Segar helped with the initial fieldwork and formulation of questionnaires. Marion Heap has carried much of the logistical workload of the surveys and the subsequent computer data processing. I am grateful to both of them. The Trollip brothers, Hilton and Denham, were an important support for the computer work which facilitated this study. Many thanks to Roger Meintjes for generously letting me use his photographs; he in turn would like to thank the Centre for Documentary Photography at the University of Cape Town for its support. Mary Starkey has been responsible for helping me turn a thesis into a book, and I am deeply appreciative of her editorial skills and expertise which she put to the benefit of my work.

Amina Jacobs, my secretary, has been a tower of strength for me during the writing up of this study. She created an 'iron wall' around me which gave me the space to read, reflect and write. I am grateful to my sons Hlumelo and Malusi for their patience, and Makgetha for ably standing in as their mother.

The study on which this book is based was made possible by the generous three-year grant by the Chairman's Fund of Anglo American and De Beers, for which I am thankful. The Carnegie Distinguished Visitor Fellowship at the Bunting Institute was important in exposing me to other women scholars and to a wide range of ideas, which helped to shape this study. I am also grateful to the Ford Foundation and the Canadian International Development Research Centre for their grants which enabled me to complete the writing up of this study.

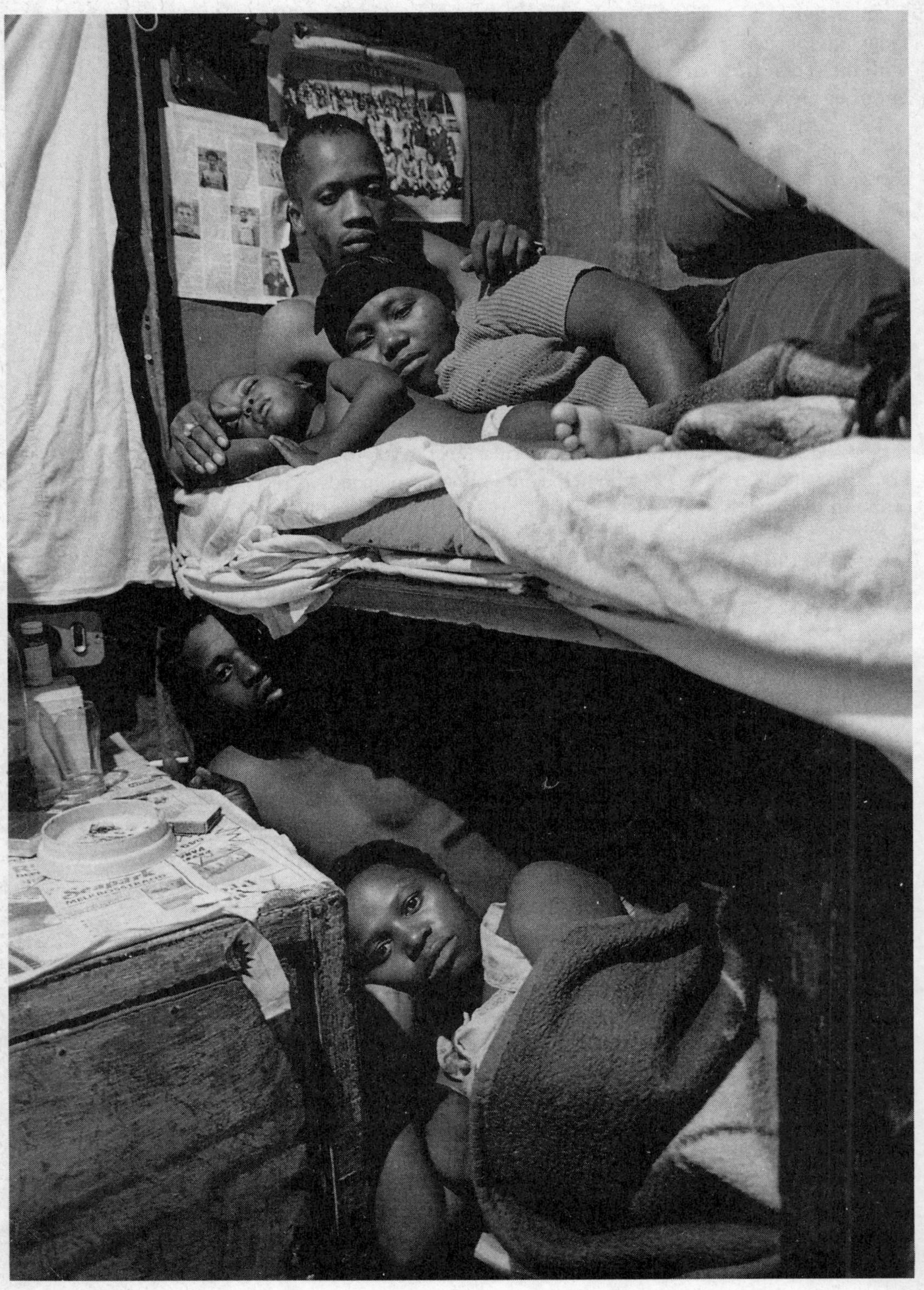

1

A Bed for a Home

An introduction

Migrant labour hostels in South Africa, particularly those in the Pretoria–Witwatersrand–Vereeniging (PWV) region, have over the last two years become associated with violence. Violent encounters between hostel dwellers and township residents, and among hostel dwellers themselves, have become a major feature of the violence accompanying political transition in South Africa. Of particular concern has been the brutal nature of the attacks on township residents, their apparent randomness and senselessness. Migrant-labour hostel dwellers have over the years since industrialisation began in South Africa lived in anonymity. They have been largely invisible, particularly to those living outside African townships, hidden, as their hostels often are, from the white public in divided South Africa. It should come as no surprise that some hostel dwellers may have chosen physical violence to draw attention to the structural violence of their conditions of life. There have been increasing allegations that recent violent attacks by hostel dwellers are being orchestrated as part of the contest for power between Inkatha and the ANC (see media reports of the Goldstone Commission, 1992).

It is, however, important not to lose sight of the fact that the majority of migrant-labour hostel dwellers are peace-loving people who have over the years developed creative strategies to cope with the limitations of their social reality. They are men and women whose major concern is to be accorded the respect due to them as human beings. This book documents conditions of life in the migrant-labour hostels of Cape Town, which has thus far not experienced the type of violence referred to above. I focus on hostels in Langa, Nyanga and Guguletu in my exploration of the nature of hostels and their impact on the lives of hostel dwellers, the complexity of skills which these hostel dwellers have consequently elaborated to survive in this environment and the long-term implications of the resultant survival strategies.[1]

We have been made conscious of migrant labour hostels as occupying impoverished, isolated and degrading spaces in the South African landscape. In focusing on hostels, one is at once confronted by the reality of space as 'political and ideological. It is a product literally filled with ideologies' (Lefebvre, in Hayden, 1984:1). Hostels are a euphemism in South Africa for single-sex labour compounds,[2] constructed to house Africans who were, until 1986 when the pass laws were repealed, only permitted to reside in the urban areas 'to minister to the needs of the white man and to depart therefrom as soon as they cease so to minister' (Stallard principle quoted in Wilson & Ramphele, 1989:192).

The construction of the hostels, and the regulations governing such accommodation, were provided for under the Natives (Urban Areas) Act 21 of 1923, which was among other things motivated by the need 'to ensure that further labour requirements be met by

1. This study is based on research conducted in the hostels of the Western Cape between 1986 and 1988. The data gathered during the course of this research are presented more fully in Ramphele (1991). For details of the research methods used, see the Appendix.

2. Francis Wilson refers to these compounds as 'labour batteries', generating labour units in the same way that chicken batteries do. See also his work on migrant labour (Wilson, 1972).

housing African men in hostels and barracks in urban areas' (Elias, 1984:26). Special attention will be paid to the nature of space presented by these hostels and the resultant quality of life of the people inhabiting them.

This study aims to address the concern expressed by Thornton about the limited use to which space has been put in ethnographic texts, as well as to expand his search for an approach 'to the nature and potentialities of space in social organisation'. His study is limited by its focus on 'a technologically simple and egalitarian society' (Thornton, 1980:1). Thornton's exploration failed to move beyond the symbolism of physical space. I hope to demonstrate the usefulness of focusing on the multi-dimensionality of space and its application to complex social settings. Insights gained by other anthropologists from analyses of physical space and the meaning it imparts to social relations will be used in this study (see Hirschon, 1970, 1978, 1981; Rodgers, 1981). Hirschon's studies focused on Greek communities in Athens and documented the use of physical space to define social relationships, whereas Rodgers's focus was on women's spaces in the British House of Commons. Coping strategies by people confronted by physical space constraints, such as women in the Greek societies in Hirschon's studies, are of relevance to this book.

The various dimensions of space

I have developed the concept of space to denote its multi-dimensional nature, and will explore the impact of the various dimensions of space on the processes of both transformation and replication of particular forms of power relations. These dimensions are physical, political–economic, ideological–intellectual and psycho-social. It is also important at the outset to draw attention to the micro- and macro-level dimensions of each of these spaces and their interrelationships at different levels. Changes over time and place in these various dimensions and levels as well as their interrelationships will be examined.

The micro-level space dimension refers to those limits within the local hostel environment which have an impact on people living in hostels. The macro-level dimension, on the other hand, refers to the larger space nationally, in South Africa as a whole, which has an impact on the lives, as well as the capacity for transformative action, of people in these hostels. Macro-level space also encompasses the global dimension, which, it will be argued, has a significant bearing on national and local level power relations. The distinctions being drawn between the various dimensions are delineated to aid my analysis, but it is important to bear in mind the interconnectedness resulting from the articulation of the various dimensions of space with one another. They form a mesh around people's lives, constraining them to varying degrees at different levels.

Physical space

Space has a physical dimension to it, which can be seen in both geographical and architectural terms. It sets the limits to one's physical location in the world and defines the parameters of the space one can legitimately appropriate for use. It also sets limits to the area of legitimate access, and by virtue of that may establish the right to exclude others from that space to ensure uninterrupted or unhindered use. The limits set by physical space also define in very clear terms inside versus outside (see also Thornton, 1980); private versus public (see Hirschon & Gold, 1982); family versus non-family; security versus insecurity; urban versus rural. Ultimately, of course, national boundaries are set using the same logic.

The concept of physical space co-ordinated with time is referred to as 'locale' by Giddens to denote 'settings of interaction – within which systemic aspects of interaction and social relations are concentrated' (1983:13). For example, in any dwelling, different social activities are associated with particular parts or rooms, such as eating–living space on one hand and sleeping space on the other. In situations where the same space is used for different purposes, time–space co-ordinates are used to define what activities are appropriate or can be anticipated in a given setting. The delineation of physical space gives and is given meaning by the pattern of social relations.

Political-economic space

This space determines the framework within which social relationships are conducted and legitimised. It could be defined as that aspect of social relations concerned with the capacity to marshal authoritative and allocative resources (Giddens, 1983:19).[1] Policies pursued by a given political and economic system set limits on choices which individuals can exercise within a particular area of jurisdiction, such as a given country or region. Formal (legal) and informal mechanisms are used to sanction and reward different types of behaviour selectively to ensure desired outcomes in social relations. Political–economic space could also be seen as the space within which discretion over who defines the various spaces and delineates their limits is legitimised. Access to political and economic resources, too, opens the way to access to other resources in society. Simkins refers to this space as 'room for strategic manoeuvre' which depends on the resources available to contending forces in a given political system (Simkins, 1988:8).[2]

Hostel dwellers, both as 'migrant workers' and as Africans, have been excluded from effective participation in the political and economic institutions of South Africa through racial discrimination policies pursued by various governments over the years. Their mobility was also circumscribed by legislative means[3] until the promulgation of the Abolition of Influx Control Act of 1986. The definition of hostel dwellers over the years as 'migrant workers' has created problems

1. Giddens sees political institutions as establishing the 'authority' structure within which social interaction is conducted, whereas economic institutions create the framework for allocating resources (1983:19). Both form part of a social system within which power relationships are defined.

2. Simkins characterises South African politics as being dominated by contending 'racial blocs' fighting for room for strategic manoeuvre. On the white side there is command of the official political apparatus with a sophisticated security system and a powerful economy. On the black side, there is control of labour power through trade unions and consumer power through access to a huge body of consumers who can be mobilised (Simkins, 1988:8–9).

3. A series of laws such as the 1913 and 1936 Land Acts, the pass laws, influx control regulations, the Suppression of Communism Act, the Terrorism Act, etc. was used to limit the political and economic space within which those opposed to the political system of this country could organise for change. It remains to be seen how much political space will open up for those at the bottom of the power hierarchy in the reform climate of the 1990s.

in relation to the delineation of legitimate shop-floor issues versus non-trade union ones.

The separation of these issues into mutually exclusive entities is of immense strategic importance to the conception and maintenance of the hostels as labour compounds. They are neither acknowledged as legitimate extensions of the working environment, nor defined as domestic space accessible to the families of those living there. Political space for those living in these environments to organise for change is constrained by the limits imposed by the dominant political order.

The exclusion of families from this space furthermore denies the reality of these hostels as domestic space. The resultant ambivalence in definitional terms has over the years significantly hampered effective challenge to this system. Changes which have occurred from the 1960s to the mid-1980s have mainly concerned beating the system at its own game, rather than redefining the rules and parameters of the game. The notion of 'decision versus non-decision' areas in power relations underlines the importance of expanding the process of transformation to areas which may be presumed to be non-negotiable in situations such as these (Giddens, 1986). For the majority of hostel dwellers, hostels have until recently represented non-decision areas.

The constraints on political space also set limits on models for alternative political and economic systems. This is in part due to curtailment of public debate as a consequence of lack of freedom of association and assembly[1] which characterised South Africa before 1990. Limited access to information on alternatives[2] has also played a part in determining the quality of debate among those involved in liberation politics (see also Simkins, 1988).

The treatment of those falling foul of a repressive authoritative system also helped create fear among the people. This fear has been an important determinant of the nature of South African politics (Biko, 1986:73–9). Fear and lack of trust between people have had the effect of driving organisations into secrecy, further limiting public debate and encouraging authoritarian practices within political organisations. The State President's speech on 2 February 1990 marked the beginning of a process of liberalisation in South Africa, opening up political space for all players.

The 'forbidden fruit' syndrome has also had an impact on South African politics, the implications of which remain to be seen. This syndrome seems to play a part in the attraction to particular social systems such as 'communism' or 'socialism'[3] which is evident in some segments of South African society. One should not underestimate the long-term impact of the support given to liberation movements by socialist countries at a time when Western countries were hesitant, however. This support has created and reinforced an association between freedom and communism which is likely to endure beyond the lifespan of the regimes which promoted it.

1. Repressive laws such as the Riotous Assemblies and Suppression of Communism Acts have eroded the political organisational space for South Africans.

2. The ban on publications and other material under the Suppression of Communism Act or at the discretion of the Publications Control Board has limited people's access to a wealth of information available elsewhere in the world.

3. The launching of 'The World's Last Communist Party' (Owen, *Cape Times*, 30 July 1990) is part of this phenomenon, and is in sharp contrast to the situation in Eastern Europe, where over the last two years communism and its symbols have been widely rejected in the struggle for democracy (*Cape Times*, 14 September 1989; *Weekly Mail*, 15–21 September 1989). See also Gorbachev, 1987 on the rigidity of ideological systems.

Ideological-intellectual space

This relates to the symbolic framework within which social interaction is conducted, and is the space within which norms are set for 'legitimate' discourses. Intellectual space can be defined as the capacity for critical awareness of one's environment and the position one occupies in the power structure of one's society. It helps individuals to demystify ideology and to limit the impact of the constraints of a hegemonic order on social relations. An overarching ideological framework such as that in South Africa between 1948 and 1990 could be characterised as a 'hegemony', which Gramsci defined as

> an order in which a certain way of life and thought is dominant, in which one concept of reality is diffused throughout society in all its institutional and private manifestations, informing with its spirit all taste, morality, custom, religion, particularly in their intellectual and moral connotations (Youngman, 1986:72).

Ideology is most effective when it remains interred in habit and has no need for words. It thus becomes a way of life without ever 'attaining the level of discourse' (Bourdieu, 1977:87, 188, quoted in Comaroff, 1985:5).

The boundaries of domestic (as opposed to public) space are determined by the dominant ideological assumptions in any social setting, and carry with it certain sanctions to enforce the notion of 'appropriate' spaces for the various members of a given social group or community. For example, the place of women and children is delineated in this way both inside and outside the domestic sphere[1] (Ardener, 1981; Hayden, 1984:212; Comaroff, 1985:43–77).

Social orders all over the world use a set of symbols for definitional purposes. These symbols include language, verbal and non-verbal; ceremonial tokens such as flags and medals; particular dress; and rituals. The struggle over ideological space is often fought over the appropriation of these symbols. For example, Inkatha and the African National Congress use the same black, green and gold colours in their flags[2] to authenticate their claim to the heritage of the Congress tradition of the 1950s. Similarly, religious factions fight over legitimacy by appropriating shared symbols (England, 1987).[3]

Language, both verbal and non-verbal, is an important symbol in South African social relations. The plurality of languages in South Africa, coupled with the designation of some languages as official and others as non-official, limits the capacity of significant segments of society to participate effectively in the political process. Communication between members of society with different language backgrounds is also curtailed.

For those with limited access to educational opportunities the language problem is particularly relevant. Of interest to this study,

1. Enforcement of this delineation takes various forms, but the most dramatic one is in the area of physical and sexual assaults on women, where victims get blamed for being at a wrong place: 'What is a nice girl like you doing out here in the street?' (Hayden, 1984).

2. The only difference in the two flags is the addition of a red band to the Inkatha flag.

3. Frank England examined this phenomenon with respect to the Anglican Church, where different factions were involved in warfare over who had legitimacy to continue to use Church symbols (England, MA Thesis, University of Cape Town, 1987).

however, is the extent to which political organisations operating across the board in predominantly black areas tend to use English as a medium of communication. English seems to have been legitimised as the language of political discourse within a significant sector of South African society. The use of English in this way excludes a large segment of society from active participation in public debates which have an important bearing on the formulation of alternative political approaches.

Language is also an important carrier of coded ideological messages. Racist and sexist assumptions are contained in the language that people use (Moore, 1986:164). Feminist scholars have been particularly successful in exposing the ideological assumptions of predominantly male scholarship and shaping academic sensitivity to this issue, as well as in drawing attention to the relationship between the command of language and the occupancy of a privileged position in the structure of society and its symbolic order (Moore, 1986:166).

Another important element of ideological space is the part played by the 'ideology' of the inhabitants of this environment, particularly the role played by appeals to beliefs, customs and 'tradition' as non-negotiable, sacred and unchanging social realities. We will examine the intersection of 'hostel ideology' and the manner in which it is used as a survival strategy to counteract the dominant ideology and to advance 'the cause'. A recognition of the importance of this ideological space is crucial to an analysis of limitations on individuals working within organisations such as the Hostel Dwellers' Association (HDA).

In the context of South Africa, intellectual space is also constrained by the dominant ideology, which promotes a world view favouring authoritarianism, hierarchy and male dominance as well as discriminating against blacks in terms of resource allocation. With respect to Africans, the basis of the barrier to access to educational resources embodied in 'Bantu Education' was unambiguously stated by H.F. Verwoerd, chief architect of apartheid and former Prime Minister of South Africa, as aimed at preventing the preparation of 'the Bantu child for greener pastures which he will never be allowed to graze in' (Hansard, 1953, as quoted in Wilson & Ramphele, 1989). Thus a deliberate strategy of intellectual impoverishment of black people has characterised the historical development of South Africa. The outcome of this intellectual space constraint has been devastating to the development of black intellectual skills and the effective participation of blacks in the definition, analysis and strategic thinking-through of the problems facing South Africa, as well as the articulation of a vision of the future. Intellectual discourse has been dominated by white males, with predictable consequences.

One of the consequences of this Eurocentric male intellectual bias has been the falling into disrepute of the pursuit of any intellectual activity in the eyes of some young black radicals. The slogan 'Freedom now and education tomorrow!' was an angry denunciation of intellectual achievement which not only excluded them from significant participation in its formulations, but which was also seen as irrelevant to their aspirations for change to the status quo. The crisis of legitimacy of intellectual discourse is reflected upon by Bookman and Morgen in their criticism of the artificial division between activism and research. They blame this approach for discrediting research in the eyes of activists (1988:19).

For hostel dwellers, intellectual space assumes enormous import, not least because of their educational status in the hierarchical structure of our society. Critical analysis of internal contradictions in their organisational structures is also constrained by the 'siege mentality' referred to by Maria Isasi-Diaz in relation to internalised oppression of Hispanic women as a marginalised group in the USA (Russell *et al.*, 1988:103). She asserts that people under siege are fearful of self-critique, and that romanticism becomes a useful survival strategy in such situations.

Caution has to be exercised in dealing with the issue of intellectual space. It does not necessarily follow that intellectuals are always more revolutionary than non-intellectuals, nor that they hold the monopoly over revolutionary consciousness (Giddens, 1982, 1986). The assumption that 'the working class' is incapable of engaging in transformative action without the leadership of a vanguard party dominated by intellectuals has serious implications (see also Connell, 1982). Intellectuals have been known to act as apologists of repressive systems based on ideologies which negate fundamental values of justice and equity. Meaning in social relations is not inherent in any particular social order, but has to be invoked through the practical activity of individual social actors. It is within this context that one should distinguish lack of intellectual synthesis from lack of practical awareness in social actors (Moore, 1986:190). The proponents of false consciousness seem to be confusing these two concepts.

Psycho-social space

This is delineated by the 'inhabited space' that one finds oneself in (Comaroff, 1985:54). It could be argued that one is given certain cues by one's environment that encourage one either to expand or to narrow one's expectations and aspirations in life. To a large extent inhabited space has a major impact on the self-image of individuals and their perception of their place in society (Hayden, 1984:40; Moore, 1986:167). For hostel dwellers, interesting questions arise about the impact of the constant assault on their dignity in the work environment, where they do menial jobs, and in their accommodation, with its squalor and lack of privacy. This combination will be examined with a view to focusing on some of the possible consequences for the sense of self-worth and self-respect of the individuals involved. Unlike the domestic workers described by Dill in New York and Philadelphia, the positive impact of 'living out' in their own homes, which she identified as an important element of the buffer system protecting against a negative self-concept, is not available to hostel dwellers (Dill, in Bookman & Morgen, 1988:47). Dill's study identified a variety of strategies used by domestic workers to protect their dignity as people, such as dressing up for their trip home after work, and the ability to assert themselves in their job situation knowing that they had the support of families at home which could be drawn upon at the end of the day.

The blurring of boundaries between working space and living space, as well as the nature of these spaces, raises the question of the extent to which hostels can be conceived of as total institutions.[1] This book will examine those elements of hostels which resemble total institutions as well as indicate some differences. Of importance in this part of the analysis will be the notion of permeability of institutions of this nature and the impact of this permeability on the coping strategies of those residing in them (Goffman, 1961:117). The reported unwillingness of some hostel dwellers in the PWV area to contemplate the upgrading of hostel accommodation into family units may be not only an indication of resistance to alleged manipulation by civic pressure groups, but a reflection of the internalisation of hostel life. Such resistance would be similar to the behaviour of long-term prisoners who may display an unwillingness to re-enter open society after being socialised into a total institutional life-style.

The overwhelming impact of the hostel environment on human dignity is captured by Mtutuzeli Matshoba's short story based on life in a hostel in Mzimhlope (Soweto, Johannesburg):

> What do you say about the very idea of building such a place, of removing men from their families after taking their livestock and what little land they had, and burying them in filth? Is that not meant to kill a man's pride in himself? (Hodge, 1987:227)

Poor self-concept and lack of a sense of self-worth inhibit the capacity for transformative action. They limit the possibility of those involved to feel worthy of challenging the status quo. On the contrary, a poor environment encourages a self-deprecating attitude, which leads the victim to blame him/herself and to negate that which is identified with this sense of failure (Fanon, 1966; Biko, 1986). This problem is captured by the Marxist alienation thesis that 'The animal becomes human and the human becomes animal' (Marx, in Giddens & Held, 1982:15).[2] Hostel dwellers' lack of freedom in their dwelling environment is a dimension that Marx, and indeed many of his followers quoting the above phrase, had perhaps not fully contemplated.

1. Goffman outlines five types of total institutions: those intended for care of the disabled; care of those perceived as dangerous to society, such as mental and infectious patients; prisons; institutions for special tasks, such as labour and military camps; and training centres or retreats. Hostels would fall into the category of institutions for pursuit of specified tasks (Goffman, 1961:4).

2. Marx, in his analysis of 'labour and alienation', was of course concerned about the impact of loss of control by workers over the production process. He thus saw workers as being reduced to being freely active only in their animal functions of eating, drinking and procreating and at most also in their dwellings and personal adornment.

Not only is the sense of failure in such situations felt by individual victims of domination, but it engulfs whole communities and nations that are made to feel less than human by other human beings. It should come as no surprise that they too lose respect not only for other human beings, but for life itself. The inferiority complex which results in such a situation was, and continues to be, an important element of the process of subjugation. One aspect of this systematic 'killing' of the pride of people was vividly described by Fanon:

> Colonialism is not merely satisfied with holding a people in its grip and emptying the native's brain of all form and content. By a kind of perverted logic, it turns to the past of the oppressed people, and distorts, disfigures, and destroys it (Fanon, 1966:169–70).

People with pride in neither their past nor present are limited in their capacity to believe in their own agency in history. This fact was recognised by the Black Consciousness Movement (BCM) of South Africa in the late 1960s and the 1970s. Taking the issue of psychological space seriously, the BCM drew attention to the need for psychological liberation as a necessary part of, and an important strategy for, transformation (Biko, 1986:29). The call by Cabral, with respect to Guinea-Bissau, for 'a return to the source' was also a recognition that culture is an essential element of the history of a people. He likened the relationship of culture with history to that of a flower and a plant, and stressed the particular relationship between culture and its material base. The level and mode of production determines the dominant cultural forms. Thus he asserted: 'A people who free themselves from foreign domination will not be free unless they return to the upward paths of their own culture' (1973:142–3).

Seen in this light, culture is a resource which can be, and is, appropriated at different historical periods by both those working for and against transformation to legitimise their positions (Thornton, 1988:24). It is thus a double-edged sword. I intend to demonstrate in this analysis how 'selective conservatism', a term referring to the tendency of people to select elements of their own 'traditional cultures' and merge them with those of an encroaching culture for the purpose of entrenching their own power position, is practised in this hostel situation (Hunter, 1936:548). This tendency imposes further limits on the transformative capacity of human beings by constricting the psychological space for legitimate non-conformist behaviour.

It is, however, clear even from this schematic outline that there are interrelationships among the various dimensions of space. The political–economic both defines and is defined by the physical, psycho-social and ideological–intellectual space in which people in a given environment find themselves. There is a constant shift in focus in social interaction from one spatial field to another. These spatial foci also interact with time co-ordinates to constitute 'locale' (Giddens, 1983:1), which could be liberating or limiting to those within their domains. The social processes which shape and are shaped by people's struggles for survival in these hostels constitute the politics of space, which is the subject of this analysis.

Empowerment – towards a working definition

Most of the discussion on space thus far has emphasised the constraints exerted on people's lives by the spaces they inhabit. The dominant theme is one of the reproduction of social forms characterised by unequal power relations, yet within these constraints people have managed to find room for manoeuvre, to cope and to survive. We must thus also recognise the emancipatory possibilities within this environment. One of the most important social and political tasks facing South Africa now and in the future is empowerment, which involves exploiting these possibilities and extending people's spaces. Empowerment is all the more important in view of the fact that the current reform process may not significantly change hostel dwellers' lives.

The concept of empowerment is based on the understanding of power as 'the use of resources, of whatever kind, to secure outcomes. Power then becomes an element of action, and refers to the range of interventions of which an agent is capable' (Giddens, 1977:348). This definition stresses the transformative capacity of human action. The resources referred to here are both allocative (material) and authoritative (political), which operate in social interaction through signification. Signification refers to the use of symbols, including social theory and its codification (the written word), to legitimise particular power relationships or else to critique them (Giddens, 1986).

The current conflict in South African politics in part reflects the operation of the 'zero–sum' notion of power, a concept based on the view that power is possessed by one person or group to the extent that it is not possessed by others (Giddens, 1977:334). This leads to the mistake of identifying power with the use of coercion and force. In fact, open force used in power relations is an indication of an insecure power base. An intolerance for different points of view by the contending parties as they juggle to position themselves in the newly opened political space indicates a desire for total control, rather than shared responsibility.

An understanding of the relationship between knowledge and power is important. The more powerful an agent is seen to be, the more likely subordinates are to submit to the agent's discretionary powers. A shift in perception of that discretion is essential to a redefinition of such a relationship. For example, the invincible power of the National Guard under Somoza disappeared when the people of Nicaragua saw fear written on the faces of the guards during the uprisings against that regime (Ruchwager, 1987:17). That change of perception radically altered the options which the oppressed people in that situation exercised, and enabled them to resist and finally overthrow the regime. Thus manipulation of the distribution of knowledge (see also signification in Giddens, 1986) is central to the perpetuation of desired power relationships. It is the classic case of a self-fulfilling prophecy. It is also in this manner that male domination, for example, is both legitimised and perpetuated in most social settings (Smith, 1975; O'Brien, 1981; Ramphele & Boonzaier, 1988).

Knowledge is widely recognised as a form of power (Reason & Rowan, 1981; Youngman, 1986). But it is also important to realise that mystification of power relations can effectively hamper an appreciation of where power actually lies. For example, involving workers in self-management schemes can give them a false sense of power, which can militate against effective trade union organisation (Lamphere & Grenier, in Bookman & Morgen, 1988:227–56). The same applies to the rhetoric of 'democracy' in extra-parliamentary politics in South Africa, which masks undemocratic practices.

Empowerment can be defined as a process which shifts the perceptions of powerless people and enables them to assume greater control over their own lives. It is premissed on the imperfection of control that the powerful have over the powerless. It can also be defined as the identification, exploration and expansion of that residue of unrestricted discretion and autonomy that the powerless have (Barnes, 1988:50). It is a process aimed at extending the limits that powerless people set to the form which the distribution of discretion can take, and embraces a spectrum of activities ranging from individual resistance to mass political organisations which challenge basic power relations in society (Bookman & Morgen, 1988:4). Empowerment is targeted at facilitating the ability of powerless people to grasp the significance of the relationship between the representation of the distribution of power and how such representation shapes the actual form which such a distribution of power takes. After all, it is the workers in a factory who possess the ultimate discretion to move their muscles to perform tasks which perpetuate an exploitative relationship with the owner of a particular factory. Empowerment occurs at that level at which the workers make the connection between their possession of that ultimate discretion and their capacity to exercise it (Barnes, 1988:50). This is not meant to suggest that powerless people wittingly and willingly subject themselves to oppression, but it is an attempt to depict human beings not as hapless victims of social structures but as active agents constantly interacting with their environment as 'informed, calculative beings' (Barnes, 1988:xiii; see also Giddens, 1982, 1983, 1986).

Empowerment expands the limits of parameters in the constant calculations people make, which determine their ultimate choices about altering their positions in life. In other words, empowerment is aimed at expanding the capacity for 'risk-taking' in those defined as powerless to enable them to transcend barriers set in the path of human fulfilment. 'Risk-taking' behaviour involves several levels of social interaction, ranging from the mainly personal and individual to the public and overtly political. Human beings are constantly facing tensions within themselves relating to resistance to or acquiescence in dominant forces and norms in their day-to-day lives. Such tensions arise from concerns for the price one has to pay, in the form of social sanctions, for choices that entail a departure from set norms and expected behaviour. The affordability of the risks involved in the context of hostels will be examined in relation to the space the various players perceive themselves to have, in a given situation.

One of the most important considerations in 'risk-taking' behaviour is the tension between the universal human need for 'community' and that of realisation of individuality. To be fully human, one needs to be acknowledged by other human beings. This characteristic is what distinguishes humans from other creatures. Constant tension arises out of the contradictory demands of the two aspects of personality: the particular, expressed by individuality and the concrete self; and sociability and the abstract self (Unger, 1975:239). This tension also raises the moral dilemma of choosing between individual freedom and considerations of 'the common good'. Attempts at resolution of this tension have occupied human beings throughout history, but neither the approach of liberal doctrine nor the various approaches by Marxists have thus far satisfactorily resolved the dilemma. Unger argues that

> The universal good is the perfection of the species nature in which he (man) [*sic*] participates by virtue of his sociability and of his abstract self-hood. The particular good is the development of the unique set of talents and capacities through which the species nature of mankind takes a concrete form in him (Unger, 1975:239).

Mercy Oduyoye, a Nigerian theologian, reflecting on her own position as an intellectual in a 'traditionalist' setting, echoes this theme and concludes that she cannot be alive in a community that ignores her humanity as an individual (Russell, 1988:49). As no political theory has yet proposed a satisfactory resolution of this tension and moral dilemma, it is essential that a recognition of the inherent contradictions of this state of affairs should inform the constant searching for alternatives and striving towards a lessening of these contradictions (Unger, 1975:289).

The data in this book indicate that people living under space constraints in all the dimensions defined above are constantly subjected to pressure to conform. Their need for acknowledgement and community would seem to be much greater because of their higher insecurity in both material and non-material terms (Goffman, 1961).[1] Gordon's study of migrant workers in Namibia also documents the pressures on inmates of hostels to conform (Gordon, 1977). There is no escape in such a physically restricted environment from physical proximity with others, and constant consideration of the needs of others is necessary due to lack of private personal space. The capacity for risk-taking is correspondingly inhibited. Empowerment in such a situation also entails making risk-taking affordable to people by expanding their perceptions of the space around them as well as actually expanding that space.

The Hostel Dwellers' Association, particularly through its health, child-care and upgrading programmes, is itself part of the process of expanding the space for hostel dwellers. This book will examine the extent to which these processes have succeeded or failed in empowering hostel dwellers and have enabled them to become transformative agents. Particular emphasis will be placed on processes within these empowerment programmes that produce and reproduce power differentials between hostel dwellers and the manner in which such differentials are legitimised, represented, negotiated and renegotiated. Whenever relevant, attention will be drawn to the similarities and differences between social relations within hostels and those of the surrounding townships. The impact of the hostel and township spatial contexts on the process of empowerment towards transformation will be examined. The HDA's goals, structure and its mode of operation will be analysed with a view to evaluating the extent to which there is consistency or contradiction between its short- and long-term goals and strategies for change. The impact of space on the capacity of the HDA to act as an effective agent of transformation will be examined. Factors influencing the direction of the dynamic processes at play in the hostel setting towards either transformative or replicative tendencies will be identified. The key inherent contradictions of the hostel environment will be explored. These contradictions arise in relation to the gap between intended and unintended consequences of policy decisions that led to the conception of hostels as single-sex labour compounds, their physical location within the African townships yet separation from them, the 'invasion' over time of these male domains by women and children, and the resultant power relations which have to be renegotiated at every level.

Soyinka's anguish, as portrayed in his *Play of the Giants*, also cautions against simplistic analyses of power relations:

> Unlike many commentators on power and politics,
> I do not know how monsters come to be, only that
> they are, and in defiance of place, time and pundits
> . . . no one has ever satisfactorily explained why near

1. Goffman noted that there is an expectation that group loyalty should prevail and that this forms part of inmate culture, which underlies the hostility accorded those who break inmate solidarity (p. 61).

identical socio-economic conditions should produce
on one hand, Julius Nyerere and on the other, an Idi
Amin[1] (Soyinka, 1984:iii).

1. It should be understood that Nyerere and Amin are projected in this play as representing two distinct leadership styles; the former more humanistic, the latter ruthlessly authoritarian.

The challenge presented by Soyinka's concern is of particular importance to the current process of reform in South Africa. What are the possibilities of long-term profound transformation rather than replication of old forms of social relations?

2 Tracing the Contours of Space

That people could come into the world in a place they could not at first even name and had never known before, and that out of nameless and unknown places they could grow and move around in it until its name they knew and call with love, and call it HOME, and put roots there and love others there ... (Grove, *House of Breath*, as quoted by Bachelard, 1969:58)

Contextualising hostels

Hostels are an important legacy of a policy of systematic racial discrimination and gross economic exploitation of indigenous people of South Africa over the last three centuries, and are a logical outcome of the process of conquest (Hunter, 1936; Bundy, 1972). This policy was pursued with varying degrees of enthusiasm and crudity by successive administrations, starting with the early settlers and culminating in the present Nationalist government. The common denominator has been the need to balance the demand for labour with the determination to deny African people access to urban resources (Wilson, 1972; Savage, 1984; Saunders, 1988).

There is considerable controversy about the nature of South African social relations. This concerns the presumed dichotomy between race and class, and attempts by analysts to accord primacy to one over the other (for detailed comment see Bozzoli, 1987; Lonsdale, 1988). Early liberal writers emphasised the contradiction between the realities of integration, which was seen as inevitable given the demands of a single economy, and the tightening of the process of segregation (Saunders, 1988).

Later 'revisionist' writers in the 1970s and 1980s (see for example Wolpe, 1972; Bundy, 1988) emphasised the functionality of segregation to capital, and some of these, notably Wolpe, went even further and suggested that industrial capital had shaped the nature of segregation. He argued that the migrant labour system in particular allowed mines, and later secondary industry, to assume that African workers had homes in the rural areas. Consequently, capital did not need to provide housing or welfare benefits for families of migrant workers. The net savings effected through this process ensured considerable profit margins (Wolpe, 1972; Saunders, 1988:22).

The focus on the essential elements of the process of conquest in South Africa dispenses with this dichotomy as well as with attempts to establish primacy of one aspect of exploitation over others.[1] The elements of conquest are defined as the plundering of indigenous resources and the exploitation and repression of those conquered. The legitimisation of this process takes different forms, including racism. Cases such as that of uMzilikazi and his conquest of southern Zimbabwe and the ruthlessness with which he dealt with in-

1. This argument was verbally presented by Moeletsi Mbeki at a conference in February 1989 at Duke University on poverty in South Africa.

digenous people of that area demonstrate that conquest has no essential colour or race preference.

Some political economists also emphasise the ambivalence of capital in relation to racism (Lipton, 1986; Terreblanche & Nattrass, 1990). Over the past three decades a large section of the English-speaking business community swapped its traditional explicit hostility to the Nationalist government for covert co-operation, which it perceived as far more profitable (Terreblanche & Nattrass, 1990:19). It is therefore important to appreciate the complexity of the historical roots of exploitation, and to extend the parameters of the debate by including the responses of the exploited. This process of inclusion will assist in replacing the analysing of 'muted' segments of society by letting them speak for themselves.

An additional issue is that of benefits derived by those in power from the ambiguities arising from the definition of the various spheres as being either primarily political or economic. These ambiguities provided, and continue to provide, space for both capital and politicians to exploit and subordinate a large number of people at the bottom of both the race and class power hierarchies. By the same token, those struggling to survive have historically been denied the space to fight effectively for their rights both as full citizens of South Africa and as workers, because of the ill-defined nature of who 'the enemy' really was. Was it the owners of capital who benefited from excess profits, or the government, or both?

Legal constraints

Legal provisions to control the movement of Africans reflect the same contradictions. Early use of legal mechanisms was given impetus in the 1950s by the Nationalist government policy of apartheid, which ruthlessly enforced segregation and exploitation of Africans. Laws such as the Black (Urban Areas) Consolidation Act 25 of 1945, the Native Laws Amendment Act of 1957 and the Black (Abolition of Passes and Co-ordination of Documents) Act of 1952 have been used as instruments to exclude undesirable Africans from urban areas. Qualification for legal urban residence hinged upon employment, duration of that employment and availability of approved accommodation (West, 1987:45; West & Moore, 1989).

The restrictions in these laws are key to the influx control regulations, which made criminals out of ordinary Africans who dared to seek job opportunities in the white urban areas. The enforcement of these regulations hinged upon the requirement to produce a 'reference book' or 'pass' which would indicate the legal status of the holder. This applied to all Africans over the age of sixteen, who were required to carry a 'pass' at all times and to show it to any law enforcement officer on demand. It is estimated that from 1916, when the first statistics were recorded, to 1986 when the pass laws were formally abolished, a total of seventeen million prosecutions for offences related to these laws took place (Wilson & Ramphele, 1989:208–9).[1] The ruthlessness of this policy was particularly felt in the Cape Peninsula, which was

> the only area where more women than men are arrested under the pass laws. There is no demographic disproportion of this sort . . . and it is clear that there is a special assault against women in the area in line with government policy of preventing Black family life taking further root in the Cape Peninsula (West, 1982:21).

What distinguished this region from others was the promulgation in 1954 of the coloured labour preference policy, which sought to protect those classified 'coloured' from competition with African labourers.

The scrapping of the pass laws in June 1986 was effected through the Abolition of Influx Control Act. In explaining the passage of this bill, the President's Council was stated to have 'discovered that influx control was being applied in a discriminatory fashion and had a severely detrimental effect on the quality of life of Africans' (SAIRR Survey, 1986:336–7). This late 'discovery' has brought relief to many who suffered the indignities of this system, but the legacy remains. The abysmal failure of this ruthlessness to stem the tide of urbanisation is beyond dispute. It is important to note that it was largely the resistance and resilience of women, in the face of considerable odds, that facilitated the 'discovery' by the President's Council referred to above.

Many hostel dwellers look back to the pass law period with a mixture of pride, anger and amusement at the strategies they used to beat the system at its own game. These included hiding in the surrounding bushes during pass raids, pretending to be legally entitled to be in the hostels through putting on a straight, confident face, or roaming the streets during the day to avoid detection by the authorities (Reynolds, 1984:9). Many were arrested, fined or imprisoned and, as a final desperate measure on the part of the authorities, men, women and children were 'bused' back to the Transkei and Ciskei (see West, 1982). Zodwa, who was 'deported' in this way, described what happened to her:

> It was an unbelievable experience, we kept on thinking that it was not true. Was it a dream? we asked ourselves. I was highly expectant at the time and sitting in the bus made my legs swell a lot. But what could we do? The long trip provided us with time to think of a way out. Some of us who had left our jobs decided to contact family and friends on arrival in Umtata and borrowed money for a return trip the

1. This means that one person was arrested on average every two minutes, day and night, for the entire period from the year before the Russian Revolution until the time of President Reagan's second term of office (Wilson & Ramphele, 1989:208–9).

very next day. Most of us were back in Cape Town in a matter of days. One just lived like a hare being chased around, hunted. Oh, not to talk about the fines, I must have paid over R2 000 in fines over the ten years or so of struggling with the pass problem.

Growing support from groups such as the Black Sash and the academic community (see West, 1982), as well as international pressure, contributed to the 'discovery' by the President's Council of the inequity of these regulations, and to the enactment of the Abolition of Influx Control Act of 1986.

Housing and urbanisation

In addition to criminalising African job-seeking activities, a deliberate policy of not providing family housing was pursued, to discourage permanent settlement of those Africans escaping the pass law net. The only approved accommodation for 'oscillating migrants' (Wilson, 1972) was in the form of hostels, or more precisely, labour compounds. Laws passed between 1879 and 1935 were strengthened by the Black (Urban Areas) Consolidation Act of 1945.[1] The Group Areas Act of 1966 and the Slums Act of 1934 consolidated this policy.[2]

This had the inevitable result of providing poor-quality housing to Africans and was the beginning of the current national housing crisis (Elias, 1984:37). The provision of other facilities for basic needs such as schools, clinics and recreational areas was also withheld by successive governments and local authorities (Kentridge, 1986). The inevitable outcome of wanton neglect and underprovision of basic facilities has been overcrowding, squatting and squalor in most areas occupied by Africans. The contrast between overcrowded townships and the world-renowned beauty of the rest of the Cape Peninsula is striking. Whatever the designs of those in power, women and children are part of the township and hostel environments and will continue to make demands on the limited existing infrastructure.

Hostels should be seen in the context of the country-wide crisis in housing. The elements of this crisis are: acute shortages of housing for those not 'classified white'; affordability of low-income housing; availability of land for housing development to meet existing and projected needs; and provision of infrastructure to provide decent living space for people at the lower end of the economic scale (SAIRR Survey, 1988/89:191–3). Estimates of the number of houses that will need to be built to meet current shortages are 1,8 million according to the Urban Foundation, with a further 2,8 million needing to be built by the year 2000 to accommodate population growth (SAIRR Survey, 1988/89:191). This implies the need to build 400 000 units each year, or approximately 1 096 units

1. This Act hampered the development of housing schemes with employer participation, because the requirements of permanent residence were only met after ten years of uninterrupted service by individual aspirant house owners.

2. The Slums Act excluded African areas from its provisions, meaning that specifications of the Housing Code such as provision of ceilings, proper flooring, damp-proof walls and internal doors are thus not binding.

each day. This is estimated to require an investment of R6,9 billion each year, which would represent 24 per cent of gross domestic fixed investment at 1986 prices (SAIRR Survey, 1988/89:191).

There is also a need to address the problem of infrastructural inadequacies in all the townships. This would involve provision of sewerage systems, water supply, electricity, telephones and rubbish disposal. Basic social service facilities such as schools, health posts, postal outlets, leisure and other recreational places also need urgent attention.

The drain on the economy by such an investment would only be made good by an annual growth rate of 17 per cent, which is unrealistic given the current growth rate of 3 per cent per annum (SAIRR Survey, 1988/89:191).[1] It is thus unlikely that South Africa will have the means to do away with the legacy of neglect of the housing needs of the poor. Even with the removal of legislative barriers of the past, the poor will remain disadvantaged (Simkins, 1988:203).

What the implications of this legacy are for those such as hostel dwellers who are at the bottom of the pile remains to be seen.

Defining physical space

The reality of physical space constraints in the hostels of the Western Cape is overwhelming to an outsider. It is difficult to know how to begin to make sense of a haphazard world which seems to defy all rules of order and logic, but which is 'home' for many thousands of people. Driving off the N2 near Cape Town's D.F. Malan airport towards these hostels, one cannot help feeling uncomfortable. The smell from the Athlone sewerage system alerts one to the turn-off into Langa, as do the billowing fumes of the Athlone power station. The temptation to hold one's breath is overwhelming, but reality precludes such action. The streets are pot-holed and teeming with people and vehicles. The 'flowers of the Cape Flats', flying bits of plastic litter, are in evidence everywhere.

The severity of the township environment is rivalled only by that of the hostels in their midst. One is confronted by drab structures set in equally unattractive public spaces. The dust churned by the howling south-easter has no barrier to cross in finding its way from public spaces into dwellings. There are no pavements, lawns or trees to be seen in the hostel environment. 'They are all simply uni-functional sleeping areas with little sense of place' (Dewar, 1984:1). Hostels have no public facilities of their own. They depend on the limited public resources of the surrounding townships for all their needs – schools, clinics, churches, playgrounds, post offices, police stations, shops, etc. The only important difference seems to be beer gardens; these have been conveniently placed at people's disposal in all areas.

The immediate surroundings of the hostels are even more unpleasant – litter overflows from neglected bins, malnourished dogs

1. The 1989 figures showed an even gloomier picture with a growth rate of 2,5 per cent (*Sunday Star*, 18 February 1990).

sleep in the minimal shade provided by car wrecks and other disused objects in need of urgent disposal. Mobile shops (shops on wheels using trucks) compete for space along the streets with the large number of people selling all sorts of wares, from food to second-hand clothes. The place is throbbing with activity. All this sets the scene for one's encounter with life inside the hostels.

The notion of bedhold

The common denominator of space allocation in the hostels is a bed. Every aspect of life here revolves around a bed. Access to this humble environment depends upon one's access to a bed; it is the basis for relationships within the hostels, between different hostels, and between hostels and places of employment. One's very identity and legal existence depend on one's attachment to a bed.

The official procedures for access to a hostel bed, which were applicable under the influx control regulations, remain theoretically in force to date (although largely ignored) in spite of the Abolition of Influx Control Act of 1986. The stipulation is that upon arrival in an urban area, and assuming that he has a job contract, a man or his employer can then apply to rent a bed in one of the available hostels. The applicant must go to the housing officer in the township in which the hostel is situated to be allocated a bed in a specified block, depending on availability. Such a man, whether married or not, is then expected to live as a 'bachelor' until he returns 'home' to the rural areas to visit his wife and children. The regulations specify unambiguously that residence in the hostels is open to 'any male Bantu over 18 years' who, amongst other things, is in bona fide employment and is legally allowed to be in the urban area (Segar, 1988).

There is a world of difference between these official stipulations and the reality, and always was, even during the heyday of influx control. People did arrive in the urban areas without job contracts, they were not all 'Bantu males over the age of 18 years', nor were they all there because of employment pursuits. There are men, women and children living there, whose sole concern is to lead 'a normal family life'. These are all members of 'bedholds'. Their access to this space is dependent on their relationship with one or other bedholder.

The nature of the relationship between the bedholder and members of the bedhold is one of patronage, with ill-defined reciprocity, which may or may not be linked to rural base interactions.[1] In some cases bedholders are cast in the role of 'landlords' with 'land' represented by the bed, but with no actual charges to 'occupants'. The following case illustrates the complexity of these relationships:

Gaba is a married man with a wife and four children living in the Transkei. They visit him from time to time, particularly over June school holidays, constituting a bedhold of a particular type during such visits. However, Gaba also has a long-term relationship with a

1. Complexities occur in male–female relationships in particular.

woman who has her own children in the Transkei, who visit occasionally. During such visits they also become part of the Gaba bedhold.

Gaba's girlfriend also has a friend and home-girl, Thuli, a divorcée, whom she has known since 1965. They both worked as domestics in Port Elizabeth until 1971, then moved to Cape Town together as live-in domestics. Thuli moved into the Gaba bedhold in 1981, together with her own daughter and granddaughter. Thuli and her family sleep on a mattress in the front room.

She neither pays rent to the patron nor depends on the bedholder in any other way, but she has to help with the cleaning chores, when it is her 'landlord's' turn to clean. (Cleaning chores are done on a roster basis, to ensure that each bedhold makes a contribution to keeping communal space clean.) She also contributes towards the paint which is communally bought to maintain the internal walls of their hostel in a reasonable state of cleanliness. She has been living in this arrangement for more than five years. She supports herself from char-work, supplemented by her daughter's wages as a waitress in a local restaurant in the city. Her granddaughter attends a local crèche.

Another variation of this patronage system is seen in the Cete bedhold, where kin and non-kin have different relationships with Cete, the bedholder:

The Cete bedhold consists of Cete's girlfriend, who takes care of all the domestic chores, his daughter, who has come to Cape Town for health reasons, his daughter-in-law, who came to deliver her first baby at a local hospital, and his estranged eldest son, who comes occasionally to visit, but lives in a back-yard shack in Guguletu.

Cete is responsible for the upkeep of all members of his bedhold except his eldest son and his girlfriend. He provides food for the upkeep of all co-residential bedhold members, but his girlfriend has to provide for her own children who live in the Transkei.

Bedholds also have varying degrees of coherence as 'viable economic units'. In some cases they resemble 'households' in their coherence, but this seems to vary greatly, even within bedholds which have close kinship ties. This fluidity is particularly marked in relation to single women, who change membership of bedholds over time and space, depending on their relationships with bedholders. Reciprocal obligations between bedholders and women dependants seem to be based on unarticulated expectations that the latter will do domestic chores such as cooking, laundry and cleaning, as well as attend to the man's sexual needs, in return for accommodation.

Woyisa resents the assumption that she is to see to all domestic chores relating to her boyfriend's bedhold. She feels that it is an unfair practice by men who are fully aware of the vulnerable position of women in this setting. She feels that she has no choice but to play along, because of the threat to her accommodation if she were to refuse.

There is also a symbolic question raised by the notion of bedholds – the very fact of defining people as members of bedholds has enormous implication for their personhood. It touches on the foundations of the definition of space and the intended and unintended consequences of such definitions. 'The house is an image of the body, of the household and of the household's relation to society; it is a physical space designed to mediate between nature and culture, between the landscape and the larger urban built environment' (Hayden, 1984:40). In this situation the bed is the image that mediates between the inhabitants of the hostels and the larger society. That human beings, as individuals or as families, can be reduced to 'bedholds' has serious implications for both these individuals and society as a whole. They have to either 'shrink' to fit this space or expand the space to accommodate their needs.

Quantifying physical space

The focus of this analysis is on hostels in the townships of Langa, Guguletu and Nyanga. There are two types of hostels in these areas: those under the direct authority of employers for the sole use of their employees and those under the jurisdiction of local authorities.[1]

There is considerable variation in both the quantity and the quality of employer-built hostels, depending on the policies of the employer concerned. The dormitories 'look more like a temporary relief disaster area than a permanent home for anyone' (Selvan, 1976:24). Others are considerably better equipped and offer more privacy and dignity than those of the local authorities. Common to all employer hostels, however, is difficulty of access for outsiders. High security fences, guards, uncooperative and non-communicative personnel are all barriers to access. The conclusion that employers are committed to keeping these hostels invisible, anonymous, isolated and out of the public consciousness is difficult to avoid.

It would be erroneous to imagine council-built hostels as uniform structures with no variation: each has its own form and character. The area with the greatest variation in types of hostel is Langa. This may be a reflection of the fact that it is the oldest of the existing areas in Cape Town allocated for purposes of accommodating African workers, and thus had to expand and diversify the quality and quantity of this accommodation to meet changing demands. There are thus Old Flats, New Flats, Zones and Special Quarters, each with different layouts and a different feel.

Another source of confusion is the concept of a hostel block, which means different things in different areas, but basically denotes a section of a hostel with a certain number of beds in it. Resi-

1. Due to insufficient data, only a brief overview of employer hostels can be presented.

dents have tried to order their environment by coining the notion of a 'door'. This is perhaps the closest equivalent to a house. On entering a 'door' one physically goes through a door, which separates a number of rooms from the outside environment.

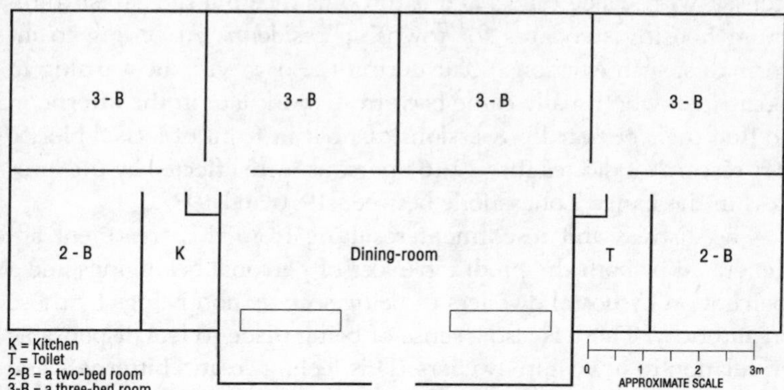

Fig. 1 A hostel 'door'

The size and number of rooms per 'door' also vary from area to area, from block to block, and within each 'door'. The common characteristic is, however, the lack of privacy. People share what limited space there is: blocks, zones, 'doors' and even beds are shared by varying numbers of people. The overall average bed occupancy rate for all the hostel types is 2,8 people per bed, but like all averages this obscures significant differences. For example, in some hostels the range of occupancy is from one to ten. How do all these people fit into this limited physical space? Studies of similar situations point to a variety of strategies adopted by people (Gordon, 1977; Hirschon, 1981; van Niekerk, 1988). Strategies include ingenious space utilisation and imagination. As one *favela* resident in Rio said: 'One has to be an artist to survive as a poor person . . . you have to imagine space where there is none.'[1]

The nature of the space which these beds represent needs some elaboration. The 'beds' are wooden bunks or concrete slabs the size of a narrow single bed, without mattress or spring. Occupants have to provide their own mattresses and bedding. The usual arrangement is for the man and his wife or girlfriend to share the bed with the youngest child they have; other young children and teenage girls sleep in between their parents' beds. The 'front room' is used as sleeping space for all other adults and teenage boys. The amount of space per resident works out to 1,8 square metres (Thomas, 1987).

1. Quote from video film on *favelas* in Rio shown by Liz Leeds at the Bunting Institute, Radcliffe College, Cambridge, USA. Neville Alexander's observations in Robben Island, during his ten years of political imprisonment (1964–74), confirm the importance of imagination in coping with space constraints: 'one creates imaginary boundaries around oneself. Body language is an important part of the strategies used. Just turning one's shoulder slightly establishes private conversation space' (personal communication). See also Goffman, 1961.

There has also been a systematic erosion of the very limited space available to hostel dwellers. This loss has been effected by a two-pronged process. First, the response of the authorities to pressure by township residents for accommodation for families, some of whom have been on waiting lists for housing for more than ten years, has over the years been to evict hostel dwellers from available space in the Zones, and to upgrade such space for family occupation. Upgrading takes the form of creating four-roomed semi-detached houses, with inside toilets and bathrooms meeting the barest minimum housing standards for township residents. According to informants, such evictions occur during the day, without warning to occupants, who usually come back from work late in the afternoon to find their personal possessions cast out in front of locked blocks. My research indicates that 29 164 persons were affected by this process in the Langa Zones alone between 1976 and 1987.

The distress and resentment resulting from this treatment are generated by both the predictable loss of personal belongings and a perception by hostel dwellers of being seen as non-beings by those in authority. There is also a sense of being made to feel dispensable in relation to township dwellers. This feeling creates bitterness and engenders a competitive relationship between hostel dwellers and township residents, with a potential for serious conflict.

The following case study gives an indication of one such experience:

Duma has lived in New Flats since being unceremoniously removed from the Zones in 1979. On that particular day he had gone to work at 6.30 a.m. as usual and, on returning to the Zones at 5.00 p.m., was shocked to find his hostel locked and private possessions of inmates scattered all over the open space in front of the hostel. In spite of searching through the scattered possessions, he could not find many of his valued clothes, bedding, and cooking and eating utensils. He assumes that passers-by must have helped themselves from the pile all day long. There was no official in sight to explain what had happened, nor was there any compensation possible. He spent that night 'squatting' with a home-boy in another hostel. It took time for him to get the present bed allocated to him in the New Flats.

He should probably count himself lucky, because others were not readily able to find alternative accommodation, as the following report from the *Cape Times* illustrates:

> Nearly a thousand illegal residents in the derelict Zones hostels in Langa township were evicted when the hostels were earmarked for conversion into married quarters. Those left homeless moved in the cold and fog into the barren, vacant area behind the Administrative Board offices in Nyanga. By 11 p.m. no

shelters of any sort had been or were being erected (quoted in Devereux, 1983:64).

The second process which has reduced available space in hostels is privatisation. This has happened particularly in Nyanga, where council hostels were sold to private employers who then upgraded them to house their own employees. Upgrading usually involves fencing off the property and installing electricity and better ablution facilities. The undoubted benefits accruing to the employees concerned have to be set against the losses of those evicted, who have to double up with other people in already overcrowded circumstances. Again, the potential for conflict between different categories of workers and hostel dwellers is considerable. According to my calculations, 6 199 persons were negatively affected by these evictions in the short period between 1985 and 1987 in Nyanga alone. Privatisation is a growing trend, threatening other hostel areas as well, and involving private housing developers.

Differentials within the physical space

It is important at this point to disaggregate physical space and to highlight some of the differences in the quality and the quantity of this space. Different areas and hostels each have their own internal logic which tunes the minds of those inhabiting them (Comaroff, 1985:54). It is also important to bear in mind the ways in which the inhabitants of the space can fine-tune it. People living in Langa Old Flats experience qualitatively different space constraints from those in the Langa Zones, and even more so from those in the Nyanga hostels. These different experiences have a significant impact on the social processes inhabitants of these hostels engage in.

Langa Hostels

Langa is the oldest of the areas set aside for African accommodation in Cape Town and has far more hostel beds than any other area. These beds are distributed in different types of hostels with varying degrees of density and configuration.

Langa Old Flats

These are the oldest hostels in current use.[1] They were built just after the Second World War, and consist of eight blocks of four-storeyed buildings of solid, polished brownish-red brick with a solid brick staircase on either end of each block. The ground floor consists of two communal rooms with well-built fireplaces, originally intended as recreational rooms. Most of these facilities are in an advanced state of disrepair, with broken windows and dust and filth everywhere. Some of these communal rooms are used as storage space by the residents, while others are still functional as recreational spaces.

1. Railway hostels in Langa are the only exception, having been built around 1896 according to Wilson (Wilson, 1972:70), but were not included in this study, because of problems of access.

Also on this floor are seven rooms which were intended as storage space and a caretaker's flat.[1] These are now used as bedrooms, providing approximately eleven beds. There is also one lavatory and two sinks on this floor as well as a laundry and bicycle parking space. There is one light in the passage, barely making a difference to the gloom. Washing-lines are outside in the surrounding open space. The other three floors are all similar, with 28 rooms leading off a very narrow, poorly lit central corridor. The poor light is a result of a combination of the weakness of four small bulb fittings and the dark brown paint on the walls of the corridor. There is an ablution block, a kitchen, a store-room and two balconies on each of these floors. Each ablution block has four toilet bowls, a urinal, two sinks and six showers. There are no partitions between showers nor is there privacy around the toilet bowls. These facilities are used by both men and women.

Each kitchen is fitted with a wooden shelf and a number of cupboards along one wall. There are a number of private fridges, chained up and secured with padlocks. Because individuals prefer to prepare their meals in their own rooms, the kitchens are used largely as storage space. The bedrooms have two beds each (a total of 225 in each block). This form of accommodation is much sought after, given the low bed occupancy of 1,8 (the lowest in all areas) and the consequent relative privacy. In addition, each room has two narrow cupboards for keeping personal effects. Despite this relative luxury, the persons–toilet ratio is 31:1. This results in frequent blockages, which residents deal with by building barriers between the floor and the lower ends of doors to prevent the flow of sewage into their bedrooms.

There is a lot of activity in and around these hostels, as they are near a major shopping area, a taxi rank and a bus rank for both local and inter-regional transport to and from the Eastern Cape. A multitude of street vendors cashes in on this hub of activity, hawking everything from food and clothing to herbal remedies.

Special Quarters

These are single-storeyed structures with 364 bedholders. They provide much-sought-after privacy for these people, as 64 rooms have one bed each and the other 150 have two. The only lighting is provided by one overhead light in each room, as most of the outside lights above the doorways are permanently non-functional. These rooms were originally intended to provide temporary accommodation to 'migrant workers' during their wives' visits and were to be used on a rotating basis to ensure access to all in need. Needless to say, those who moved in first devised ways of staying on indefinitely.

The superior quality of sleeping accommodation in this area is offset by the poor ablution facilities, which are in a separate block

1. The system of employing caretakers for these flats has been discontinued for some years. There is at present one man, who is the overall caretaker for all the Old Flats. He lives in one of them, but also has a township house.

with no pretence at recognising the need for privacy and decency. There are neither doors at the entrances to these facilities nor partitions between the toilet section and the washing areas. There is one light bulb in each of these ablution rooms. Special Quarters are adjacent to family housing in Langa, and the residents use the adjoining shopping area across the street, the Langa Post Office half a kilometre away and a Day Hospital across the street, as well as other public facilities such as schools and churches. The surrounding open spaces are wind-swept dust bowls with a few palm trees along the main road.

Langa Zones

These are single-storeyed brick structures built in long rows constituting 'streets', very close together with the spaces in between cluttered with car wrecks, chickens, rubbish heaps and people of various ages going about their daily business. The Zones are by far the worst accommodation amongst the council-built hostels in Langa.

The Zones are situated near the Old Flats, on the outskirts of Langa, near the main road leading to the industrial area of Epping, where some of the inmates work. There is a lot of activity around informal markets where various wares are hawked, from offal, sheep's heads and chickens to home-brewed beer and second-hand clothing. Some residents also keep a few goats.

Although the Zones are sturdily constructed they have grim, dark interiors, with few windows and a layout which allows very little light between the structures. Most units comprise three bedrooms – two with three beds and one with two beds, an ablution area with one toilet bowl, a urinal and shower, and finally a small kitchen area. The kitchen area is also the hostel entrance room and the only common sitting area; it is narrow, unlit and unequipped except for a sink and a tap in one corner. Approximately twenty-two people share each unit.

The bedrooms each have one overhead electric light. In common with most other hostels, there are no wall sockets. The rooms were built without ceilings, and makeshift ceilings have been fashioned by the residents from cardboard or plastic sacking. In search of a semblance of privacy, some residents have made cloth or sacking curtains between beds.

New Flats

These were built in 1969–72, to relieve the overcrowding in the Zones. Despite their 'newness' they compare unfavourably with the Old Flats, because of the poor quality of construction. Major structural defects are evident everywhere in these hostels, which have all the indications of a general state of dismal disrepair.

The New Flats are two-storeyed structures on the outskirts of Langa, bordering the N2 highway to the D.F. Malan airport. Each block consists of four units or 'doors', the upper level being reached by a set of outside stairs at each end of the block. These stairs are made of concrete slabs, often broken and replaced with wooden blocks. The area under the stairs is put to ingenious use: chicken runs, storage and, in one case, a fish and chips shop complete with a fryer and other equipment. Mops, brooms and other cleaning equipment often hang from the sides of the stairs. There is a washing area for laundry in front of each block, which has a cold water tap, concrete slab and drainage area. Doing laundry out there is a risky business, given the not infrequent chance of having sewage waste splashing on one from leaking drains above.

Each 'door' leads into a 'front room', which is the communal recreational and eating area. These rooms are fitted with two fixed tables, a metal sink with cold running water and an electric wall socket. There are remnants of coal stoves in various states of disrepair in some of these rooms, originally intended to provide heating in the winter. Additional furniture such as benches and fridges are provided by the residents. These rooms are used during the day for cooking and eating, washing up, personal washing, light laundry work and social interaction. During the night 'front rooms' serve as additional sleeping areas for teenage boys and other adults without bed space in the bedrooms. Various forms of bedding are spread on the cement floors.

Each unit has a toilet and a wash-room with a basin and cold running water. There is also a kitchen, which comprises a small room with a wooden bench along one wall and one electric socket. Most cooking is done with paraffin stoves, the private property of residents, which give off a constant cloud of soot and smell. There are six bedrooms leading off a central narrow passage-way, four with three beds and two with two beds each. Thus for every sixteen beds there is one toilet, three cold water taps and two electric wall sockets. Given the average bed occupancy rate of 2,4, approximately thirty-eight people share these facilities.

The surroundings are dusty and littered with overflowing garbage bins and car wrecks. These spaces also provide trading areas for food, clothing, home-brewed beer and various groceries, sold from stalls or from mobile shops operating from parked trucks. The area teems with people during the day. Children use the surroundings as playing space, entertaining themselves with home-made toys and odds and ends reclaimed from the surrounding litter.

Guguletu Hostels (KwaKiki)

These hostels are in an area of Guguletu bordering the railway line serving the Cape Flats. Also known as 'Zones', they are single-storeyed structures with 'doors' similar in layout to the Langa New Flats, and have been constructed in oblong shapes so that a group of hostels faces into a dusty central 'courtyard' with washing lines and residents' vehicles in varying states of roadworthiness. There is one central area set aside as a market, which is constantly thronged with people and is a meeting place for buyers and sellers as well as for friends to share beer or the latest information.

The residents have improvised ceilings and partitions between beds, and provided decorations such as painted walls, pot plants and shelving with colourful paper linings. The average bed occupancy rate is 2,7, and 43 people thus have to share three cold water taps, one shower, one toilet and two electrical wall sockets.

Nyanga Hostels

These are similar in structure to the Langa Zones – rows of single-storeyed brick or concrete slab buildings, slightly more spaced out than those of Langa. The number of beds in each 'room' varies from two to four, yielding approximately twenty-eight beds per hostel. Facilities in these hostels are particularly bad – there are no kitchens, common rooms or electricity. Ablution facilities, two toilets and communal showers are outside the bedroom blocks, approximately 300 metres away. The persons–toilet ratio of 56 : 1 results in unbearable pressure, and showers are used as relief toilet areas. There are also sinks with cold-water taps outside these ablution blocks for laundry purposes.

Between the rows of hostel blocks are washing lines, which provide some colour in this dreary atmosphere of dust and filth. They are, however, used by vendors of offal to hang washed portions for draining off excess fluid. This offal attracts flies as well as staining the lines. Also littering these spaces are old cars. Small market stands with vegetables, fruit and other wares as well as a number of home-brew beer stalls, another sore point among residents, are everywhere in evidence.

Children play in and around these spaces, using whatever they can lay their hands on: stones, sand, sticks, used soft-drink cans, bottles, etc. They constantly have to move out of the way of adults going about their day-to-day activities.

General comments on physical space constraints

The dismal conditions in the hostels are the result of poor initial planning and wanton neglect over the years. Judging from the accounts of residents about responses to their complaints, there does not seem to be much concern in official circles about the serious state of disrepair and overcrowding in these hostels. This official attitude is a serious source of frustration for residents, who are acutely aware of the relationship between their health status and this environment.

Hostel accommodation is undesirable, both aesthetically and conceptually (see also Lamont, 1987). The physical space which hostels represent is an affront to the dignity and well-being of residents. It is also important to accept that these hostels are likely to survive the historical process that has led to their establishment. Experience in countries such as Zimbabwe demonstrates just how difficult it is to erase the legacy of deprivation, given the realities of a post-colonial economic situation (Ramphele, 1986).[1]

Hostels represent physical space that is not only limited but limiting. It is limited at a number of levels. The quality of the facilities, such as the state of the buildings, leaves much to be desired. The squalor of the surroundings, with unpleasant odours and overflowing garbage cans, could hardly be said to meet minimum standards of health requirements for residential areas. The inadequate ablution facilities and the overcrowding are indicative of degrading facilities. The limited facilities also do violence to the primary purpose of housing, which is to delineate domestic space as opposed to public space. By failing to delineate private, personal space, hostels are a symbol of the denial of the personhood of the people housed in them.

The notion of a 'door' in this setting could also be seen as a desperate measure by the residents to create 'a boundary between the foreign and domestic worlds' (van Gennep, 1960:20).[2] However, the fact that bedholders have to share rooms with others negates this intention and forces the inhabitants to face the reality of lack of privacy.

Hostels are also limiting as physical environments. They can be seen as a special type of 'total institution' for the purpose of ensuring a compliant labour force (Goffman, 1961:4). The process of systematic mortification of the 'self' starts with formal recruiting, whereby one is assigned a number and gets treated as such, thus losing one's own identity. Naked parades in the course of medical examinations and other humiliating experiences were, until recently, part of official procedures for acceptance into the urban and hostel environment (see also Mtutuzeli Matshoba's account, 1987:209). The practice of 'batch living', the stripping of any semblance of respect and privacy in the hostel environment, can be seen as part of the control mechanism used by those in power to break down resistance in these workers (see also van Niekerk, 1988). Finally, the housing of 'migrant workers' in hostels defines them as 'outsiders' and hampers their access to the resources of the Cape Peninsula at many levels.

1. I visited Harare in November 1985, and saw the old migrant hostel still there on the edge of Ambare, inhabited by families living in appalling conditions. The Zimbabwean authorities simply didn't have the resources then to upgrade them into decent family units.

2. Quoted by Thornton, 1980:39.

Taxi rank

Climbing on employer's truck

Khikhi

Women return from a nearby farm with chickens to slaughter and sell at the market

Early morning, No. 56

3 Demographic Profile of Hostel Dwellers

General demographic features

The majority of people living in the hostels are originally from the Eastern Cape. A significant proportion of this population originates from the Transkei and Ciskei, and oscillates to and from rural bases there. The dominant language spoken is Xhosa, with a sprinkling of South Sotho speakers from the Matatiele area. It is, however, important to emphasise the peripheral position of language differences in social interactions in this population. There is a liberal mixture of English and Afrikaans words thrown into everyday conversational Xhosa, without any fuss (see also Wilson & Mafeje, 1973:34).

The total hostel population was 16 per cent of the overall African population of Langa, Guguletu and Nyanga in 1988, according to the Cape Town City Council (TMS planning report). There is also evidence of a declining masculinity ratio from 4:1 in 1911 to 2:1 (see also Selvan, 1976). Only one-third of the total hostel population is made up of bedholders; the rest are dependants – men, women and children who are under the authority of the bedholders. The overwhelming majority of bedholders are male, a not surprising feature given the regulations, which allow only male workers to rent beds. The exceptions are women who 'inherited' their beds from men, under whose names they continue to rent.[1]

The myth of hostel dwellers as 'migrants' persists in the minds of many Cape Town residents.[2] This ignores the reality of the length of stay of some of these bedholders, which in a significant number of cases exceeds 25 years. In some cases beds have been handed down from father to son, going back a generation or two. Xola is a case in point:

He came to join his father 27 years ago as a 16-year-old schoolboy. This was the age at which, as an African, one became liable to being arrested for 'failure to produce' (a euphemism for failure to show one's pass book). He remained registered as a school pupil while staying with his father in one of the hostels in Nyanga, until he completed his Standard 8 and got his pass book permitting him to work in Cape Town.

He still occupies the same room, which his father left him when he died in the late 1960s. He has devised a strategy of having the room to himself, by paying rent for a nominal room-mate. The room is neat, with many modern conveniences such as a gas lamp, stove, telephone and a cupboard bed. He is a store clerk, one of the few employed in a meaningful job. His own son is now getting too old to be adequately disciplined by his wife in the Transkei, raising the possibility of a third generation coming into this room.

The average length of stay in Cape Town is 26 years for male and 12 for female bedholders, while the corresponding figures for dependants are 5 and 6 years for males and females respectively. This variation seems to be related to age; the older residents tend to have been in the city longer than younger ones. There is also a relationship

1. The inheritance of beds ranges from being temporarily in charge of a particular 'bedhold' during leave periods of the person renting the bed to being left with the bed when the authorised user retires.

2. This includes some local authority officials, who attempt to use this as justification for not according priority to provision of family housing for hostel dwellers. The term *amaguduka*, literally meaning 'those who go home somewhere else', is still widely used in the townships to refer to hostel dwellers.

between bedhold status and age, as those who are older and have been in the city longer tend to secure access to the limited beds available.

A closer examination of the nature of this population is important at this stage to enable the reader to gain some measure of understanding of the people living in this limited space. The following diagram shows the total demographic profile of the group studied (Ramphele, 1991), depicting the proportions of males and females as well as children and adults:

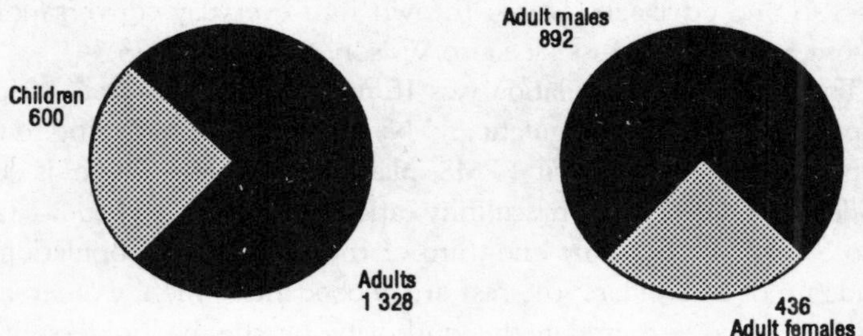

Fig. 1. Demographic profile of adult hostel dwellers

The networks of kin and non-kin relationships between people in the hostels are represented in Figure 2. These relationships are important for survival of individual hostel dwellers as well as providing order and meaning in social relations in an apparently disordered context.

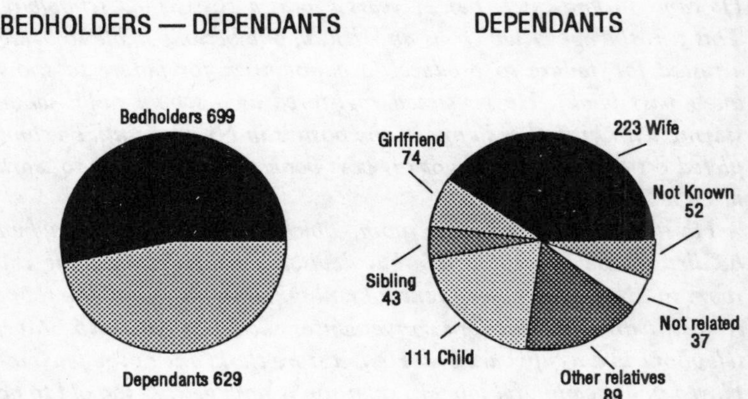

Fig. 2. Adults and their relationships

The highest proportion of bedholders is aged between 50 and 69, and concentrated mostly in the Old Flats and Special Quarters in Langa. These areas provide qualitatively better accommodation than others, and access here for older bedholders is a reflection of the increasing privilege which comes with age and a greater capacity to 'work the system'. This 'working the system' includes the bribing of those in authority.[1] Amounts changing hands in such deals for beds in these better hostels apparently range from R20 to R60, depending on the level of desperation of the applicant and the demand for the particular bed, which then goes to the highest bidder.

Less desirable areas such as Nyanga have younger populations. Most older people are said to have moved out to the better areas, including surrounding squatter settlements.

Education profile

The level of education of this section of the population reflects their disadvantaged position in society. This low education level is both a cause and a result of their limited political–economic space. Limited space is also reflected by their occupational status. Dr Verwoerd's policy of keeping Africans off 'the greener pastures' of South African opportunities seems to have had its desired effect: 12 per cent of the adult hostel population has no education at all, while 23 per cent has Standard 3 (five years of schooling) and 46 per cent has Standard 6 (eight years of schooling). A mere 18 per cent has achieved a higher education standard, with 15 per cent having Standard 9, 3 per cent matric and 1 per cent a post-matric qualification (Ramphele, 1989:398).

Figure 3 highlights some of the differences and similarities between men and women.

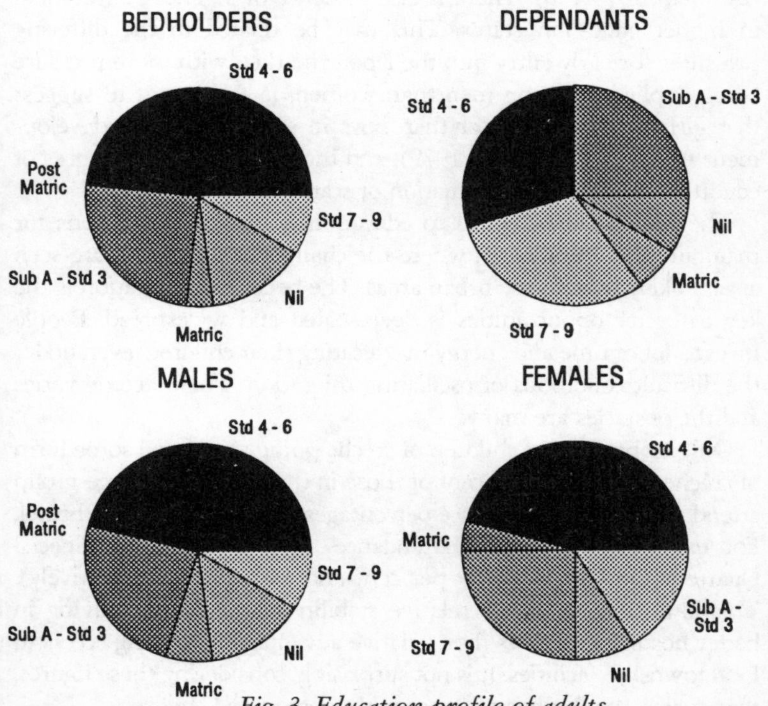

Fig. 3. Education profile of adults

1. The 'authorities' at this level comprise *izibonda*, who are the equivalent of headmen in the villages. See Hammond-Tooke (1975) and Thomas (1987) for further details.

The low education level of hostel dwellers is a reflection also of the relative poverty of the rural areas, which have been systematically impoverished through years of migrant labour and underprovision of basic education facilities (Wilson & Ramphele, 1989:197). Poverty forces many rural children to drop out of school and search for income-generating activities to help support their families. Low education status is also in part due to disruption of family life by the migrant labour system, and the consequent poor performance of children at school without the presence and support of both their parents. The presence of a large number of young people of school-going age in the hostels clearly shows the destabilisation of children's education by this system.

Some features of the education profile are indicators of gradual change in opportunities for, and attitudes to, education. Bedholders, who are the oldest members of this community, have a higher illiteracy rate, comprising 71 per cent of those with no schooling at all and 62 per cent of those with a level of education below Standard 4. Overall illiteracy figures thus include 12 per cent of the sample who have had no schooling at all, and a further 23 per cent who are functionally illiterate.[1] This means that effectively a third of this hostel population is illiterate.

The hostel education profile is indicative of a growing trend towards higher education among this group, in keeping with other similar populations, where education is seen as a route out of poverty (Perlman, 1979:148). There is also evidence of a gender differential in higher education status. This may be related to the differing pressures for early entry into the labour market, with more pressure being applied to young men than women. It also seems to suggest that girls tend to do better than boys in early intellectual development (Gilligan & Murphy, 1979), and thus enhance their chances of educational progress in a situation of scarce resources.[2]

The high value accorded to education is one of the reasons for maintaining a 'rural base', where the chances of disruption are seen as less likely than in the urban areas. The belief that education is the key to better opportunities is deep-seated and widespread. People invest a lot of time and energy in educating their children, even under the difficult conditions of oscillating migration. The outcome varies and the obstacles are many.

Only 15 per cent of children of crèche-going age attend some form of crèche, and just 42 per cent of those in the school-going age-group attend school. The attendance percentages vary from hostel to hostel. For example, the highest attendances were recorded for Special Quarters and Old Flats (89 per cent and 64 per cent respectively). This is a function of the relative stability of the families living in better hostels, as well as their relative advantage in gaining access to local township facilities. It is not surprising, considering these figures, that during the day hostels teem with women and children.

1. Functional illiteracy is defined as a state affecting people who have less than six years of schooling, and who are not exposed to active reading and writing opportunities over long periods of time (Wilson & Ramphele, 1989:138).

2. A recent study in the USA argues that lower expectations of black males in terms of educational attainment is having a negative impact on outcome: Gibbs (1988).

Employment profile

Most hostel residents are low-income earners who do unskilled work. Fields of employment include transport, manufacturing, commercial, fishing, hotel and domestic sectors. Women predominate in domestic service, but men also participate, particularly in the public sector such as hospital and prison service cleaning.

There are a few people who have progressed from low-paying jobs through merit promotion over a number of years and are in semi-skilled positions. There are also younger people with matric and post-matric qualifications who entered the labour market at a higher level. Most of these exceptional people are employed in clerical, lower management and technical jobs.

Income sources of bedholders

Most bedholders (78 per cent) are formally employed with average weekly incomes at the time the survey was conducted of R100. The 5 per cent in self-employment earned on average R62 per week (see Ramphele, 1989:397). Caution needs to be exercised in interpreting the difference between formal employment income and that derived from self-employment. First, there are true differentials in favour of formal employment, due to the uncertainties of the kinds of income-generating activities most self-employed people are involved in, such as hawking. Second, there is widespread underestimation of income from self-employment due to the illicit nature of some of the activities involved, such as selling dagga (marijuana) and other intoxicating substances, including alcohol. Alcohol sales are high in the hostels: one shebeen king admitted to a net income of R400 per week. He also disclosed on closer questioning that it had paid him to resign from his job, where his wages were less than half the amount he now makes, in order to concentrate on his business.

Pensioners and grant recipients constitute 6 per cent of the hostel population. In order to understand why septuagenarians would be 'choosing' to reside in these hostels instead of retiring to the dignity of their rural 'homes', it is important to realise the effort required to secure and retain access to pension pay-outs in the rural parts of South Africa. Some people are 'dropped by the computer', a useful device for 'homeland governments' under increasing strain of limited resources, whereby a certain percentage of pensioners are simply erased from the list of those entitled to receipts (Nicholson, 1984). In addition, in cases where people have pensions from retirement benefits, the unreliable postal system in the rural areas makes transfer to a rural address risky (Human Awareness Programme, 1984).[1]

Income sources of dependants

The average income in the late 1980s of all dependants with a non-zero income was R57 per week (see Ramphele, 1989:398). There are various points of distinction between dependants and bed-

1. In some rural areas post is simply left lying in the open for people to check through and take what belongs to them.

holders. Bedholders are older, they have been in Cape Town longer than their dependants and in contrast to the relatively high employment rate for bedholders (78 per cent), only 26 per cent of adult dependants have any source of income.

It is also important to note that few if any dependants are in receipt of pensions or grants. It would appear that pension and grant recipients not previously connected with hostels tend to stay away from them completely. The main reason appears to be that this category comprises older people who find conditions in the hostels too shocking. In particular, elderly people would find the lack of privacy, noise level and rowdy behaviour prevalent in the hostels intolerable.

There are also interesting differences between male and female dependants. Female dependants, particularly the wives of bedholders, tend to oscillate more often between urban and rural areas. They tend to stay in Cape Town longer than male dependants, wives and girlfriends, averaging ten years compared with five years for their male counterparts (Ramphele, 1989:399). Women are less likely than men to move out of their dependency status into independent accommodation, and are also more likely to be dependent on bedholders for both income and accommodation, making them more subject to control: 70 per cent of female dependants (compared with 52 per cent of the men) had no income of their own. This is at least partly because more job opportunities are open to men than to women, and women's childbearing and other domestic responsibilities tend to limit their ability to take advantage of such opportunities as do exist.

The average weekly income of female dependants is less than that of males, partly because of the higher formal employment rates of 47 per cent for male dependants (compared with 19 per cent for females). Female dependants are also more likely to be involved in self-employment activities, such as beer brewing and selling, or the hawking of food. These activities generate more income for women than does formal employment – an indication that employment opportunities for women are limited mainly to low-paying jobs, predominantly within the domestic service sphere. The average income from self-employment for male dependants is interestingly much lower than that of self-employed women. This is partly accounted for by the tightness of this avenue for newcomers, who often lack the requisite networks to establish themselves; women have a decided edge on men in this. It also reflects the nature of the activities involved, which most men find demeaning and thus avoid.

Children in hostels

Hostels, as labour camps, are not supposed to house children (Reynolds, 1984), but in reality there have been children there since the 1960s. The perception remains strong among hostel dwellers that hostels are not 'places for children'. This is because of concern for the 'corrupting' influence of this environment on children. The ideal of childhood as a period of 'innocence' persists in spite of the fact that both urban and rural children are increasingly involved in social situations which are a far cry from innocence (Wilson & Ramphele, 1987).

The definition of a 'child' in this setting, as is the case in similar situations of deprivation and low socio-economic status, is very fluid (Burman & Reynolds, 1986). There are 'children' who are income earners at the age of 10, having been out of school for two or more years, as well as 'children' in their twenties, who are at teacher training college and visit their parents during school holidays. Given the requirement which once compelled African children over the age of 16 to carry identification and the fact that welfare child support ceases at this age (Burman, 1988), 17 will be used here as the cut-off point for a working definition of a 'child'.

The hierarchical structure based on age, however, requires those who are younger to defer to older people. It is thus not unusual for adults to refer to themselves as children when addressing their seniors or for the latter to dismiss opinions of younger adults as 'child talk'. It is also common for men to justify their tendency to exclude women from decision-making processes by labelling them children, with limited capacity for critical thought processes.

The dismissal of younger people's and women's opinions as 'child talk' is evidence of the manipulation of language as one of the symbols legitimising a particular social order. This manipulation enables older men to control access to the means of communication and to limit the process of negotiating new forms of social interaction – 'it is men who command language, and as such they occupy a privileged position in the structure of society and in the structure of the symbolic order' (Moore, 1986:166). Many men still insist on taking the wages of their sons, who may be in their twenties, for communal needs, or at the very least, on being informed, with proof provided, of disbursements such as savings (Reynolds, 1984).

A number of children are permanently resident in the hostels; for some, hostels are the only 'home' they know. Many children below the age of 17 have been conceived in these hostels, as a result of the increasing trend, since the 1970s, for women to come to the city. Even more have been born there, due to the preference among women for urban births (Ramphele, 1989). Many other children accompany their mothers on visits to fathers and other relatives, but older children also come on their own to visit during the school holidays or for special reasons such as health (see also Jones, 1990). Older children, who are neither employed nor at school, are particularly prone to boredom. Most of them start their days by helping out with domestic chores, and spend the rest of the time playing cards or soccer in the dusty spaces (boys only) and occasionally reading magazines or newspapers, whenever they can lay their hands on them. Younger children spend their time playing wherever they can find the space to do so. In the mornings and evenings or on rainy days, they play in the front rooms while adults are engaged in some activity or other around the common table.

Conclusion

The picture of hostel residents provided by this demographic information shows them to be a severely disadvantaged population at many levels. The physical space constraints are considerable; overcrowding, filth and lack of privacy are constant assaults on the dignity of the inhabitants of this space. The pressure on limited facilities is immense, along with the potential for conflict among those competing for access. The noise level to which residents are exposed is overwhelming; there is no quiet moment during which one can gather one's thoughts in peace. Withdrawal from the constant noise and intense human presence is impossible within the confines of this physical space. The fact that some semblance of human community is possible in such an environment is remarkable and a tribute to human ingenuity.

The combination of poor education opportunities and lack of positive recreational facilities creates and perpetuates a level of intellectual impoverishment that can only limit the horizons which the inhabitants of these spaces set for themselves. This is particularly significant for children growing up in this situation and for the young people whose days are endlessly boring (see also Jones, 1990). Hostel dwellers are thus subjected to a combination of physical, economic–political, intellectual and psycho-social space constraints.

This book explores the coping strategies employed by the inhabitants of these spaces to enable them to survive under such severe space constraints. It also attempts to examine the social cost of such coping strategies of hostel dwellers for themselves as individuals, and for society as a whole. To what extent are such people, who have to sacrifice so much of their own individuality for the sake of survival, able to recapture their creativity and become agents of transformation?

4

The Quest for Wholeness

Human beings are integral with human problems
(Sarpong, 1985:9)

Introduction

The correlation between socio-economic status and health status indicators is beyond dispute (Sanders, 1985; de Beer, 1984; Wilson & Ramphele, 1989). Hostel dwellers are particularly hard hit by the combined effect of poor environments and the instability of their life circumstances; this limits their capacity to gain access to health care facilities in the urban setting of Cape Town, which are world renowned for 'excellence' (Yach, 1986; Benatar, 1986).

This chapter explores the complexities of health problems confronting hostel dwellers due to the space constraints they have to contend with. I will pay particular attention to the variety of strategies which individuals elaborate over time to cope with the challenges of their circumstances. Communal health care strategies often emerge as cumulative wisdom forged through experience, and constitute a pool of folk wisdom which provides sustenance in the face of challenges confronting individuals.

Stories of ordinary hostel dwellers illustrate the nature of challenges faced by people living in this environment, and indicate the variety of responses hostel dwellers are capable of.

Vuyo is a 58-year-old man who has been in Cape Town since 1953. His wife lives in the Transkei with the youngest of their three children, who is in Standard 8. He remits regularly from his R300 per month income. He describes himself as a very sick man. His problems started in 1980 when he developed swelling of his body and painful bones and joints. He has tried all the available health services in Cape Town: he started with general practitioners, who referred him to the Day Hospital, from where he was referred to the Provincial Hospital. He understands the nature of his illness quite well, which he says is 'sugar disease (iswekile), *rheumatism* (irumatiki) *and impotence* (ukungavukelwa)*'. He articulates his dissatisfaction with suggested forms of treatment so far very clearly. First, general practitioners are too expensive, 'they charge up to R62 for a quick fix, which doesn't work'. Second, the Day Hospital requires him to observe a strict diet to reduce his weight (over 120 kg) and to control his blood sugar level, but he argues that he cannot have a fixed eating timetable. He has to eat all the time, to keep himself awake given the requirements of his job as a 24-hour watchman of a mobile shop in the hostels. He sleeps for very few hours in the early part of the morning before the 'shop' opens. He also has very high blood pressure of about 240/130. His job constrains his ability to go for a monthly medical check-up, which would take up at least two hours of his working day. Third, he regards traditional healers as 'crooks who take your money for nothing'. He even consulted 'a famous one' in the Transkei to no avail. He is currently on 'no treatment,' because he is 'through with all healers'.*

Vuyo's case raises a number of issues which need to be elaborated: the sick role and its affordability; problems of life-style and chronic illness; conflicts between personal well-being and other responsibilities; and the hierarchy of resort in the event of sickness.

The sick role and life-style implications

Health and sickness are commonly viewed in a complementary sense (Temkin, 1973), sickness being 'negative' in relation to health (see, for example, Barth in de Gruchy, 1987). Together they can be viewed as a continuum in the range of human experience, and in the event of an illness episode people take action to regain health. Sickness is the acknowledgement by others that the person is ill (Young, 1976). Acknowledgement by others legitimises the adoption of the sick role, which Janzen views as

> a way of defining and mobilising rights and duties within a community of persons who take responsibility from the sufferer and enter into brokerage relationships with specialists (Janzen, 1978:7).

The concept of the sick role has an important bearing on the 'affordability of illness' for some people and thus on their capacity to acknowledge being ill and to seek help. For some people without the necessary material and social support, sickness may be a luxury they cannot afford (see, for example Segar, 1982).[1]

In Vuyo's case, he initially acknowledged his illness and sought treatment, but as his perception of his illness changed from that of an acute temporary problem to a chronic one, his evaluation of the affordability of his 'sickness' shifted. He could no longer 'afford the luxury' of adopting the sick role. This shift does not imply loss of insight into his health status, it simply implies that he has come to terms with the fact that the quality of his life is likely to remain poor. His focus is thus shifted to doing what he can to fulfil his responsibilities as head of a household and breadwinner within the limitations of his health status.

Finally, the prospect of lifelong treatment with pills is not an attractive one, even in the best of circumstances. Few people are disciplined enough to pursue such a course of action without default. In the hostels, with their overcrowding and lack of private space, such an achievement is beyond the reach of most people. The option of effecting a change in life-style, which has been demonstrated to alter the course of illnesses such as diabetes and high blood pressure significantly without recourse to drugs, is unfortunately not easily attainable for people such as Vuyo, who often search for other healing systems.

1. Segar's study demonstrated the large discrepancy between the amount of sick leave taken by black and by white workers, with the latter over-using their access to medical aid and sick leave benefits, which the former did not have.

The hierarchy of resort

Available health care resources comprise the biomedical, folk and popular healing systems (Kleinman, 1978:85–93; 1980:50). The term 'biomedical' system of health and disease is used in this chapter to denote a model that tends to regard the human body as a biological organism that develops malfunctions requiring mainly technological (and occasionally other) interventions (see also Kriel, 1989).[1] It also tends to view the human body as consisting of various organs and systems which, in spite of being seen as part of a whole, are often treated as discrete entities by various specialists.

'Folk' healers are generally regarded as those practitioners whose frame of reference differs from the above and, in particular, are seen by some (or many) biomedical practitioners as being of questionable value in health care (see also Kleinman, 1980:56). The historical link between the biomedical system of health care and the ruling classes in most countries has also served to entrench this system as the norm in health care, and thus defines others as aberrations from this norm. This category includes homeopaths, chiropractors, spiritual and traditional healers, and many others whose popularity seems to have flourished in recent years (Health for Africa, 1987 and 1988). Finally, there is the popular domain, comprising informal networks of support providing valuable advice and health resources to individuals in need (Kleinman, 1978:85–93; 1980:50).

Vuyo's approach to health care followed a definite sequence: general practitioner, Day Hospital, Provincial Hospital, folk healers and finally giving up hope. But how representative is Vuyo in terms of his strategies for health care? We conducted a survey among hostel dwellers during 1986 and 1987 using semi-structured interviews as well as conducting an epidemiological investigation into their health status.[2] The data collected give indications of the size of the pool of wisdom from which people such as Vuyo draw.

Certain points need to be noted from the demographic profile of the responses in Table 1. First, all male participants are bedholders, but overall there is a fairly even distribution between male and female participation. The preponderance of bedholders among male participants is a true reflection of their status as a major component in this group. The participation by dependants was slightly higher than that of bedholders (dependants, 55 per cent; bedholders, 41 per cent), which is possibly an indication of the fact that bedholders' participation was limited by their full-time employment status in comparison with dependants (see Chapter 3 on demography). The 'children' listed in Table 1, who comprise a small percentage of the responses (4 per cent), are people between 6 and 16 years, who did not qualify for the specific health questionnaire for children 5 years and younger. Children were also not subjected to the objective measures (blood pressure reading and blood sampling), which were part of the adult survey.

1. In an article in *South African Family Practice*, Kriel looks at patient dissatisfaction with medical care as linked to the philosophical assumptions of this profession, particularly the technocratic approach.

2. For detailed information on this aspect of the study, readers are referred to a special issue of the *South African Medical Association Journal*, Vol. 79, No. 12, 15 June 1991.

TABLE 1.

Demographic profile of respondents to the health survey, by sex, by bedhold status.

'Bed' status	Sex		Total	%
	Male	Female		
Bedholders	172	0	172	41
Dependants	25	206	231	55
Children (5 –17yrs)	7	10	17	4
TOTAL	204	216	420	100
%	49	51		100

Our respondents indicated a number of health problems they had experienced at the time of the survey, what help they had sought and where from, as per Table 2 below.

TABLE 2.

Treatment sought in the event of disease by resort.

Resort	Disease conditions					Total	%
	TB	STD	Diabetes	BP	Other		
G P	1	1		4	23	29	26
Clinic	5	1			2	8	7
Industrial clinic				2		2	2
Private clinic					1	1	1
Day Hospital	2		1	13	15	31	26
Provincial Hospital			3	6	13	22	20
Indigenous healer					2	2	2
District surgeon					1	1	1
Out of town					1	1	1
No treatment		1	1	2	11	15	13
TOTAL	8	3	5	27	69	112	*100

*This is an approximation computed from rounding off small percentages.

Biomedical healers. Day Hospitals and general practitioners are the commonest resort for hostel dwellers seeking treatment. Of our 112 respondents, 52 per cent indicated that they used these two health care facilities equally as their first port of call. The general practitioners have business premises in the 'coloured' townships adjoining Langa and Guguletu. The Day Hospital organisation provides a general service from 7 a.m. to 4 p.m. Monday to Friday as well as a morning session on Saturdays for emergencies. General practitioners tend to be open until late in the evening and in some cases provide after-hour services at an extra fee. Provincial Hospitals are also fairly well used by hostel dwellers for sickness as well as injury. For treatment purposes, they are the only in-patient service available to hostel dwellers.

The efficacy of treatment for acute episodes is the main attraction of biomedical healers. The administration of injections and other medicaments is the most important consideration – the 'quick fix' Vuyo referred to. General practitioners are particularly popular, because of convenient and flexible working hours, shorter waiting time and the perceived liberal prescription of injections and medicines in their treatments. The latter point is in agreement with other studies (Mfenyana, 1988:141; Kennedy, 1980) and reinforces the image of doctors as problem solvers who use medical remedies for complaints brought to them. Kennedy is particularly critical of this medicalisation of human problems, because it ignores the fact that a significant number of people seeking medical attention are simply unhappy and lonely, needing someone to talk to. Mfenyana also discusses the change in expectations that occurs in people as their experience of biomedical healing grows, in particular people's preparedness to accept advice as adequate management, without medicaments.

TABLE 3.

Complaints by institution and therapist.

Complaint	Institution/therapist						Total	%
	GP	PH	C	DH	H	IC		
Not examined	0	0	0	2	0	0	2	5
Lack of communication	0	0	0	3	0	0	3	7
Long queues	1	3	1	9	0	0	14	34
Expense	17	1	0	1	1	0	20	49
Lack of transport	1	1	0	0	0	0	2	5
TOTAL	19	5	1	15	1	0	41	100

GP = general practitioner; PH = Provincial Hospital; C = Clinic; DH = Day Hospital; H = Hospital; IC = Industrial clinic

Respondents were asked if they had any complaints about the services to which they had access. The responses to specific questions echoed those elicited from earlier in-depth interviews and group discussions. These are listed in Table 3.

The main complaint people have is cost of health care, particularly private general medical practitioners (49 per cent), where the cost per consultation averaged R15. In contrast, low-income earners paid R1 at the Day Hospital during the same period in 1987. Of particular significance is the fact that people who are low-income earners were prepared to pay these high fees rather than use Day Hospital facilities.

Hostel dwellers encounter significant barriers to gaining access to Day and Referral Hospitals in the wider Cape Peninsula. Long queues are a particular problem. There is also a perception by many that they are at a disadvantage compared to township dwellers, whom they perceive as well connected, with friends and relatives working in the health services as resources to 'beat the system' and jump queues. The validity of this claim may be questionable, but the existence of such a perception acts as a barrier to access by creating a feeling of being outsiders. The 'outsider' perception also undermines the capacity of hostel dwellers to challenge what they perceive as unfair practices and poor service provision.

It should be noted here that the time budgeted by the Day Hospital organisation for consultation is 5,5 minutes per patient. During this period a patient has to state the presenting problem (often through an interpreter), undress for examination, be examined, have a discussion about the cause, nature and possible course of the problem, and finally have treatment prescribed and explained. This time restriction results in many corners being cut by health workers in this situation, and accounts for the complaints by patients of lack of examinations and inadequate communication.

This brief consultation should also be compared with the average waiting time for people before being seen by the health-care professionals. Informants stated that in order to ensure a favourable place in the queue, one had to be up at 6 a.m. and be standing at the hospital gates by 6.30 a.m. at the latest. This means that by the time the first patient is seen at 8 a.m., that person would have been waiting for an hour and a half. On average people spend five hours at the Day Hospital, of which only 2 per cent is spent in consultation.[1]

In general, hostel residents face considerable difficulties when seeking treatment in the event of an acute and severe episode of illness or injury. First, there are few accessible and working telephones in hostels in general. During my research period, I only came across four functional telephones servicing all the hostels in Langa, Nyanga and Guguletu. These were private services, which were sometimes made available for emergency use. Public telephones installed in some of the hostels were out of order most of the time. Second, general practitioners and ambulances are reluctant to go into townships, especially hostel areas,[2] particularly during periods of heightened township violence. Finally, taxis to the nearest hospitals are expensive. The following case study illustrates some of the difficulties encountered.

Tobeka sells fish and chips from a small 'lean-to' attached to the hostel block where she lives with her husband. Late one afternoon

1. This information was collected by me over a period of one month, October–November 1987, at Guguletu Day Hospital where I worked as a Medical Officer.

2. This unwillingness is related to the perception that the safety of health workers cannot be guaranteed, particularly during periods of civil strife, or 'unrest' in official language (see Yach, 1986 MRC report).

she accidentally spilt boiling oil over the right side of her body. Her husband had not yet returned from a purchasing trip in town when the accident occurred. Friends carried her to the police station, because ambulances would not enter the hostel area. There she waited for over an hour before she was taken to Conradie Hospital, where she was admitted for three days. On discharge she was referred to the nearest Day Hospital for daily dressings. She was still unable to walk and for the two-week period during which she was required to go for daily dressings her husband had to organise and pay for a taxi at R7 per time.

Folk healers. For the purposes of this analysis, folk healers include herbalists, and spiritual and traditional healers. Our survey indicated a very low use of these healers, contrary to expectations based on other studies in comparable situations, as well as conventional biomedical wisdom in certain circles. One such study (Olivier, 1987), for example, indicated that 24 per cent of poor urban Africans consulted traditional healers as a first choice in illness episodes, compared with 4 per cent and 3 per cent for psychologists and psychiatrists respectively. Olivier's study has many methodological problems relating to sampling and the phrasing of survey questions, which weighted the responses in favour of folk healers. The conclusion drawn from this study, without any reference to available health services in the areas of study, that 'the Xhosa faces unique problems in which the traditional and faith healer have a definite place' (Olivier, 1987), is surprising to say the least.

Siyavuma, the organ of the South African Traditional Healers' Council (SATHC), claims that the Council has eleven million members consisting of both patients and healers, with the latter numbering 1 200. It quotes their National Secretary as saying:

> Before a person visits a hospital he or she will consult a traditional healer. The patient must find out whether the disease is connected with an ancestor. A modern doctor is not able to do this (*Siyavuma*, Feb. 1988:5).

This is a surprising claim which presupposes that ordinary people are incapable of making a decision about appropriate responses to illness episodes (see Frankenberg & Leeson, 1976; Kleinman, 1978). Research indicates that people employ a hierarchy of resort in search of healing and that this hierarchy is developed in relation to available healing resources, with evidence of a facility to adjust to changing realities. It would thus be surprising if Africans in South Africa adhered to 'traditional' practices in their choice of healers in spite of their changing socio-economic circumstances.

Our data show that people have developed their own skills in this process of decision making, Vuyo being a case in point. It appears that the above claim and the sudden growth in the number of 'traditional healers' require more systematic analysis. They could be related to a confluence of interests between the need to legitimise the role of the SATHC and the response by certain people to an increasingly tight job market in the ever-expanding urban settlements, rather than to a sudden abundance of the gifts of 'traditional healing powers'. In the Western Cape alone there are 400 healers registered with this organisation. This development has no historical precedent; on the contrary, traditional healers are regarded by some scholars as rare and specially gifted people (Ngubane, 1977:147; Heap, 1989:143).

The claims of widespread use of traditional healers should also be seen against the background of the cost of consultations. In the Cape Town area, for example, costs in the late 1980s were on average R10 for divination, R40 for treatment of minor ailments and several hundred rand for major problems such as *ukutwasa*.[1] Given the income levels of people in the hostels, few people would be able to afford these services without making extraordinary sacrifices, which would be appropriate mainly in exceptional situations and where all other options have failed. This cost factor was seen by all, including one traditional healer, as prohibitive. It had cost her over a thousand rand over a period of three years to complete her course of *ukutwasa*. Another participant went as far as to say that she defied a diagnosis of *ukutwasa* because of the cost factor and is none the worse for it. She sees this outcome as a vindication of her view that 'they just wanted my money for training'. Lock and Scheper-Hughes point to the role of healing systems in controlling social relations (see Lock & Scheper-Hughes, 1990:47–72).

It appears from interviews and group discussions that traditional healers were used only in special circumstances such as *mafufunyane*,[2] *idliso*,[3] cancer of the breast and special family problems. These were regarded as conditions biomedical healers were unable to treat.[4] In particular there was unanimity about the negative outcome of operations to treat cancer. None of our informants knew of anybody who had been successfully treated for cancer and all felt that if they were to be affected by it they would not submit to biomedical treatment. It would appear that the lack of positive experiences with cancer therapy and the negative impact of mutilating operations associated with it are major factors in influencing people's choices.

In particular, cancer of the breast poses many problems for women who have not been exposed to public and personal campaigns to identify cancer early and thus improve the chances of a positive outcome. None of our informants were aware of the need for self-examination of breasts on a regular basis. It was also difficult for people to comprehend how a painless lump could pose a threat to life, given their experience of the association of pain and serious illness. The

1. This term is a Xhosa word for the culmination of a ritualised process prescribed by healers for one deemed to be called by the spirits of ancestors to undergo training for healing. The literal translation of this term is 'to emerge'.

2. This term is used in both Xhosa and Zulu to refer to possession by evil spirits, which is deemed to be brought about by evil-doers or witches; see Ngubane, 1977 for further details.

3. This term refers to disease attributable to having been 'fed' or 'made to eat' (a literal translation of a common Xhosa and Zulu term) a harmful substance by evil-doers.

4. I acknowledge the biomedical bias of the study this book is based on as a possible explanation for low rates of consultation of 'traditional healers', but believe that the level of rapport with individual respondents was sufficient to counterbalance the bias to some extent.

psychological impact on a woman of the removal of a breast should not be underestimated; some people may choose death rather than a gross distortion of self-image without guaranteed results.

One of our informants, a healer, listed the diseases that she dealt with most often as sexually transmitted diseases *(idrop* or *gqushula)* after being treated with injections by biomedical healers,[1] some children's diseases, cancer of the oesophagus *(umhlahla)*, some forms of tuberculosis *(iTB)* and diabetes *(iswekile)*. Asked to define 'some forms of tuberculosis and diabetes' which she dealt with, she stressed that these were mainly cases which were resistant to conventional biomedical treatment. This information adds weight to the argument above that limited use is made of traditional healers for conditions which are seen to be adequately dealt with by biomedical services.

Spiritual healers seem to be popular, the main attraction being the lack of stipulated charges; one gives them whatever one can afford. There is also a perception that spiritual healing can be used as a cheaper alternative to *ukutwasa*. Spiritual healers are more accessible in terms of distance and communication. However, there are people who are sceptical of their claims of assistance, with unemployment in particular, where holy water and purification are supposed to rid one of bad luck and thus increase the chances of acceptability to prospective employers.

It would appear that on the whole spiritual healers are important in helping people living on the edge of survival to cope with anxieties and feelings of worthlessness.[2] The preoccupation with 'cleansing' is also a significant indicator of the acute awareness of living in a polluted environment. Pollution is perceived both in the physical sense of a filthy environment and in a symbolic sense of being thrust into the company of people one may not necessarily be comfortable with or choose to live with. Other people's *izithunzi* (literally 'shadows') end up weighing heavily on one, with potential ill effect. One would thus need to cleanse oneself regularly to maintain some sense of integrity and wholeness, and to prevent misfortune. The symbolism of healing ceremonies creates a 'soul clinic' atmosphere, enabling ordinary men and women to find a rewarding and not too painful existence, while they cope with an imperfect world (Dubos, 1977:32).

An important feature shared by traditional and spiritual healing is the capacity to turn weakness into strength by enabling former patients to become healers themselves, the 'wounded healer' being seen as better able to have empathy for others in distress. In addition, the care disturbed people receive from their supportive relatives and friends, as well as the shifting of the blame for ill-health from the victim to some external force, lessens the burden of the affected person (Ngubane, in Whisson & West, 1975:56). The following case contains some of these elements:

1. Her logic was that although biomedical injection (presumably penicillin) is the treatment of choice for STD, there is a place for cleansing rituals to protect the victim from future vulnerability to such attacks.

2. The popularity of the Zion Christian Church (ZCC), which attracted over a million worshippers to the Easter 1992 service in Moria, northern Transvaal, is a further indication of this phenomenon.

Zoliswa is a 39-year-old woman who recently qualified as a healer. She had a very unhappy childhood in the Transkei, feeling discriminated against by her stepmother and neglected by her father. She dropped out of school in Standard 4, because of lack of family support and fatigue from domestic chores. From that time on she developed headaches and sore throats which defied diagnosis and treatment by biomedical doctors. She later entered into an unhappy marriage with a man who is an alcoholic and abuses her. Her illness worsened, forcing her to consult a traditional healer, who prescribed ukutwasa *as the only cure. After initial resistance due to the cost and the lack of supportive relatives, she finally relented.*

For many months while going through training, one has to be celibate to allow the spirits of the ancestors to find their way into one without disturbances and impurities. Dreams play an important part of the training programme. These have to be related in detail to the trainer, at whose abode the trainees reside. It is through dreams that one learns about causes of illnesses and one is 'pointed' to specific remedies by one's ancestral spirits.

She has now found inner peace, which enables her to tolerate her husband's problems. The income she derives from her practice also affords her independence.

It is interesting that Zoliswa admitted to having kept some of her dreams away from her trainer because 'they learn new skills from you and if you are not careful you end up enriching them with the wisdom of your own spirits. One has to keep back some of the secrets passed on in dreams.' Here she is learning to resist control even by her trainer–healer.

The need for abstinence from sexual intercourse is not surprising, but must have been particularly convenient for Zoliswa, who probably experienced enormous frustration at this level. Sexual intercourse on a regular basis is not easy for a migrant labourer's wife, who experiences long periods of separation. Also, an alcoholic husband could hardly be a good sexual partner on the few occasions that they were together. The elevation of abstinence from sexual intercourse to being part of the healing process helped to restore Zoliswa's sense of her own worth as a person – putting her in control of when to have sexual intercourse rather than being at the mercy of her alcoholic and abusive husband.

It is also interesting to note the role of 'embodiment' (see Lock and Scheper-Hughes, 1990:47–71) in the cause of illness and the traditional healing process Zoliswa underwent. 'The body in health offers a model of organic wholeness; the body in sickness offers a model of social disharmony, conflict, and disintegration. Reciprocally, society in 'sickness' and in 'health' offers a model for understanding the body.' Zoliswa's body was thrown into disharmony, manifested by continual sore throats and headaches, due to difficult family relations in her unhappy childhood and later in her stressful marriage. Wholeness was restored through a healing process which allowed her to take control of her own circumstances through the strength she derived from perceiving herself to be acting as an agent of her ancestors. This restored her broken family ties which had caused her to feel rejected by her stepmother and her own father.

Zoliswa has been transformed from a nobody into a somebody, and is able to help others to find their own wholeness in the difficult circumstances of the hostels where she is practising. Her life circumstances have changed somewhat, but of greatest importance is the confidence she now has to face those aspects which cannot change without her being overwhelmed by them. Similar stories were told by women spiritual and other healers in the hostels.

There are various interpretations by anthropologists about the significance of a predominance of women in 'traditional' healing roles. Gluckman (1955), Hammond-Tooke (1962) and Lee (1969) all contend that these roles primarily provide avenues of escape in a male-dominated society, while Ngubane sees these women, among the Zulu, as fulfilling a function determined for them by society for its own benefit (Ngubane, 1977:148). It would appear from our informants, and from West's analysis of spiritual healers in Soweto (West, 1975), that women are not simply 'fulfilling roles set for them by society', but are striving to find a way of surviving in a tough environment, in which male domination is one of the major problems they have to contend with.

The consequences of a society 'in sickness'

The disease profile of hostel dwellers reflects the 'sickness' of South African society. It is only a sick society that can require the separation of families, and tolerate the 'immersion of people in filth' and without any privacy.

The following data give an indication of the health status of hostel dwellers.

TABLE 4.
Prevalence of TB, diabetes, hypertension, sexually transmitted diseases (STD).

Disease	Sex				Total	%
	Male	%	Female	%		
TB	3	1	5	2	8	2
Diabetes	3	1	2	1	5	1
Hypertension	13	6	13	6	26	6
STD	2	1	1	0.4	3	1
Other	34	17	34	16	68	16
TOTAL	55		55		110	

There are interesting differences between the information gathered from direct questioning of the respondents and that obtained from clinical measurements. On objective measure (see Table 5) the prevalence of hypertension in particular is higher (10 per cent) than that reported (6 per cent). The same discrepancy appears in relation to sexually transmitted diseases (STD), which are approximately 1 per cent and 6 per cent respectively. This suggests that there are some chronic conditions for which hostel dwellers in this sample are not seeking therapy or which they are unaware of. It is also plausible that they may have elected not to disclose these to the research team for a variety of reasons, some of which will be explored later in the chapter.

TABLE 5.

Prevalence of hypertension, liver damage and sexually transmitted diseases, by objective measure, by sex.

Disease	Sex				Total	%
	Male	%	Female	%		
Hypertension	23	13	43	18	66	10
Liver damage	25	13	13	13	38	9
STD	8	8	16	16	24	6
Diabetes	2	1	2	2	4	1

Note: Statistics refer to those examined by an objective measure and who show results outside acceptable normal limits. The following was taken as indicative of the condition:

Hypertension: diastolic >90
Liver damage: Gamma GT >40
STD: VDRL, Reactive on laboratory report
Diabetes: Sugar one to four +s glucose in the urine

Tuberculosis figures show the same underreporting compared with actual notification figures from the local authorities. The figures in Table 6 also enable us to compare the health status of hostel dwellers with that of surrounding township residents.

Only 1 per cent of our respondents reported having been on TB treatment, compared with 3 per cent estimated from notification figures in Table 6. This underreporting is partly a result of our small sample, but may also be an indication of unwillingness of hostel dwellers to disclose such illnesses.

Table 6 suggests that hostel dwellers have a risk of being on the notification list for TB almost three times higher than their township counterparts, this risk being considerably higher in Langa than in Guguletu. These differences are in proportion to the level of overcrowding in the living spaces affected people have access to. The Zones area of Langa hostels, in particular, is much more overcrowded than any of the Guguletu hostels (see Chapter 2 on physical space). Although townships are very crowded, they still compare favourably

TABLE 6.

TB notification rates per 1 000 of the population for the Council-built hostels of Langa and Guguletu for an 18-month period: January 1987–June 1988.

Location	Population	Notifications	Per 1 000
Hostels			
Langa	17 400	525	30
Guguletu	7 540	434	17
Langa & Guguletu	24 940	659	26
Township (excluding hostels)			
Langa	55 100	402	7
Guguletu	143 460	1 390	10
Langa & Guguletu	198 560	1 792	9
Township (including hostels)			
Langa	72 500	927	13
Guguletu	151 000	1 524	10
Langa & Guguletu	223 500	2 451	11

Source: Notification rates – City of Cape Town Medical Officer of Health
Township population figures – Cape Town City Council, TMS
Council-built hostel population – Conditions of Life in the Hostels of the Western Cape Project

with hostels. Unfortunately, figures for Nyanga were not made available to us by the health authorities, but it can be assumed that the notification rate for Nyanga hostels would have been the highest, given their higher bed occupancy rate. Of all the health problems facing hostel dwellers, three reflect their circumstances most clearly: tuberculosis *(iTB)*, sexually transmitted diseases *(izifo za bafazi, idrop* or *gqushula)* and alcoholism *(isifo so tywala)*. The two diseases in this category, TB and STD, provoke considerable interest among hostel dwellers, who have a good understanding of the circumstances under which these conditions take root and flourish. They are also of particular concern to medical professionals, because of public health implications. TB is reaching epidemic proportions in Cape Town: 1 in every 130 persons was expected to contract TB in 1988 (*Cape Times*, 29 June 1988). The AIDS scare has also focused attention on all forms of STD. Alcoholism, although not regarded as a disease in the ordinary sense of the word, was specifically singled out as a major health problem by our informants, because of the association in their experience between alcohol abuse and diseases such as TB. In particular, it is believed that brandy is exceptionally potent in causing a rapid decline in health status and severe TB.

Sexually transmitted diseases (STD)

For both men and women STD is higher on VDRL result than reported prevalence (see Tables 5 and 4). On VDRL result alone the prevalence is higher for women than for men (16 women, 8 men). The VDRL results for women in comparison with reported findings suggest that those with a positive VDRL may not be seeking treatment. Several reasons may be advanced for people not seeking treatment. Attendance figures for the STD Municipal Clinics suggest that female attendance is generally lower than that for men. Overall in 1986, women comprised only 37 per cent of all those receiving treatment at Cape Town STD Municipal Clinics (Cape Town City Council Annual Report of the Medical Officer of Health, 1986:174). Lower attendance by women may be related to the nature of some sexually transmitted diseases and their presentation. The main features to note are the asymptomatic nature, or lack of dramatic symptoms in women compared with men, of some of these conditions. For example, gonorrhoea (a bacterial infection of mucus membranes, *idrop*) presents with such discomfort and a discharge of such proportions in affected men that it is impossible to ignore, whereas in women there may be only vague discomfort which would not be seen to warrant serious attention.

The Medical Officer of Health's report referred to above suggests that there is differential attendance by women in the Cape Town area at the STD clinics. Of the total female patients attended to, Africans comprised 26 per cent, whites 11 per cent and 'coloureds' 63 per cent. STD is not a notifiable disease (MOH report, 1986). If a white woman from a higher-income group visits a general practitioner in preference to a Municipal Clinic in the event of STD, this attendance would not be reported or reflected in official reports. However, for poor people the free service of the clinics would be a more rational economic choice. The higher percentage of 'coloured' women attending STD clinics is a reflection of an effective referral system from the more numerous and relatively superior ante-natal services in the 'coloured' areas (Coetzee, Senior State Health Officer, personal communication). Of the 23 obstetric units for the Cape Town population, the majority of which are in the 'coloured' townships, only one is located in the African areas.

Access to adequate and regular ante-natal care, which includes routine VDRL examination, is particularly difficult for hostel women. Ante-natal care may be commenced in the Transkei or Ciskei, where it is doubtful whether VDRL is routinely carried out, given the inadequate laboratory facilities in the area. Towards the end of pregnancy women move to Cape Town, where they prefer to deliver in better-equipped hospitals. But there is little formal contact on antenatal care between the health care services of the 'independent' Transkei and Ciskei and those of Cape Town.

STD is also an interesting category of disease because of the social perceptions, myths, fears and taboos associated with it. Conventional wisdom associates STD with 'unclean women' and makes men shy away from the sexual partners they associate with their infection. This leaves women out of the therapeutic process. There is also a general feeling among informants that contact between men and prostitutes, who are not subject to any regular medical checks, perpetuates a pool of infection in the community.

The subject of sexuality does not lend itself to full discussion, on account of the reluctance of a significant proportion of members of society to deal with it openly. Few people find it easy to talk freely about genitalia and any sexual problems they may encounter, yet there is an expectation that health workers should be able to sense the need to have this area explored during consultations. Innuendo and hints are used to draw attention to problems related to genitalia or sexuality (Murray, in Whisson & West, 1975:58–77). There are serious public health implications of this social attitude, given the growing AIDS epidemic. It may be partly responsible for the difference in the numbers of men and women seeking treatment for STD. Few men openly discuss sexual problems with their partners in the hostels (partly due to lack of privacy), leaving those women in the dark about possible infections. Infidelity in relationships, exacerbated by separation of families through the migrant labour system, further complicates this situation (Ramphele, 1989). The 100 per cent response rate of people with positive VDRLs and their partners to advice to follow recommended treatment indicates that people do respond positively to targeted health campaigns.

There is wide acceptance of biomedical treatment for STD. Informants are unanimous in their perception that STD treatment is acceptable and effective. The major strength is seen to lie in the short-term nature of the treatment course and its ability to prevent the perceived threat to fertility and sexual performance associated with these diseases. This view was shared by a traditional healer whom I interviewed. She stated that she always insists on treating people with STD only after they have been given an injection or equivalent treatment by doctors or clinics.

Tuberculosis

The level of self-reported cases of TB from our respondents is low in comparison with the official statistics reflected in Table 6. A possible reason for the low reporting of TB may be the fact that our survey dealt with the materially better off in a particularly impoverished group of people. TB is generally associated with extreme poverty. The poor tend to be hidden from society, which means that they are also hidden from health care services and service providers. They are the least likely section of society to volunteer for a health survey.

Another important factor may be the perception of the implications of being diagnosed as having TB. The long hospitalisation which used to be associated with TB treatment is seen as a threat that looms large in the minds of insecure, unskilled workers, who run the risk of losing their jobs. The perceived unsympathetic attitude of employers in the case of ambulatory treatment presents a real disincentive to seeking help early on in the disease process (Cornell, 1984). Welfare assistance for victims of the disease is hopelessly inadequate to provide alternative support for affected families, as illustrated by the following case:

Zolile, a middle-aged man with a wife and six children ranging in ages from 12 to 1 year old, contracted TB in 1985, which cost him his job. He also suffers from diabetes, which lowers his resistance to infections of any kind, rendering his TB more difficult to control in spite of regular treatment. He is now an invalid and cannot conceivably hold another job in the future. The cumulative effect of inadequate nutrition, overcrowding and depression from constant want has resulted in his whole family contracting the disease. The support they get in welfare grants is mainly foodstuffs, some of which they are forced to sell to buy other essentials such as soap.

The picture of misery shown by this family and many others in the same predicament frightens fellow hostel dwellers, encouraging them to deny the possibility that they might be affected until it is too late. Indeed, even when the truth is known, the option of treatment might be too costly. 'I am forced to kill one child to feed the others,' said a woman in Kgano (QwaQwa), faced with a similar predicament, in which the only breadwinner had contracted TB but was forced to continue working in order that his family could survive (Sharp & Spiegel, 1984:15).

Alcoholism

It is of particular interest to note that the condition which the hostel dwellers identified as a major problem revealed one of the highest prevalences: 13 per cent of respondents showed indications of liver damage associated with alcohol abuse;[1] men constituted 65 per cent of those affected (see Table 5). Although caution should be exercised in interpreting the result of high Gamma GT, given other causes of liver damage in this environment, there is a close correlation between the result and volunteered information on alcohol intake. This information will be presented in a section of Chapter 5 dealing with life-style.

Alcohol abuse is one social problem which has defied the tendency of biomedical professionals to 'medicalise' human problems. It is also not easy to legitimise as a 'sickness' because of the tendency of the affected people and those close to them to deny it such a status. In the context of the hostels, high alcohol consumption can also be seen as a health strategy in itself. For example, many women who would otherwise be totally destitute rely on brewing and selling alcohol for survival. In addition, alcohol provides solace for people

1. A Gamma GT test is a crude indicator of liver damage, which cannot be relied on to identify alcohol abuse on its own. This test was used in this study to corroborate our qualitative data.

brutalised by poverty and dehumanising living and working conditions (Ndaba, 1984:9).

Even if some of the affected hostel dwellers were prepared to undergo therapy for this problem there would be major barriers to access to appropriate facilities. The Alcoholics Anonymous Association has indicated a willingness to assist anyone with a drinking problem, but there are some basic practical difficulties which have to be faced. Limited access to therapy in this case would be related to a lack of telephones, language difficulties and problems with means of transport to meetings, which are an important part of the therapeutic process.

Conclusion

The above data indicate that health strategies of people in the hostels are often the result of rational decisions appropriate to their circumstances. The contribution of experience with various healing systems and their relative efficacy to the choice of healers is also indicated. Forms of treatment whose efficacy is proved and accepted encounter little resistance. Barriers to access to existing biomedical health services for poor people seem to be the major constraint to the implementation of rational decisions in this regard. These barriers relate to affordability, distance, working hours and communication.

This lack of communication occurs at various levels in the hospital and clinic situations. At the reception stage, patients are often just told to move from queue to queue without any serious attempt by the overextended and poorly motivated health workers to explain the process and the rationale behind it. Procedures carried out in the waiting area are often conducted with little sensitivity to the anxieties and dignity of patients. Something that looks innocuous to a health worker, such as passing urine into a small container, may be highly embarrassing for many ordinary people. There is also the language question; health professionals find it difficult to explain processes in ordinary simple language. Medical jargon finds its way into patient–doctor conversations. In addition, in most out-patient settings used by hostel dwellers, few doctors can communicate in Xhosa, which is the home language of most patients. Finally, the non-verbal communication of most health workers dealing with the poor conveys little respect for the human dignity of patients.

I found no significant evidence of people defaulting from biomedical management in favour of 'traditional' healing; on the contrary, there is a lot of confidence in the biomedical system in those areas where it has proven efficacy, but people do use traditional healers in areas where their expertise is established. The same observation was made in a study in Zimbabwe (Chinemana, 1988:14). There also seems to be little difference between people in the hostels and poor working-class people anywhere in the world (Sanders,

1985:157–213). The preoccupation with 'the African view of disease' and the more subtle notion of distinguishing between the 'First' and 'Third' World sectors of South African society distract biomedical healers from the essential task of searching for appropriate ways of addressing the problems of care in a situation of socio-economic and political differentiation.

It is not surprising that most of the people identified as suffering from chronic illnesses such as high blood pressure end up defaulting on treatment and, in spite of remotivation by the research team, few of them went back for treatment. Vuyo, whose case we studied earlier in this chapter, is therefore not an exceptional case: how could he be expected to give up his job in search of personal care at the expense of his family responsibilities?

Whatever one may think about Vuyo's approach to his health problem, one must concede the logic of his choice of strategies for dealing with his illness. He did make efforts to find a solution or cure, but has so far met with no success. His disease is incurable and the only treatment the biomedical system can offer him is palliative and the maintenance of an ideal blood sugar level. This option demands of him time, adherence to a strict diet and a change in life-style, all of which he perceives as being beyond his means. He has no illusions about the long-term outcome of his illness, but has chosen to maintain his dignity by continuing to be an effective breadwinner for his family for as long as he is alive. He deals with his depression by eating his favourite food, meat and gravy, and drinking soft drinks. Alcohol has little appeal for him; he cannot afford to be drunk on duty. He has found his own way of maintaining 'wholeness'.

The constraints of space in the hostels at all levels act as positive incentives to ingenuity, but also limit transformative action in a creative sense. The necessity for survival also poses a threat to risk-taking behaviour in terms of the patient–healer relationship. Patients tend to 'vote with their feet' rather than challenge individual healers or health services to provide better-quality, affordable and accessible care. The power of the biomedical profession is overwhelming, even for well-off, sophisticated people; how much more must it be so for hostel dwellers?

Finally, the data in this chapter indicate that constraints of space in all its dimensions have an adverse effect both on hostel dwellers' health status and on their capacity to respond with effective health strategies. Their ingenuity and intuitiveness are impressive. It is however only when society confronts its own 'sickness', as indicated by its wanton neglect of the well-being of hostel dwellers, that true healing and wholeness can be restored to all.

ata Mboto, Nomachule, Mgwayi and Mamfene, No. 29

esidents in the Prebuilt Co. Hostel

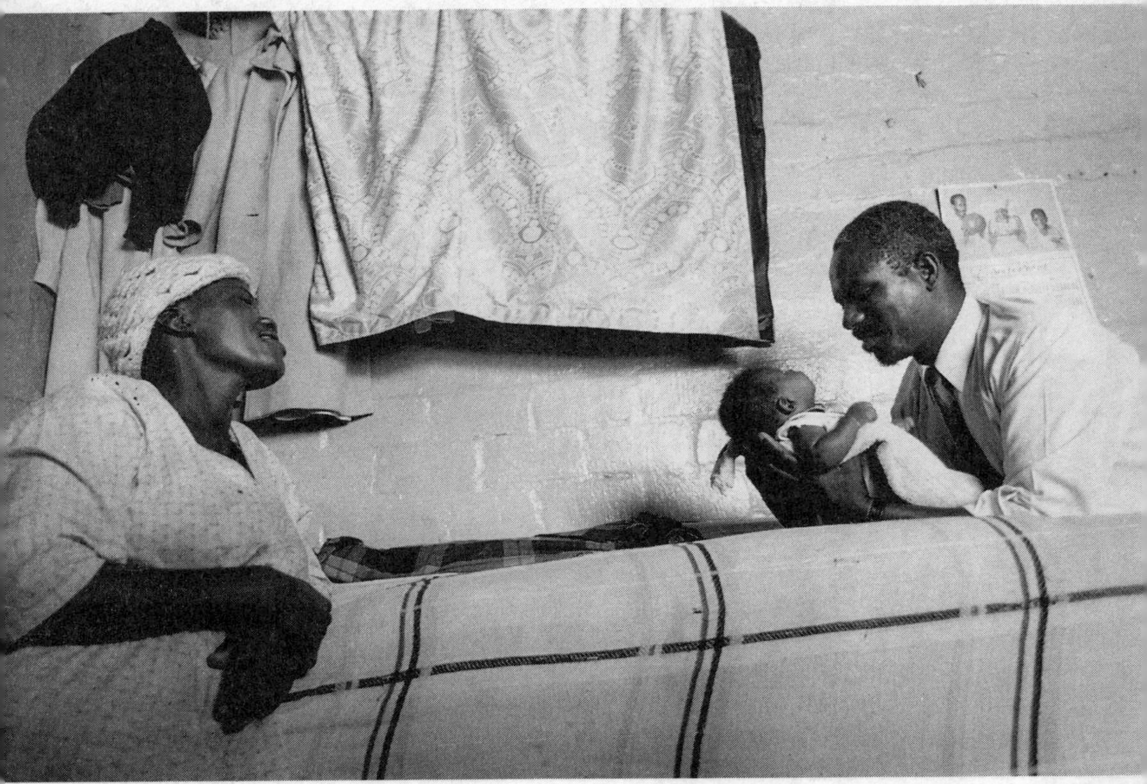

Mr. Jama with his niece Nomlungu and her chi

Inmates of the I & J Co. Host

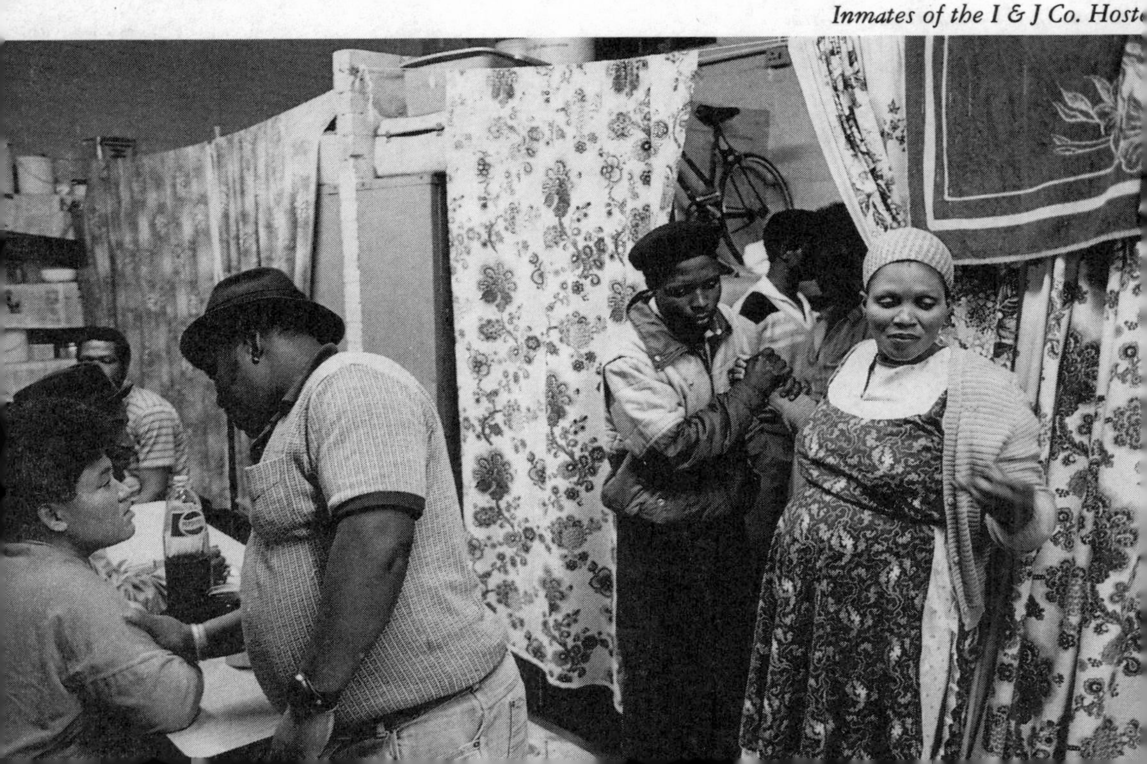

Mamiya in her room

Some of the residents of No. 4

Mr. Nosam and Bongani Marulub

5 Social Organisation

Together, space, time and money intersect to establish the physical settings where all events of life will be staged. Whether they are harmonious or discordant (Hayden, 1984:39)

Introduction

The nature of contemporary relationships between hostel dwellers has changed significantly since the entry of women and children into the hostel environment in the late 1960s and their increasing numbers since the promulgation of the Abolition of Influx Control Act of 1986 (Wilson & Mafeje, 1973; West, 1982; Reynolds, 1984; Seleoane, 1985). What was essentially a 'man's world' has been changed into an environment accommodating men, women and children in a mixture of configurations of 'bedholds'. The quality of life before the arrival of women and children in these hostels was evidently pretty grim. Men would have to wake up as early as 5 a.m. in some cases, and wash as well as they could; sometimes the pressure on limited facilities precluded proper washing, because of the fear of being late for work. For those in hostels near places of work, a few minutes' walk was all that it took to get to work. For others working far away, commuting by bus and train was, and still is, the order of the day, taking up to an hour or two in each direction.

After coming back tired from uninspiring menial work, most residents found cleaning their personal physical space and preparing a reasonable meal were often difficult. This resulted in many of these men 'living in filth' (Matshoba, 1987:227) and eating whatever ready food they could buy from hawkers. One man described conditions as follows: 'We lived like animals – sleeping in the same unmade bed for days on end. It was no different from a rabbit in relation to its burrow.' Laundry and cleaning of rooms were done mainly during weekends. However, it would seem that some people still managed to keep tidy beds and to cook reasonable meals for themselves, either alone or in conjunction with 'home people' *(amakhaya)* sharing chores and resources (see Wilson & Mafeje, 1973:47–73).

The quality of life also varied from hostel to hostel, depending on the support networks individuals had with friends and relatives. Older men generally acted as mentors for younger people from their villages to ensure their protection from 'the evils of the city', and discouraged them from visiting local township folk for fear of exploitation, which was reputed to be rife. Exploitation related mainly to relationships of convenience with local township women, who were said to fleece vulnerable 'rural bumpkins' mercilessly. Unwary hostel dwellers also fell victim to exorbitant rentals charged by the relatively better-off township residents to hostel dwellers for use of backyard shacks during emergency visits of family members from rural areas. In many cases mentors went as far as keeping all but a small allowance of the earnings of their charges, to effect savings for the end-of-the-year visit 'home', in addition to regular remittances. Some hostel residents attribute the ability to save from meagre incomes and the relative stability of many of their families to this mentoring system.

Others fell through the cracks due to lack of support or refusal to be controlled by others, alcoholism or loss of contact with the rural base, and final ruin resulted. They became known as *amarumsha*, those who have lost touch with Xhosa customs. Some of the *amarumsha* ended up *be tshiphile*, totally lost to the city. Some of these individuals are today inhabiting the Langa and Nyanga 'old-age homes'.[1] These are men and women in the dusk of their lives. They have no family to go back to and are too old or disabled to care for themselves. Some of them wept unashamedly when asked about how they coped with the lack of contact with their families. Others refused even to discuss the issue. For example one old woman said, 'It is too painful to even think about it, let alone talk about it. I am praying for death to come soon to release me from this torture.' Most of the men in these old-age homes are former inmates of hostels around the Cape Peninsula, while the women are largely retired domestic workers who used to live in the backyards of their white employers, and lost contact with their families over the years. They are all victims of a system that has treated them as labour units, and has now discarded them as obsolete. Other informants are quite philosophical about the turn of events:

Dumo is a 70-year-old man, with severe alcohol damage to his liver and peripheral nervous system. He has been in Cape Town since the late 1940s. He started off as a 'garden/kitchen-boy', living in the backyards of white suburban homes. Over the years, his fortunes changed when he found better-paying work in the hotel industry. Life was good then; he mixed with the best guys, dressed well and had a lot of lady-friends at his beck and call.

He cut his ties with 'home-boys' in the hostel in which he resided and became a 'city-wise' person. He lost contact with family at home and sank his roots deeper into the city. He says he has no regrets now that he is in this state, musing that he did have a good time. He believes that he deserves the manner in which he has to end his days. He still enjoys his drinks, whenever he can afford the means to purchase liquor, especially after his R150 old-age pension pay-out[2] every two months.

To capture the essence of current social interaction in the hostels, one would have to live there for a period of time and observe interaction over 24-hour periods. The space constraints of this setting preclude this form of study, but partial participant observation has been done (Ramphele, 1991) and complemented by other data sources.

1. The facilities of the Nyanga home are very humble, comprising a converted semi-detached eight-room house of the same quality as the Nyanga township houses (see Ramphele & Meiring, 1986.)

2. In terms of the 1992/93 national budget, the old-age pension is now R293,12 per month.

Daily routine

A typical working day starts at 5 a.m., with competition among 38 people for use of the same toilet and shower. For those too late to wait, basins with water warmed on primus stoves are used for washing in the front room or 'bedrooms'. Those sleeping in the front room have to be up to make room for workers to move around. Teenage boys, who generally sleep in the front room, help with the chores of warming water for relatives, making coffee and later cleaning the front room on a roster basis. Women workers have logistical problems in getting ready for work, because of lack of privacy. In some hostels, only men are permitted to use toilets and showers in the mornings, because they are said to have a prior claim to them historically.[1]

The other women and children rise later, and prepare breakfast at leisure before starting their chores for the day. Breakfast, normally consumed between 9 a.m. and 10 a.m., consists for most people of mielie-meal porridge, bread (sometimes with margarine and jam) and coffee or tea. There is a fair amount of communal eating among the women and children. Almost all the women who are single heads of households engage in some income-generating activity for most of the day. Their wares range from home-brewed beer to sheep's heads cooked or raw, offal, vegetables, fruit and second-hand clothing. The tempo of these activities picks up as the day wears on, in preparation for workers coming back from work.

Children spend most of the day outside with their mothers, playing in and around the open spaces. They have to be kept outside and reasonably quiet to allow night-shift workers arriving back in the mornings to sleep for a while. This is often a friction point between those who feel that their space is being invaded by noisy women and children and those who live with their families.

For those people not engaged in income-generating activities, chores such as laundry, mending, shopping and tidying up take up most of the day. The late afternoon activities centre around preparing the evening meal in time for returning workers. A lot of social interaction takes place during the preparation of meals and their consumption. Food most often consumed includes samp and beans with or without vegetables. Meat of varying quality (always the cheapest varieties, such as offal, chicken feet or low-grade red meat) is consumed at least once a week. The front room and the kitchen are both used for cooking. The front room is generally reserved for men to have their evening meals and meetings. Women have to use either the bedrooms or the outside area to have their meals. The enforcement of this rule varies from hostel to hostel. Rules about bedtime also vary, but generally 10 p.m. is considered time to switch off lights to allow workers to get enough sleep. The front door is then locked to ensure the security of front-room sleepers.

1. This is yet another example of tradition being used to defuse a difficult logistical problem with inadequate facilities to cater for men and women.

Weekends are mainly devoted to relaxation, cleaning, shopping and laundry for those working during the week. In Langa Old Flats, for example, only men are allowed to use the laundry and to hang their clothing out on the line during weekends. The reasoning is that women are at home during the week and should not compete with men who have no other time to do their laundry. This ignores the needs of the 19 per cent of the women who are formally employed, and is only one example of the contradictions between the 'old ways' and the demands of the new situation with the presence of women and children in the hostels as a permanent reality.

In such a situation, it would be reasonable to assume that the potential for conflict is high. There are, however, relatively few reported incidents of violence among the residents of these hostels. This may be because a lot of violence is simply taken as normal and is never reported, but research suggests that there is a semblance of order kept in most of the hostels (Ramphele, 1991). One has thus to examine the system of internal governance and its role in ordering relationships in this setting. The description just given of day-to-day life indicates some rigidity imposed by rules and regulations governing social interaction in these hostels; an authority structure has in fact evolved over the years to oversee this process (see Wilson & Mafeje, 1973; Thomas, 1987).

The traditional authority structure

Hostel administration and governance is regulated under provisions published in the Government Gazette of 14 June 1968, which provides for a hostel superintendent to set up a structure to assist him in managing these hostels. The primary function was to control movement in and out of these places and to minimise conflict between inmates (see Thomas, 1987).

The structure involves the election of representatives of 'doors' from among the occupants. These are, on the whole, elderly men, known to their fellow residents for wisdom and fairness. These men are termed *izibonda*,[1] and their functions are similar to those people of the same designation used by white governments to control villages in the rural areas (Hammond-Tooke, 1975:80; Gordon, 1989:41–65). These *izibonda* are subject to review and replacement if they fail to meet the expectations of their fellow residents, but in general they tend to remain in office until retirement or movement back to the rural 'home'. Their responsibilities revolve around keeping the peace. They are in charge of the roster for cleaning the communal space, making sure that people adhere to set sleeping and lock-up times, and they arbitrate in disputes around these and other issues. In conjunction with the hostel superintendent, they also regulate access to empty bed-space and expulsion of undesirable elements from the beds under their control.

1. This is a common Xhosa word (singular *isibonda*, which refers to a man set in authority over a local area). These men are also known as headmen.

Most of these functions are carried out with the assistance of other residents who sit in on arbitration hearings and jointly mete out punishment to guilty parties. It is thus to some extent a participatory system of justice, as far as men are concerned. Fines normally range from R10 up to R20, with higher fines imposed on multiple offenders. Recalcitrant offenders are reported to the superintendent and may be expelled. Such people can either find alternative beds or exchange with others willing to live in their hostel and abide by its rules.

Offences viewed in a serious light are foul language, noise, 'disturbing the peace' (if one can imagine peace in this environment) and assault with resultant disturbance of the peace. Women are not recognised as persons in this system of justice, except in their capacity as complainants in relation to their husbands or boyfriends. They are not eligible to participate in the hearings, and some men do not even bother to address them about matters in dispute. Women are deemed to be the extensions of their menfolk, who are held accountable for their offences.

This 'non-person' status is a source of distress for many women, who feel abused by some of the men. For example, some women claim that certain men deliberately litter the communal spaces or soil toilets while the women are attempting to tidy up. When challenged by the women, they simply ignore them or retort: 'I don't speak to *amabhinqa* (women)[1] on such matters – your man can raise that issue with me if he likes!'

There is a high level of compliance with the rules and regulations as well as with the system of justice. There is also a wide range in the quality of relations between the residents and the *izibonda*. In hostels such as the Old Flats where the *izibonda* have become entrenched in their positions, there are tensions between them and those under their authority. Conflicts of interest arise in relation to corruption around allocation of beds and access to recreational facilities.

The effective operation of this system of traditional authority depends to a large extent on the legitimacy it derives from 'tradition' and custom as a resource (see Thornton, 1988; Spiegel, 1988; Gordon, 1989). There is a fairly widespread transfer of imagery, metaphors and idiom from rural Eastern Cape 'tradition' to hostels, both as an expression of people's roots and as a cushion against total violation of self by a hostile environment (see also Keesing, 1981). Great pride is expressed, often with racist connotations, in enjoying enduring *amasiko* (customs), in contrast to *aMalau* (a derogatory term, used by Xhosa-speakers to refer to those classified 'coloured'), who are seen as lost, without any tradition to cushion them in times of need.

Men control language, as is the case in most societies (see Moore, 1986:164; Ruether, 1983:47–71; Heilbrun, 1988:17–31), and it is through this that they choose which metaphors, idioms and social processes are legitimate or illegitimate. It is mostly older men who

1. The expression used in Xhosa is even more telling than the translation here would suggest – *ibhinqa*, as a term for a woman, is meant to remind her of her status in relation to men; she is meant to wear a towel or other cloth around her waist *(ukubhinqa)* to show respect, particularly to men.

are in this position of authority. An extreme example of language control is embodied in the *hlonipha* (respect) language, which some rural Xhosa women in the Eastern Cape are forced to adopt to avoid using terms, syllables and names which may in any way be related to their in-laws' names, especially that of the father-in-law, as a sign of respect (see Finlayson, 1985). Failure to observe this practice is seen as a sign of total disrespect. The use of the *hlonipha* language is to be found mainly among the newly arrived women in the hostels. Most others have discontinued the practice, but some admit that they have to be on their guard when they go back 'home' and relate to sensitive in-laws.

Leisure activities

'There is nothing to do here – this place is very boring,' laments an 18-year-old, echoing the sentiments of many young people in the hostels. What leisure facilities exist within hostels and how accessible are outside facilities to hostel dwellers? What amount of leisure time do people have? Are there differences in this between men and women, or between people of different age groups? Do hostel dwellers see leisure facilities and time as issues deserving attention? If so, how do they cope with the constraints they experience with regard to leisure?

Wilson and Mafeje's study (1973:125) concluded that sports and other leisure facilities in Langa were inadequate for the population of that time. In 1954, for example, only 30 acres were available for fields for a population of 44 300 Africans, which compared unfavourably with standards in the United States and Germany, where 220 acres would be required for a comparable population size. There has been no significant change in this situation over the years. The provision of a few additional facilities has failed to match the population increase.

The quality of township leisure facilities in Langa, Nyanga and Guguletu varies from area to area, but is generally poor. There are three stadiums, all open-air, used mainly for rugby and soccer, except in Langa, where cricket is catered for. All the tennis courts are disused and the only two swimming pools in the area are poorly maintained, if not outright dangerous from a public health point of view. Community centres are under a lot of pressure, offering mainly indoor games, boxing, ballroom dancing and netball as well as being used for meetings and choir practices. Conflicts are inevitable under such circumstances. The Nyanga community centre was torched in the civil strife of 1986, but was restored in 1988. Guguletu has more community centres, including a good-quality one built by the Urban Foundation. There are neither theatres nor cinemas in any of these areas, the nearest place offering such facilities being Athlone. There is also inadequate provision of playgrounds in all the areas. For example, in Langa township playing facilities for younger children were non-existent, except for those provided for by five crèches, until 1988, when the authorities put up one play area in Church Street, Langa, which is predictably over-used.

The inadequacy of facilities should be viewed in the light of the total township and hostel population, which is conservatively estimated at 223 500 for Langa and Guguletu only (Cape Town City Council Report, 1988), but which in reality could be anything between 500 000 and 750 000 people for all three areas. The need for greater psychic space for those living in limited physical environments is well documented (see Dewar, 1984; Heilbrun, 1988:114), but seems to have been ignored in these townships.

There is, however, an added problem for those living in hostels; they are further discriminated against by their township neighbours who see them as outsiders, *amagoduka* and *oobari*, terms referring to those who periodically go home and are therefore not seen as part of Cape Town in a permanent sense, and to country bumpkins (see Wilson & Mafeje, 1973:113–36). This discrimination has changed only marginally over the years, and while hostel dwellers are well represented in rugby, as members of Mother City Club, and in soccer clubs, they do not take part in cricket, netball and indoor games. There are also different choirs for hostel dwellers and township residents. Many hostel residents see the inadequate provision of leisure facilities as an important problem, particularly in relation to weekends. There is also a difference between the perceptions of men and women. Women tend to find more things to do than men, given their tendency to engage in domestic chores during weekends.

Some of the younger people spend their leisure time playing cards indoors in the 'front rooms', or outside in decent weather. Many lamented the lack of reading material, the only matter available being old magazines and newspapers brought in by workers on an irregular basis. Others play soccer in the open spaces around hostels, listen to the radio or watch television if fortunate enough to have access to a set. Those with the financial means occasionally go to the local cinemas and other entertainment places. This involves a considerable financial outlay, given the low income status of hostel residents. The taxis stop running after 9 p.m., creating difficulties for those returning from evening shows, and the risk of violent attacks associated with walking home in the dark. Fears of violent attacks are well founded. According to the then Minister of Law and Order, Adriaan Vlok, Cape Town's position as the crime capital of South Africa, and of the world (see Wilson & Ramphele, 1989:153), remains unrivalled. In particular, Guguletu is reported to have the highest assault and murder rate per 100 000 people in the world. Some older men spend time gambling, a pastime particularly common in the Old Flats. Gambling involves card games, playing draughts and throwing dice.

The scarcity of facilities generally, the concentration of communal rooms in the Old Flats and the predominance of people with long-standing ties to Cape Town in these Old Flats have occasionally led to violent conflicts, centred around competition for communal rooms, which are a scarce resource. Some residents want them to be used for gambling purposes, while others prefer to hold meetings in them. On one occasion, this culminated in such a violent confrontation that the police were called in.

The high alcohol intake by hostel dwellers has been linked by some to boredom and poor recreational facilities. Others explain that abuse of alcohol is also related to the need 'to dull the pain of humiliation'. The process of dehumanisation has gone so far in some of the alcohol abusers that they have almost been reduced to an animal existence. One hostel resident expressed this view thus: 'They live for nothing else; they simply work, eat, drink and sleep – they are dazed most of the time. Talking to them about anything else is a waste of time.' Some residents have also identified dagga (marijuana) smoking as a problem among bored young men, and were particularly concerned about its contribution to violent behaviour.

Life-style

The results of a survey conducted among hostel dwellers (Ramphele, 1991:270) showed that 28 per cent admitted to nicotine usage, with a higher prevalence among older people (56 per cent among the 70–79 age group compared with 33 per cent among the 50–59 age group). These results are in line with other studies which have suggested an inverse relationship between smoking and socio-economic status (Yach, 1984; Yach & Townshend, 1988:391–9; Strebel, Kuhn & Yach, 1989:428–31).

In the same survey (Ramphele, 1991), alcohol consumption was admitted to by 25 per cent of the respondents. These responses are likely to be gross underestimations, given the biomedical bias of the study and the general unwillingness of people to admit to practices which may be seen as indications of weakness.

Dagga consumption figures were difficult to compute because of the unwillingness of respondents to disclose this information, but concern was expressed by many respondents, who felt that dagga smoking was a problem in the hostels. Particular concern was expressed about the simultaneous smoking of dagga and alcohol intake, which residents said made the consumers severely intoxicated and violent.

It would seem that on the basis of the alcohol intake and tobacco smoking, hostel dwellers have a high-risk life-style. Such a life-style has health and social implications, but it is important to see this as a consequence of a survival strategy which people living under difficult circumstances have had to devise. It is in this context that I would like to examine the social support networks which help cushion people against total disintegration in a hostile environment.

Social networks

Religion

The practice of religion is often seen as a way of creating meaning in one's life in a painful world (Marx's concept of religion as the 'opium of the people' could be interpreted in a positive light in this context). People expect the church to provide spiritual and material support in a harsh social environment (Wilson, 1971:66; Wilson & Mafeje, 1973:91–103; West, 1975). Church membership in the hostels covers a wide spectrum from the 'established' to the 'self-made'[1] (African Independent) churches. Involvement ranges from active participation to passive membership.

There is a widely held perception that the established churches discriminate against poor people in general and hostel dwellers in particular, and that they are biased in favour of prominent members of society, *ooscuse-me* or *izifundiswa*[2] (see Wilson & Mafeje, 1973). Some hostel residents have even stopped active participation in the established churches because they do not see the point of paying their church dues 'for the privilege of being insulted'.

A source of particular distress to hostel residents is the churches' failure to minister to them in sickness, or to comfort them when bereaved. They have to face the added problems of having most of their dead buried in the rural areas.[3] The church could lessen the pain engendered by the pathetic sight of coffins having to be rested in the dusty hostel surroundings before being loaded onto rural-bound transport by allowing them the dignity of church send-offs, which are accorded to more respected members of the same churches.

The unavailability of priests for hostel dwellers contrasts painfully with their perception of priests' readiness to preside personally over important people's 'trivial occasions', such as children's birthday parties. One resident said that she would rather go to a trade union meeting on a Sunday than waste her time in church, because at least she could see the value of the former in relation to her conditions of service. She added that she still enjoyed church services in her rural home base, where she experienced fellowship.

Others persevere as active participants. Zuma is a case in point:

He is a middle-aged churchwarden at an Anglican parish in one of the townships. He contracted TB in 1985 and was hospitalised for three months. Neither the priest nor his fellow churchwardens enquired after him during the entire period of his absence and illness. Upon his discharge he reappeared in church, where his priest casually asked where he had been all the time. To add insult to injury, no apology was ever offered to this man. He has quietly resumed his duties.

1. This is a derogatory term used by those belonging to 'mainline' churches.

2. *Ooscuse-me* is a term derived from the use of the expression 'excuse me' by those who appear sophisticated (Wilson & Mafeje, 1973:15), and *izifundiswa* refers to those seen to be holding themselves up as more educated than others.

3. This practice is observed by those who feel that they do not have sufficient roots in the urban setting to bury their dead there. This custom is costly in all respects: mortuary charges for many days while arrangements are being made, wakes in town and the rural home, and transport costs for the corpse.

There are, of course, exceptions to this inadequate pastoral care: the existence of the Hostel Dwellers' Association is the outcome of the caring ministry of an Anglican church chaplain. It is also important to remember that some of the problems hostel dwellers experience with established churches are a reflection of a general crisis in ministry within the churches in the townships (Ramphele, 1989:177–90). This crisis relates to the difficulties African ministers in particular experience in their attempts to be good pastors, in the context of the socio-economic, intellectual and psychological constraints imposed on them by their position as members of an oppressed group in South Africa. It also reflects the problems which the church as a whole will have to confront to free itself from the trappings of its colonial history and its tradition of patriarchal, hierarchical relationships.

Members of the African Independent churches are, in contrast, generally satisfied with the service they receive from their churches. These include spiritual support, healing and a feeling of being protected against evil and supported in a difficult world. Some members of established churches derive comfort from healing services of these Independent churches in emergency cases or when faced with problems defying other healers. Such people sometimes switch permanently from established churches to the Independent ones.

It is, however, important not to romanticise African Independent churches. They have a tendency towards hierarchical relationships, with men as leaders or bishops and women as the healers and junior partners. A healer of the St John's Church, for example, who is the leader of the church in Cape Town, has to go regularly to the Transkei to report to her bishop and deliver all the funds collected, out of which she is then given a stipend. She does not complain at all about this arrangement, but sees it as the natural way in which things are done.

Other support structures

There are various networks of support used by hostel dwellers for a range of needs. These networks range from individual friendships and loose groups such as those comprising self-employed women or people living in the same 'door' to formally structured groups such as burial societies, credit associations and so on. These support structures have varied success rates.

Burial societies' importance is a reflection of the high priority people accord to a decent funeral. Those who do not enjoy much respect and dignity in day-to-day life place their hopes on being redeemed by a dignified funeral. However, the custom of burying the dead in the rural home base imposes a considerable burden on limited economic resources, which necessitates reliance on others to make ends meet.

Burial societies are generally organised along 'home-people' lines, involving a formal structure with an executive committee responsible for proper administration of the affairs of the society. Funds are contributed on a regular basis to ensure liquidity, but lump-sum contributions are made in the event of death affecting a member or a dependant of a member. The society also rallies around the bereaved, organising prayer services, the wake, purchase of the coffin and final transportation of the body home in the supportive company of some elected members. There is general agreement about the essential service performed by these societies, and most hostel residents belong to at least one such.

Credit clubs or *imigalelo* are a popular form of saving and capital accumulation, as well as a source of rotating credit in Cape Town's African townships. They differ in size, level of contributions and sophistication. Some people belong to more than one such group. The bigger groups tend to involve long-term investment in funds for those unfortunate members who have their names drawn at the end of the line. The period of waiting could be up to five years, with little real benefit, when inflation and the opportunity cost in lost interest rates are taken into consideration. For those landing an early draw, the benefits are considerable: a low-interest lump-sum loan, payable over a period depending on the cycle of operation of the particular group. Allegations of corruption abound (see also Thomas, 1989).

Hostel dwellers belonging to *imigalelo* tend to gravitate to smaller groups comprising fellow workers, where the level of trust is high, to limit the risk of losses through defaulting members. Smaller groups also obtain quick returns, so that everyone gets a draw at least once a year.

Conclusion

Despite the obvious resilience of hostel dwellers, creativity (in dealing with inadequate leisure facilities, for example) seems to have been eroded by years of battling against continual obstacles. There are, of course, still creative individuals, but their influence is limited by the magnitude of the problems around them. Constraints of physical, economic and political space take their toll. The space to 'dream' and let one's imagination run away is not available to hostel dwellers.

6 Social Relations

Deprived of their natural guides, children of migrants (and all other poor blacks) grow through an insecure, uncertain childhood to an adult life whose sole preoccupation may be to escape the system. There must be a harvest of aggression, with the weeds of violence growing rank within it. The dreadful society is the community of the careless, of those who, treated like boys, behave like boys; of those who, having no responsibilities laid upon them, owe none to any man [sic]. *In that chill climate will there be any place for trust? Any hope for human intercourse at all?* (Barker, 1970).

This chapter explores the particularities of relationships between men, between men and women, between women and other women, and between adults and children.[1] These distinctions are important because of the different resources available to the various participants, and their effect on the quality of negotiated outcomes. Social relations in this context constitute the politics of space.

Gender relations

Relationships among men

Relationships between men are characterised by hierarchy legitimised by 'tradition' and based on age differences. Younger men defer to their elders who are supposed to have more wisdom and to be more reliable in their dealings with others. They are also more likely to occupy positions of authority as *izibonda*. Kinship and 'home-boy' groups are important reference points in terms of appropriate behaviour and networks of support. These networks are a source of support for newly arrived work-seekers, in the form of accommodation, food and placement in jobs. People from the same home village also help and support one another, especially in times of bereavement, sickness and important ceremonies such as circumcision and marriage.

Clan names, *iziduko*, are commonly used in addressing fellow residents, in preference to first names or surnames. These clan names serve several social purposes. First, they are used as a sign of respect for elders: one does not call elders by their first names. Second, they facilitate clan identification for the purposes of maintaining the incest taboo (among others), and also to invoke kinship obligations (see Hunter, 1936:51–9; Wilson & Mafeje, 1973:76).

People talk glibly of 'my brother' or 'my uncle' while referring to others whose only connection with them is a common clan name. It is thus a significant resource. In the long term, the issue of nepotism is also a major concern, as experience elsewhere in Africa has shown (for example, Hyden, 1983). If one is in a position of power it makes economic sense to ensure that one's kin have access to jobs

1. Most of the data for this chapter form the basis of an article, 'Dynamics of gender in the migrant labour hostels of Cape Town', published by the *Journal for Southern African Studies*, Vol. 15 No.3: April 1989, pp. 393–414.

rather than bear the burden of financially supporting large numbers of extended family members. This 'economy of affection' is a double-edged sword (Hyden, 1983:8) but seems to be successful as a coping strategy for survival in a difficult world.

The pattern of interaction in the hostels also encourages conservatism and conformism, as older men have a vested interest in the perpetuation of a system which gives them considerable power. Nor, strange as it may seem, is there any evidence of a concerted attempt by younger men to challenge this system. Several factors may contribute to this. It is easier to hold on to the known rather than experiment with the unknown (Havel, 1985:36–7). It is also true that human beings in general are creatures of habit, and monotonous environments encourage rigidity in people's habits (Koestler, 1964:44). The present system seems to work well for the men, and there is no reason why they should change it. Reverence for age is part of the world view of most people in this group and is reinforced throughout their socialisation period, culminating in circumcision. Circumcision also represents the final severance of the umbilical cord: one is reborn into the world of men. There is a strong argument by many people in the hostels for maintaining circumcision which, they feel, is central to 'the Xhosa tradition'. This includes women, who feel that uncircumcised men would have difficulty in fitting into the world of custom and ritual, and would therefore be unacceptable as partners.

The presence of women in the hostels seems to create problems for some men, who had got 'used' to living as 'men alone'. The redefinition of relationships between men necessitated by this 'invasion' has led to a variety of responses. For example, one 'door' in Langa has a policy of excluding all women, including the lawful wives of inmates, from the hostel, except as day-time visitors. The rationale behind this exclusion is that it is an expression of their commitment to a 'clean Christian life' and their desire to maintain a spirit of 'brotherhood'. Allowing women to sleep over in the hostels would threaten this moral purity, create points of conflict between the men and set a bad example for younger residents. All residents of this hostel are said to be 'born-again Christians' and thus support this approach.

The contradiction between this 'purity' approach and the Christian principle of keeping married couples together could not be satisfactorily reconciled by a resident with whom I discussed the question; instead, he fell back on the fact that it was illegal for men and women to live together in the hostels anyway, and he did not want to break the law. His own wife lives in a hostel nearby, and visits him during the day. They visit relatives in the township whenever they want to spend a night together. This example is an extreme demonstration of 'selective conservatism' (Hunter, 1936).

Interaction between men and women

Gender relations involve both individuals and groups. In this context I differentiate between single and married women, because of the different ways in which men relate to them, and also because of the different strategies they adopt to cope with male dominance. It is also interesting to examine how women interact among themselves, given their set gender roles. Specific case studies illustrate how some individuals deal with particular problems or conflicts. It has been well documented that African women pass through the control of different men throughout their lives (Simons, 1968:281). This system, which has been further reinforced by the legal provisions of successive South African white governments, confers the status of perpetual minors upon African women. Over the years there have been some changes in the degree of control, but the loosening of the screws has been a function of the success of individual women's struggles against this system. The role played by such women in challenging the system of control over their lives stresses the importance of individuals in either perpetuating or transforming systems of power and control over their lives (Giddens, 1981, 1983; Havel, 1985).

The cornerstone of 'traditional' control of women by men among Africans in most parts of South Africa is the system of *lobola* (bridewealth), which is used to secure control of the reproductive power of women. *Lobola* also plays an important role in ordering relations between men, both as individuals and as groups. Money has by and large replaced cattle as a unit of exchange for women. However, the symbolic importance of cattle remains in the form of the ceremony of being made to eat *amasi* (sour milk), which a young bride undergoes as a sign of acceptance into the new family. This is apparently still a widespread practice that takes place at any time from a few months to a few years after entry into the husband's family. The concept of marriage is variable and changing: women I spoke to in the hostels are participants in a variety of unions which they characterise as marriage. In some cases these unions imply the full process of *lobola*, a wedding ceremony in front of a magistrate or priest, the woman being taken to the man's home by her relatives, and final incorporation into the man's family. Variations of the above apply, but in some relationships people simply live together without going through any formal procedures.

Some of the relationships in the hostels can be seen as 'marriages' even if the man has another family in the rural areas. It is also important to distinguish between the obligations of marriage for men and for women. A woman marries into the man's family, whereas the man remains unattached to the woman's family, beyond the responsibilities of *lobola* and occasional economic contributions. Marrying into a family is the mechanism for bringing the woman into a system of control that ensures the perpetuation of patriarchal family relations. She is given a new name to signify the family's expectations of her contribution.[1] In this cultural setting, women are given the responsibility of socialising the new bride into her marital role. This begins the process of control by the mother-in-law and sisters-in-law (*iindodakazi*, literally meaning 'female husbands') over the newly wed woman, with all the rights and privileges that go with the resultant power. The system is guaranteed perpetuation by the psychological and economic benefits that senior women derive from it. This creates divisions between women instead of fostering supportive relationships. The level of intensity of this control varies from household to household, depending on the degree of independence of the new wife's accommodation from that of the rest of the extended family and the nature of the mother–son relationship.

One young woman, a 21-year-old, defied her mother-in-law when she came to Cape Town to join her husband. Her case is not typical, but indicates some of the ambivalences experienced by young couples in terms of parental expectations and control.

Nosakhele arrived in Cape Town in 1984, having been married in 1983. She describes her mother-in-law as an unpleasant person, who drinks a lot. She also feels that her mother-in-law does not approve of her as her son's wife, because she had already set her sights on a former girlfriend of her son as the chosen one.

She struggled to conceive because of her husband's irregular visits to their rural base, and so defiantly went to stay in the hostel, where she became pregnant.

Her husband does not drink alcohol, but smokes cigarettes. She regards him as a stubborn person who listens only to his mother. He has taken to regularly visiting his mother in the rural areas, a departure from his practice in the past. Nosakhele is forbidden by the mother-in-law to accompany him, because she says that the travelling could induce a miscarriage. Nosakhele, however, feels that the real reason for her exclusion is the desire of her mother-in-law to break their marriage.

Unfortunately I could not interview Nosakhele's husband to ascertain his side of the story. It sounds, however, like a case of lack of trust between the various parties. What may be genuine concern by the mother-in-law for the safety of Nosakhele's pregnancy is seen as an excuse by the latter for her exclusion. The man in the middle is likely to be confused by the competing claims over him. It must be difficult for him to choose between his mother and his wife. Two points which are relevant to the understanding of the relationship between mothers-in-law and daughters-in-law are important here. First, the mother-in-law perceives herself as a kingmaker in relation to her son. She derives power out of successfully installing him on a throne as man, husband and father. Part of the purpose of social-

1. Examples of such names are: Nosakhele (the one who is to build the family home), Nobantu (one who will hopefully be 'people-centred') and NoWise (indicating concern by in-laws about those newly weds (*omakoti*) perceived to be potential rebels).

ising the newly married woman into the workings of her adopted family is precisely that installation. Second, there is a real threat posed by the daughter-in-law to the economic benefits the mother was deriving from being the likely sole recipient of remittances from her son. It would apppear that resolution of this economic conflict determines the quality of the relationship between the two women, thus defining to a large extent whether the kingmaker becomes an ally or a hostile competitor.

Although many of the rituals relating to marriage are not carried out in the hostels, attempts are made to maintain respect for the associated customs and obligations within the hostel setting. Older women who may or may not be kin take on the role of supportive in-laws in relation to younger married women. Younger married women, in turn, act with deference towards the 'home-people' of their husbands as if they were their actual in-laws.

Men and their wives. Most of the married women in the hostels oscillate between town and country. They are torn between the responsibilities of looking after the rural 'home', bringing up children and fulfilling wider family responsibilities on one hand, and maintaining a personal relationship with their husbands on the other. In some cases married women are also driven by economic necessity to come to the city to demand support or seek income-generating opportunities.

There is often good reason for maintaining the rural 'home', given the lack of proper housing in urban areas and the undesirability of the hostels for the bringing up of children. It is, however, an issue which creates considerable tension between many young couples. The women often feel that they are left to shoulder the burden of responsibility while their men have the best of the two worlds, and the men think that their wives' insistence on the short-term gratification of living together jeopardises their chances of a better and more secure future.

For those women coming from independent rural households, care for their school-going children during their absence poses a serious problem. Younger children tend to be taken along to town, which explains the high percentage of them in the hostel population. In some cases desperate women even take school-going children with them, thus disrupting their education.

There are some relationships which seem to be functioning well in spite of the constraints of long separations and hostel life, while others are highly unstable or totally dysfunctional. The stability of a relationship appears to be a function of the security of the man's employment, his remittance behaviour, the level of communication with his wife and how well the couple has adjusted to periodic contact. Unstable relationships, on the other hand, are marked by unsatisfactory remittance behaviour, as a result of either employment problems or loss of a sense of responsibility for the family at 'home'. More often than not, such men will have alcohol abuse problems or involvement in long-term extra-marital relationships.

Thuli's marriage collapsed under the burden of separation. She had been married young and had supportive in-laws. Her husband stopped communicating with her after the first few happy years of marriage. In 1972 she was encouraged by her in-laws to come to Cape Town to find him and redeem the relationship.

She discovered that he was living with another woman in Nyanga Hostel and he gave her a cold welcome. She would be left alone while her husband went out with his girlfriend. On many occasions, police came and arrested her for pass offences. Her husband would never pay her fines, and she had to serve prison sentences of up to three months.

She was convinced that her husband's girlfriend had something to do with her arrests. She recalls that on the last occasion she had just come back from prison when the girlfriend came in and said, 'Oh, you again!' Shortly after the girlfriend left, the police came in and arrested her again. She was at that stage five months pregnant and decided that she had to leave Cape Town after her release. She was cautioned and discharged and left immediately for the Transkei and out of the marriage.

Married women who come to the hostels move into either a warm welcoming environment or a cold, indifferent and sometimes openly hostile one where they are seen as intruders by their husbands. Women who are made welcome are likely to visit regularly and stay for as long as they can. Those who are not, however, are likely to come only as a desperate measure to save their families from disintegration or starvation, and they employ various strategies to legitimise their visits. The most common one is the adoption of the sick role by the woman or one of her young children, whom she then accompanies to Cape Town.

There are strong pressures on a man to take responsibility for the care of sick family members. His wife and children are an obligatory responsibility, with rituals and traditional healing ceremonies that simply cannot proceed without the man of the house. In addition, the inequalities in the distribution of health resources between urban and rural areas justify the move to Cape Town for health reasons.

Dlamini used to send money regularly to his family in the Transkei after his arrival in Cape Town in the 1960s. This stopped after 1980, when he also stopped visiting during the December holiday period. When his teenage daughter went to seek him out in 1984, she found him living with another woman, whom she blames for her family problems. This woman treats her well, but she hates and fears her and remains angry. She had come on this visit because she had developed mafufunyane *(possession by evil spirits; see Ngubane, 1977:144) and her mother had sent her so that her father could take responsibility for her treatment. Her condition improved significantly after her arrival in January 1986. She is also frustrated by her mother's inability to confront her father. She feels that her mother's lack of education and her feelings of inadequacy in relation to her father contribute to her unwillingness to deal with this problem decisively.*

She insists that she will not marry until she has a profession, so that she can be free from the type of dependency she perceives her mother to be trapped in. Her mother has instead opted out, and now relies on her eldest son for financial support.

This approach to the problem of an unfaithful husband should be seen in the context of the available choices. The wife could theoretically sue the husband for maintenance, but common sense supported by research[1] indicates that the costs of winning such a case far outweigh the uncertain benefits of such a venture. In addition compliance with court orders is very poor. Another option is divorce, which would require the woman to go back to her natal home. The feasibility of this depends on the willingness and capacity of her family to accept her back and successfully fight off the inevitable demands of her husband's family for the return of bride-wealth. Few women are fortunate enough to get such support from their families. Confrontation with the husband is another option, but that requires more courage than many women can muster. In any case it is a risky operation, because a wife could be thrown out of the hostel by her husband and have to find her own way back to the rural area.

The decision to use illness as a way of reminding a husband of his responsibility is thus often the most practical course. An illness such as *mafufunyane* is ideally suited to such a purpose, as it requires rituals as part of the healing process, and it is obligatory for the father of the affected child to participate. Thus in this case 'tradition' is a useful tool for the woman. Some women, however, choose confrontation. They take the risk and come to town to demand support. In some cases it pays off, but for others it is a struggle that only the very persistent win.

Zoliswa, 39 years old, first came to Cape Town in 1986 to demand support from her errant husband. She has been coming to the hostels two or three times a year to get money from her husband, who is an alcohol abuser and irregular remitter. She sometimes gets assaulted for her troubles, but remains determined.

She has two children, one from a pre-marital relationship, born in 1967, and the other born in 1971 from her marriage. She feels that her husband must be forced to cater for the needs of their son, who is doing well at school in the Transkei. She is tired of living on debts to neighbours to support her family while her husband drinks his money away.

1. Burman and Barry's study showed just how difficult it is for poor women to get sustained maintenance from ex-husbands (1984).

She times her last visit of the year to coincide with bonus month, November, to secure his lump-sum payment. She acknowledges that it is a humiliating exercise, but thinks that it is worth the effort in the end. (See Chapter 4 for another side of her story.)

Older women tend to choose this route when all else has failed. Newly married women feel too vulnerable or insecure to attempt this without risking loss of whatever support they might have from their in-laws or their own parents. Those older women who are prepared to take the risk to renegotiate their relationships often become unstoppable in their ability to utilise all the vulnerabilities in their partners to secure positive outcomes.

Lusanda is a middle-aged woman with a pleasant personality. She comes infrequently to the hostels because she can't stand the filth and lack of privacy. She is satisfied with her family arrangements, in terms of which she is responsible for the rural base. She refers to this base as her 'own palace', where she is fully in control. She does not need to interfere with her husband's life in Cape Town: he can be his own boss in the hostels. She has a big house, her children are at school and progressing well.

Her husband has been working in Cape Town since the early 1960s and is supportive. His greatest weakness, in her opinion, is infidelity. She doesn't make a fuss, but has warned him that should there be any sexually transmitted diseases in the family, he will be held personally responsible. She feels that the AIDS scare has added a new dimension to their discussions on this issue. 'It may well be a blessing in disguise for women,' she says. 'Men are afraid to die, so they may well stop being unfaithful.'

Thoko, another middle-aged woman, had to confront a different dilemma, but seems to have found a strategy which works for her.

Thoko recently married a 60-year-old man after a long widowhood. Her husband lives in the hostel where women are not allowed to sleep overnight. He is in fact the leader of the residents who defend their stand on this issue on the basis of the need to maintain good morals and to prevent conflict between men over women.

She does not seem perturbed by the problems this stand poses for their relationship. They visit friends or relatives in the township whenever they need to spend a night together as a couple. In the hostel she prepares meals for him, washes his clothes and generally attends to his needs.

Her sights are set on a decent house, which she feels is more accessible to her as a married woman than to others. She is prepared to put up with the contradictions of her present domestic arrangements in her quest for this goal.

Heilbrun noted that 'women, when old enough to have done with the business of being women and can let loose their strength, must be the most powerful creatures' (1988:128). Few such women have emerged in the hostels. One of the reasons for this may be the dependence of women on male bedholders for accommodation, which gives men enormous power over women, making it truly a 'man's world'. This power manifests itself in various ways, but it permeates every facet of life. For married women this means that they may only stay in the hostels for as long as their men allow them to do so. Pleasing one's husband has become an essential survival strategy for married women who want to prolong their stay or indeed be allowed to live there permanently. There is of course nothing wrong essentially with pleasing one's spouse, but the equating of subordination with pleasure inhibits personal development and self-respect. Many women adopt a submissive role as a strategy to ensure their stay, especially in those situations where they have come in desperation after a period of neglect and irregular remittances.

This necessary submissiveness results in an inability to question the wisdom of certain decisions taken by the man because, however ill-advised they may seem, this might invite displeasure. For example, the open spaces of the hostels are cluttered with old cars in different states of disrepair, which women refer to as the 'corpses of our men's toys'. There is both despair and amusement in the women's voices. These are second-hand cars, often bought from dubious dealers with hard-earned annual bonuses plus savings, which fail to pass the test of making it beyond Sir Lowry's Pass or Du Toit's Kloof *en route* to the Eastern Cape as a trophy to show off to rural kin and friends. There seems to be a great need by these men to restore their self-image, which is under constant attack in their daily lives. The apparently senseless acquisition of property has been seen as an attempt to ease psychological deprivation in an oppressive class structure.

The demand for unquestioning obedience on the part of women is recognised by both educated and uneducated men as central to the maintenance of patriarchal family relations. One has to be seen as a 'real man' or be laughed at by one's friends and neighbours. There is, however, ingenuity in the apparent powerlessness of many of these women. They are much more likely to get what they want out of marriage if they are seen to possess the 'traditional' female virtues of modesty and deference. They are acutely aware of the fragility of the egos of their men and the need to make their men feel like 'masters in their own domains'. In some cases women have to submit to the humiliation of having sexual relations with their drunken men without adequate attention to a semblance of privacy, such as is afforded by darkness. Women have ambivalent feelings about allowing themselves to play this docile role, but see the risks of not complying as too high to take.

The differing expectations of men and women concerning marital fidelity create another problem. Complete faithfulness on the part of their wives is non-negotiable for the majority of men, irrespective of their own behaviour. In spite of the availability of protection against unwanted pregnancy, many men use the risk of 'having children fathered by the open veld' as the main reason for disapproving of extra-marital relationships for their wives but not for themselves. Some have gone so far as to prohibit their wives from using contraceptives, as a device to control their sexual activities. It seems that these women face a threat to their right to control their own fertility, which is an issue of interest not only to feminists but to all those interested in population growth patterns. Many women do use contraception, the commonest type used being 'the injection' (Depo Provera). Depo Provera is chosen for ease of use, a three-monthly injection, unlike 'the pill' which requires daily dosage.[1] Depo also offers protection from detection for those using contraception against their partners' wishes.

Ironically, it is around the issue of reproduction that the hostel environment presents some of the most interesting aspects of human interaction. One would have thought that, given the lack of privacy, the period around childbirth would be the most difficult for women living in this environment, but in fact they have an overwhelming preference for giving birth at the hostels rather than at their rural homes. Although access to health facilities is a contributory element in this preference, the support women get from their husbands during this period is the deciding factor. In the villages, childbirth is a woman's affair, and ritual prohibitions relegate the father of the child to a minor role.

In the hostels, however, the father is the only person morally obliged to support the mother and child. In addition to sharing the limited bed space with the mother and newborn baby, the man has to ensure that hot water is available for bathing, that breakfast is cooked for the mother and that when the woman is unwell the nappies are washed. This is in stark contrast to the treatment she would be likely to receive from her in-laws, who would be reluctant to 'spoil' her and in some cases would compel her to engage in household duties as early as a day after delivery.

A critical question remains – how do adults make love in the presence of others, and strangers at that? Many hostel dwellers say that they wait for midnight when others are asleep to make love to their partners. But if almost everybody is waiting for midnight, who is fooling whom? Others say that they rely on the partitions between the beds for a semblance of privacy, but these are mostly flimsy curtains or sackcloth. Some admit that one has to grit one's teeth and either pretend to be asleep when others are at it, or feign deafness. One woman said that one has to lower one's sensitivities to survive in this setting. The long-term implications of these lowered sensitivities for self-respect, mutual respect and values central to human decency could be far-reaching (Turnbull, 1974).

1. There are dangers in using Depo Provera which has many side-effects and has been at the centre of controversy between feminists and those dumping Depo on poor women without due regard to its dangers.

One is reminded of the comment of a hostel dweller in Reynolds's study when asked about the indignities of hostel life: 'We are spilt just like water on the ground' (Reynolds, 1984:11).

These dingy hostels are turned into 'castles' by the men, who lord it over their women; the constraints of physical space add considerable intensity to human interaction. The separation of men and women by legal decree, although formally removed, has left a legacy of distorted family relations by limiting space for the development of mutual trust and respect.

Men and single women. Interesting and varied relationships exist between men and single women in the hostels. These are widowed, divorced or never-married women, most of whom have children and have come to Cape Town in search of ways of securing a source of income with which to support their families. Survival is the motivating factor behind their every move. Relationships with men are determined mainly by the need to secure access to accommodation, although other considerations, such as financial support and occasionally affection, play a part. As one woman put it: 'People have boyfriends mainly because they need a place to stay. Some do it for the sake of being supported by these men, but they are a minority. Most people hate the system of *ukuhlalisana* (living together) but they have no choice, because of accommodation problems.'

There is general agreement among both men and women that most of these relationships are characterised by mutual abuse, and that both partners derive whatever benefit they can while they can. The benefit for men is mainly that of having a 'domestic slave' to attend to their laundry, cooking and cleaning, in addition to providing an outlet for pressing sexual needs. Such women are constantly reminded that they are dispensable. 'I know the face of my wife' is a common saying of married men to their girlfriends whenever there is an argument. Single women are also disadvantaged by the stiff competition for supportive males – a scarce resource. This competition limits their ability to bargain for a better deal. They know that there are countless other desperate women waiting to replace them.

There are, however, some ingenious women who take out of life as much as they can. They literally and figuratively jump from bed to bed in search of optimal benefits. Sisi Buli is a case in point.

She was widowed in 1978 with four children, and came to Cape Town in 1982 as a work-seeker. After a short spell as a live-in domestic worker, she was fired because she did not have a proper pass. She then moved to Langa Hostel where her sister was staying with her husband. She used to sleep on the floor on a sponge mattress, between the beds in her brother-in-law's room. She made a living by selling vegetables from a stand outside their hostel. She soon found a boyfriend with whom she moved to another hostel in

Langa. She has a child by this man, but had to move out in 1985 when his wife came to stay with him. She moved next door where she had a relative, and again slept on the floor between beds. She has now secured another boyfriend, a successful shebeen king, and helps him run a 'mobile shop' parked outside their window. Her youngest child is thriving and is the only one of her children who has not suffered from malnutrition. Her views on relationships are very clearly expressed: 'I feel that relationships with men are a matter of convenience. One takes what comes and moves on when the time is right. There is a lot of competition amongst women for men's attentions and, once involved with one, one must ensure that one keeps their attention.'

She is one of many women who have elected to stay single after the end of their marriages. She tried the respectable way of earning an income, as a domestic worker (one of the few avenues open to poor African women), but the ruthlessness of the pass laws of that period put a stop to it. Her story also shows some of the networks in the hostels that enable women to gain entry into this supposedly male preserve. Relatives, acquaintances from 'home' and friends all serve at some stage or other as useful contacts. Men are seen in this context as useful resources, thus making competition inevitable. Manipulation of sexual and reproductive capacities is a major part of the 'survival kit'.

There are, however, others who have 'satisfactory' relationships, which seem to work well for all parties. They live together in relative dignity and encourage each other in fulfilling their respective responsibilities to their rural family bases. One woman involved in such a relationship went as far as to say that her boyfriend's wife is eternally grateful to her for the positive contribution she has made to the stability of their married life. She is employed as a domestic worker and, although she has borne him four children she does not make undue demands on his income.

Relationships among women

These relationships are characterised by competition, notably between married and single women. The former see the latter as potential or current objects of their husbands' attentions and consequently a cause of neglect of family responsibilities. The latter resent the lack of respect which married women tend to display towards them and feel strongly about being blamed unfairly for the irresponsible behaviour of married men. There have been numerous instances of physical fights between women over these issues; in rare instances, these end in death. One such case involved a woman who arrived by bus in the early hours of the morning, having received a tip-off from another woman who had been visiting her own husband. She found her husband's girlfriend asleep in his bed.

He was on night duty. She had come prepared for a showdown and was armed with a knife. In the ensuing struggle the girlfriend got hold of the knife and stabbed the wife to death. Many families have broken down under the stresses of triangular relationships. Such cases are quoted by people who condemn single women as destructive elements in the hostels.

There is also competition among single women for the attentions of potential partners. Attractiveness becomes a matter of survival, and central to a woman's looks is the colour of her skin. Women feel that, even if they run the risk of damaging their skins, it would be suicidal to stop using skin-lightening creams. When the problems of long-term skin damage are mentioned, a typical response is: 'Let that day come when it comes; for now I can't stop and take the risk of losing out. In any case it might happen when I am too old to bother about my looks.' Many of the older women have severe skin damage from this practice. The active ingredient of these skin-lightening creams destroys the upper layer of the skin in the long term (see Hemsworth, 1983). To complicate matters, those so affected tend to use stronger creams with higher concentrations, in the vain hope of reversing the ugly, rough, dark appearance. (The offending chemical is hydroquinone and the creams used with high concentrations are *He-man*, *Super Scotch*, *Ambi for Men*, etc.) Some resort to desperate measures such as using bleach, shoe polish or cortisone cream – but to no avail.

The issue of skin-lightening creams raises two important points. First, it is a product of a racist environment that denigrates anything that is not white. Lightness of skin colour is thus equated with beauty, or alternatively with higher socio-economic status (Biko, 1986:63). It could thus be inferred that Africans are at the bottom of the socio-economic ladder, because of the colour of their skins, which correlates with genetic inferiority. Second, it is a reflection of the sexual objectification of women's bodies, turning them into playthings owned by men.

There are some circumstances in which women support one another. These relate mainly to periods of distress or illness. There is also significant support given to mothers with newborn babies, in the form of warm meals for the mother, washing of nappies and running of small errands. This is by no means a substitute for the father's role during this period, but is seen as being complementary to it. Women also rally to the support of others during periods of grief, sickness of relatives and assault by male partners. With respect to the last-mentioned, support takes the form of alerting other men to restrain the offender. Such cases are said to have decreased significantly over the last five years, due to the heavy penalties meted out to offenders by the disciplinary system of the *izibonda*. According to residents, assault of women resulting in disturbance of the peace is punishable by fines.

There are interesting points raised by the system of discipline and justice. It appears that a man is free to assault his female partner as long as he does not disturb the peace. Some men take their partners to the open veld where they assault them without falling foul of the disciplinary code; only the uninitiated women fall prey to this. Women are tipped off by others to refuse to go out after arguments and, if forced, to threaten to scream. It also shows how women have learned to exploit an instrument of male domination for their own protection. The louder one screams, the greater the chances of other men in the hostel intervening to stop the fight. In the cases of assault, women close ranks and temporarily forget their competitive relationships to ensure protection of the victim.

The apparent inability of women to organise effectively as a group and fight for a better deal is surprising, particularly considering how much time they spend together while most men are at work. Several factors contribute to this. First, one has to recognise the reality of the lines that divide women in this setting, namely age, marital status, length of stay in Cape Town and degree of economic dependence on men (see Cole, 1986). These lines of division are stronger than the ties that bind them by virtue of their common oppression.

Age differences are important dividing lines between women. Senior women, 'who are done with the business of being women', become honorary men controlling younger women, instead of being 'models of deviance' for them (see Ramphele, 1989b).[1] This divide-and-rule strategy, used successfully by oppressive systems, functions successfully in gender relations as well. Second, there is the fear of taking risks, which is a feature of most exploitative and oppressive systems. This fear also undermines the capacity to establish relationships of trust between the oppressed individuals. The establishment of common purpose is further complicated by the atomisation of women in their individual relationships with men. These are very personal, and each man exploits and subordinates in a unique way within the parameters of such relationships. Third, power relationships between individual men and women are more complicated than, for example, those between employers and employees. The individuals concerned are also bound by an emotional bond, which cannot be discounted in drawing battle lines between men and women. Individual men and women have to negotiate the thin line between being 'lovers' in a personal sense and being 'enemies' in the gender power game. Last, the totality of oppression also takes its toll by conditioning the oppressed to actually believe that their best interest is served by acquiescing in the demands of the oppressor (Brittan & Maynard, 1984). The result is that, when women do organise, they do so in ways reinforcing their nurturing roles and not in those promoting their interests as people in their own right.

There are a few women who in many ways transcend the bounds of these power relations. Some do this through playing the men's

1. I use this concept to refer to individuals whose approach to life deviates from the norm in a conformist social system.

game with tongue in cheek while undermining it; others choose defiance. As an example I cite two important stories of women struggling against a powerful system. Their stories are neither typical nor uncommon, but are part of a wide range of possibilities that women grapple with.

Woyisa was born in the Transkei in 1940. Her mother was one of two wives, and the son of the other wife eventually inherited all her father's considerable livestock, a source of ongoing bitterness for her. Her mother died in her childhood, and she had a bad relationship with her half-brother, whom she brands as selfish.

In 1960, having completed Standard 6, she went to work in East London at a textile factory, where she married a man 'for the convenience of having my pass fixed'. To limit future obligations, she refused to have him pay lobola *for her, but elected marriage by Christian rites in an Anglican church, of which she is still a member. She had three children from this marriage, one of whom died; the others are grown up and married.*

She admits that she deliberately fomented problems which ended in her divorce in 1973. She then took her children to her natal home, where a maternal aunt looked after them while she continued to work. She built a home of her own both for her children and to provide an escape route for her younger sister in case of marital problems. She improved her educational qualifications and completed Standard 8 through correspondence studies.

She arrived in Cape Town in 1979, using various cousin bedholders until she set herself up with her present boyfriend. She has a cynical view of men and their tendency to exploit women, and is quite certain that marriage or long-term relationships with men are not an option for her. She sees herself as a 'free spirit'. What matters most to her is her children: 'There is no proper home without a mother to keep the children in check; even when grown up and married, they need a mother's advice and wisdom.' She works at a local textile factory where she is a union shop-floor steward and she proudly relates the battles won and lost and many more that lie ahead. 'The conditions of work are unhealthy – many people are getting brown-lung and asthma' is her parting comment.

It is worth noting that in her thirties this 'free spirit' also defied a divination prescription to heed the call by the ancestors to become a healer. She is also the only woman in my dealings with hostel dwellers who enjoyed the freedom to don full traditional regalia and join in vigorous dancing with all-male impromptu dance groups on festive occasions. Other women said they were too shy to do that. She is obviously a woman who 'is done with the business of being a woman' and has become a 'powerful creature'.

Nomsa is an exceptional woman in a different mould. She embodies all the elements of resilience, but retains an attractive vulnerability.

Nomsa's first arrival in Cape Town was in 1966, having cried and screamed herself hoarse in a car after being abducted from her Transkei village, where she was a 19-year-old school pupil. She was a victim of a forced marriage to a man who was living in one of the hostels. Despite her protests, the marriage was formalised by payment of 'forgiveness money' and lobola *to her parents.*

She then lived with her husband, alternating between a shack in Guguletu and her husband's bed in the hostel. After being an oscillating wife from 1967 to 1975, she insisted that the family joined other people who established Crossroads squatter camp in 1975. She weathered the storms of patriarchal politics of this squatter camp as a member of the women's committee (see Josette Cole's study of Crossroads, 1986).

She finally divorced her husband because of irreconcilable differences, and faced the struggle to support their four children. She suffered a nervous breakdown in the process, but managed to recover with the help of friends and relatives. She was employed for a while as a health worker in Crossroads, in a community development agency. In 1984, she moved into a house in New Crossroads, which is her present home.

She completed the full circle of emancipation by taking up a job with the Hostel Dwellers' Association in 1986, as a health worker with special responsibility for organising women for full participation. She had a chequered career, which ended in her resignation towards the end of 1987, because of fundamental differences with the leaders over their attitude to the role of women. She is now creatively employed elsewhere.

Both these women, like many others in similar situations, have to confront multiple, interrelated problems of power relations: sexism, racism and poverty.

Adults and children

Relationships between adults and children are confined to the local constraints of time and space, but the pattern followed is heavily influenced by 'tradition'. Most children are treated with gentleness and tenderness by both parents during infancy. The sharing of the same bed by all three, which goes against all rules of 'tradition', may perhaps be a facilitating process for the bonding which occurs. The father cannot turn a deaf ear to a crying baby right next to him, whereas it is easy to do so if the newborn and mother are secluded in a different room or hut with other women for support. In this case space constraints are a positive force for transformation of attitudes. This changes at the toddler stage, with increasing demands being made on the child for responsible behaviour and help with domestic chores. The teens and early adulthood bring more demands and less intimacy.

The arrival of siblings tends to break the closeness, particularly between the father and the child, which has then to be relegated to a floor-bed next to the parents' bed. This can result in sibling rivalry, which is ingeniously dealt with by making the older child responsible for the protection of the new arrival against any possible harm – such as the myth of strangers coming to take away unloved babies. The nurturing of the older sibling's sense of responsibility is also an important part of the process of socialising children for later communal responsibilities.

The demonstration of the loving care of parents towards their offspring is inhibited in the hostels. The lack of private space for families also limits their capacity to function as a coherent unit in day-to-day social interaction. Working parents have too little energy left at the end of the day to play with their children or engage them in story-telling to encourage closeness. Women, even those not employed, are also burdened by domestic chores and tend to demand help from their children early on (see also Reynolds, 1989). The greatest difficulty occurs when children are sent back to the rural areas to start school (see also Jones, 1990). Most families (women claim it is their husbands who insist on this) opt for the woman to live in the rural area to keep the home warm for the children. Others ask a relative to look after the children, with the promise of regular remittance (see Reynolds, 1984). Such children tend to come into the hostels as visitors during school holidays or see their parents during their annual visits home.

Children are not granted automatic right to the limited physical space available. They are in the same category as women when scarce resources are allocated, and have to wait until the men have finished (see Sidel, 1986). There is thus greater warmth and closeness with mothers than with fathers as children grow older, particularly when the mother spends more time in the rural areas than in the hostels (see Reynolds, 1984:16–18). The father becomes more estranged and his presence is sometimes resented, coming as it often does with the tightening of discipline.

This does not mean, however, that fathers lose their traditional importance in the lives of their children. I would suggest that circumcision as a ritual not only perpetuates patriarchy, but in some way it symbolically and violently severs the bond between mother and son, and re-establishes the father as the central figure in a young man's life in spite of earlier physical separation. Even children born out of wedlock seek out their biological fathers or their paternal relatives to perform this ritual successfully. Other rituals, such as *imbeleko*, performed earlier in childhood, strengthen the paternal bond. *Imbeleko* is a ritual performed widely in both the urban and rural areas, any time between birth and teenage years, to introduce the child to its ancestors. A goat is slaughtered and the child is made to eat a selected piece, before others can partake of the festivities.

Children negotiate the difficult terrain of the hostel environment using different strategies at different stages of their development. The very young have recourse to tantrums, pestering, ridicule and adoption of the sick role. Older children tend to vacillate between acquiescence and resistance, sometimes using exaggerated humility to get their way.

Young children's games are both a reflection of their interpretation of their environment and a strategy for coping with it. Impersonation of adults takes the form of 'mother–father' games with appropriate gender role play as these roles are perceived in the hostels. Children also poke fun at adult drunken ways, the quarrels, the harsh punishment of kids and so on, using the same medium of play. There is a lot of improvisation, because of lack of toys. Bottles, bottle-tops, stones, rags and tins, all find their uses in games.

There is sometimes an overbearing, patronising, authoritarian attitude towards children, particularly from men, who seem to assume authority over any child they encounter. On one occasion, I witnessed a man chasing children around with a whip to punish them for alleged disturbance of his chickens, which are kept in a makeshift fowl-run under a flight of stairs. However, I have found no evidence of the high level of violence against children reported by Jones in his Lwandle hostel study (Jones, 1990:213–36). Children are subjected to corporal punishment regularly, but in the form of a spanking or smack, rather than the frenzied attacks by angry adults reported by Jones. On the whole, however, children are valued by hostel dwellers. They are loved for what they are – a joy to their parents.

It is also important to note the high value placed on children as a sign of virility for men and fertility for women. Parents need children to feel whole as people, and their status in society is also enhanced by having offspring. The pressures on infertile couples (infertility is usually interpreted as the fault of the woman) are enormous. This is partly due to the fact that children are also perceived as a resource by the poor, who have little prospect of owning much else; adults see children as an insurance policy for their old age or in the event of disability (see Wilson & Ramphele, 1989:63–9). People go to great expense to seek relief for infertility, but adoption is not seen as an option. The response to direct questions relating to the reasons for this resistance to adoption tends to be: 'How can I deal with a child whose lineage I know nothing about? It is alien blood that can only bring problems.' Childless marriages rarely survive, but where they do, the couples adopt children of relatives. Women submit to the pressure of being blamed for infertility and in some cases actually accept responsibility for childlessness.

Relationships between hostel dwellers and outsiders

Relations with informal settlement residents

The relationship between hostel dwellers and residents of informal settlements seems to be ambivalent for several reasons. Many former hostel dwellers have moved out into informal settlement areas such as Crossroads in search of privacy and physical space for their families (see Josette Cole, 1986). Some people who have been disillusioned with the failure of hostels to be upgraded into family housing have moved out into these areas, and they are seen as deserters from the cause by members of the HDA. Others hedge their bets and own a shack in one of these areas, while retaining a bed in the hostels.

There are also strong kinship and 'home-boy' ties between the two residential communities. These are strengthened by perceived discriminatory practices on the part of township residents – 'the common enemy'. Hostel dwellers and informal settlement residents are both looked down upon as *amagoduka*, and share the feeling of being treated as outsiders. They also feel that they are not fully consulted and included in existing political and organisational structures dominated by township residents. The ties between residents of informal settlements and hostels are, however, weakened by competition for land, which is a scarce resource.

Relations with township residents

These are problematic, to say the least. The problems are long standing and reflect the difficulty of dismantling relations based on apartheid legislation, which defined hostel dwellers as 'outsiders' and township dwellers as 'insiders' (see also Wilson & Mafeje, 1973). The resultant divisions have been consistently exploited by those in authority, especially the security forces, who encouraged the actions of vigilantes (popularly known as *witdoeke* from the white cloth they wear as headgear for identification during battles) from the ranks of 'outsiders', such as happened in 1976 and 1977 in Langa and Nyanga. Further possibilities of vigilante action by hostel dwellers were forestalled by the formation of the HDA.

Conflict also centres around scarce resources, for example leisure facilities, but it is over land that most bitterness has arisen. This is likely to escalate in the future. Township residents seem to feel that they are more entitled to housing to relieve the overcrowding they experience, even if this is done at the expense of hostel dwellers.

Commercial activity is another source of tension between hostel dwellers and township residents. All the shops and most of the mobile ones (trucks fitted with shelves and stocked with goods, parked at various vantage points near the hostels) are owned by township residents. There are complaints about inflated prices of goods sold to hostel dwellers, as well as unfair competition with hostel dwellers who would otherwise benefit from such trade. The most serious accusation relates to the running of shebeens by township residents, which are said to promote excessive alcohol usage. Shebeens are seen as undermining both the health status of hostel dwellers and their social fabric.

Although it could be argued that there is no reason to prefer hostel dwellers' claims to relief over those of township dwellers, there are several distinctions between the situations of the two segments of this poor population that should be made. First, although the physical overcrowding of sleeping accommodation may not be different in terms of the ratio of people to rooms, township residents are likely to be sharing these limited facilities with kin and friends rather than total strangers. Second, hostels are institutions and not homes. There is no sense of ownership, or hope of such ownership in the future. Township residents have recently been given the option to buy and own their dwellings, however humble these may be. The motivation to keep dwellings clean and tidy also contrasts with that pertaining to the hostel situation, where people feel no attachment to the impersonal space. Even shack dwellers have been noted for the care with which they decorate their humble dwellings with colourful magazines and trimmed newspaper linings. All this contributes to a positive self-image.

Hostel dwellers have developed various coping strategies to protect their self-respect, ranging from manner of dress to language usage and apparent aloofness. It is remarkable to see just how meticulously some of these men and women dress, even for casual shopping outings: the struggle to affirm their humanity in the face of constant assault is unceasing. The issue of language is also an important one. Hostel dwellers, faced with a world where English is the dominant language of political[1] and other social discourse, display a remarkable facility to learn some of the common phrases.

Some of the hostel dwellers have completely 'liberated' the English language from its rules of grammar and happily converse in 'English through the medium of Xhosa'. One outcome of this 'liberation' is in the field of interpersonal etiquette. Hostel dwellers often introduce themselves as 'Mr So-and-so', in settings which are totally inappropriate to such a formality. This manner of introduction usually embarrasses everyone involved, except the beaming 'Mr So-and-so'. It is a way, I suppose, of saying to a world which does not seem to care: 'I am.'

Aloofness, easily mistaken by outsiders for apathy or lack of understanding, is also an effective defence mechanism. People learn to keep their opinions to themselves, unless assured that they are valued. Steamrolling proceedings, as so commonly happens in 'community meetings', end up being rewarded by silent resistance (see also Havel, 1985). Silence becomes a form of power to resist domination.

1. This applies even in meetings held in predominantly African areas or where the audience is predominantly African and poorly educated. It seems to escape political activists that the essence of political organisation lies in effective communication.

Conclusion

Social relations within hostels are characterised by tensions at every level. These tensions contain opportunities for creative transformation, as well as the danger of defensive rigidity. There is tension between the formal regulations defining hostels as a 'man's world' and the reality of the presence of women and children within the hostel environment. There is ambivalence on the part of men in relation to this 'intrusion', reflected in the persistence of exclusive control structures. Some men seem to have adapted too well to living in single-sex hostels and find change difficult to cope with.

There is constant tension between the 'ideal' and the real in all aspects of social relations. 'Traditional' parenting patterns, marital relationships, gender roles and adult–child relations are under constant attack by the combination of space constraints and the challenges of changing times. 'The ideal' is appealed to, to provide some semblance of continuity and security for those threatened by change. The need to defend oneself against the constant assault on human dignity in this situation provides added impetus to idealising the past, 'the home base' and 'Xhosa tradition'.

The difference in standards of accommodation from hostel to hostel creates tensions among residents. This differing quality in hostels also presents interesting opportunities for the operation of a system of privilege and competitive relations, which acts as an additional control mechanism by those in authority (Goffman, 1961:61). For example, those living in the Special Quarters and Old Flats see themselves as better off than those in the other hostels, making the forging of unity and the adoption of common strategies against the hostel system difficult.

There are also tensions throughout the system itself. The inherent contradictions within the migrant labour system make hostels permeable to influences from outside, thus frustrating the creation of truly isolated 'total institutions'. But hostels as living spaces are a type of environment which not only represent an assault on human dignity, but have created a legacy that South Africans have yet to come to terms with.

Washing in the front room

Vuyisani in his room, No. 29

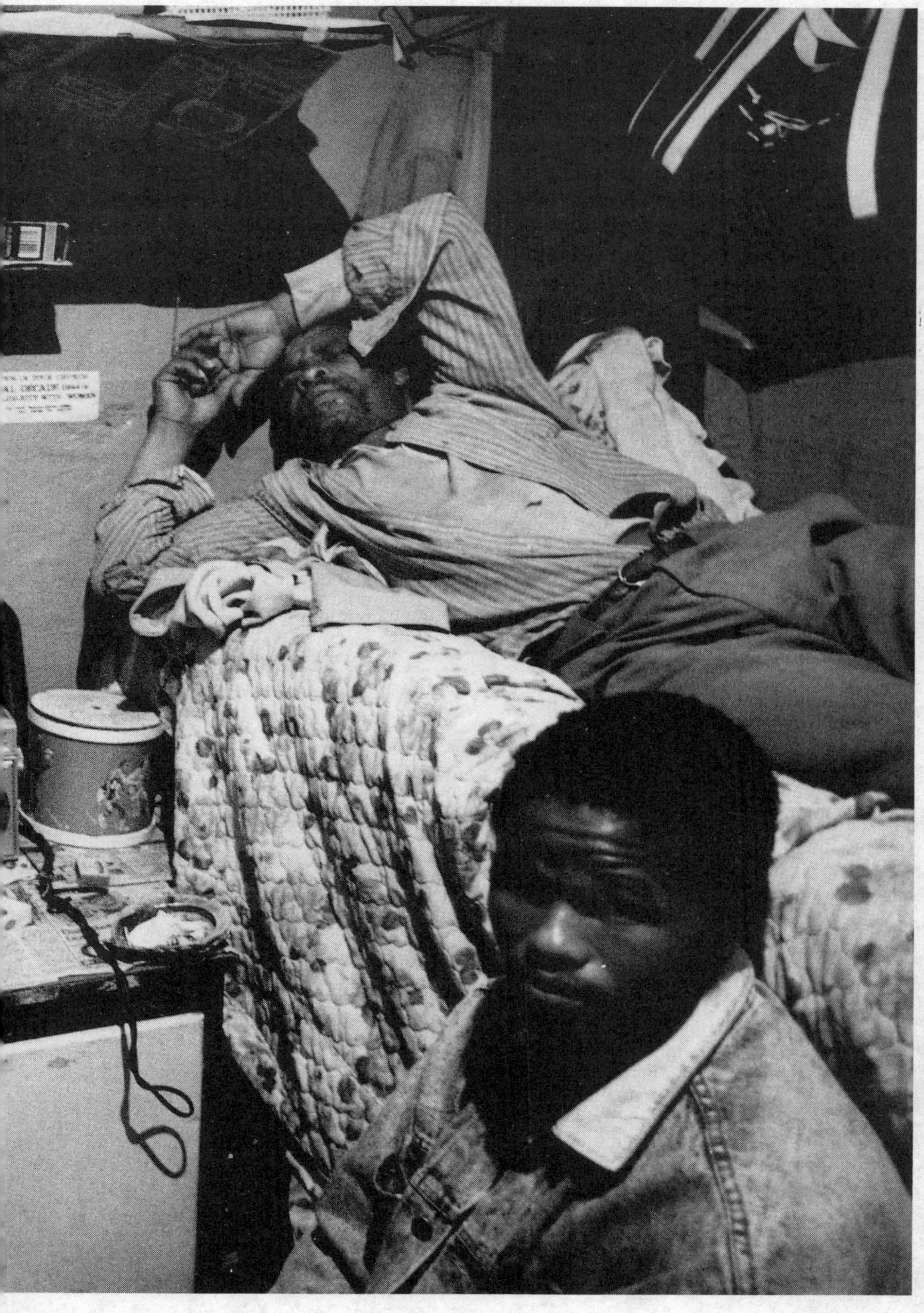

Showering in the Southey Painters' Hostel

Shebeen

7 The Hostel Dwellers' Association

The poor are often inconspicuous, inarticulate and unorganised. Their voices may not be heard at public meetings in communities where it is customary for only the big men to put their views (Paul Devitt quoted in Chambers, 1983:18).

Historical background

The HDA is a direct outcome of the Ministry to Migrant Workers project of the Cape Town diocese of the Church of the Province of South Africa (CPSA). The purpose of this ministry, which was headed by Father David Russell from 1976 to 1986, was to provide pastoral ministry to individuals, building a spirit of self-reliance in tackling needs, solving problems and healing the wounds caused by the migrant labour system (Russell, 1984). An additional incentive for the formation of the HDA was to prevent a repetition of the events of December 1976, when hostel dwellers were allegedly used by government security forces to attack township residents. This attack was directed at the youth who were locked in a struggle against the Bantu Education system. The episode had echoes in other parts of South Africa, and was seen as a strategy by the government, which manipulated existing divisions between various categories of Africans to fan the fires of conflict, using vigilante groups (see also Josette Cole, 1986).

The idea of forming an association was discussed with men in the Nyanga Hostel. These discussions were given further impetus in 1981 by the threat posed by the decision of the local authority to grant a permit to a township resident to convert a disused ablution block in Nyanga Hostel into a dry-cleaning depot. This decision, taken without reference to those affected, was seen as further evidence of disregard by the local authority of hostel dwellers' needs. The successful challenge to this decision, launched by a group of individuals from Nyanga Hostel, encouraged them to work for greater unity among hostel dwellers.

Launching the HDA

The Western Cape Men's Hostel Association was formed in 1983 with the goal of working for the general welfare of all who reside in the hostels. It was formally launched on 1 June 1985 in the Presbyterian church in Nyanga. There were an estimated thousand hostel dwellers at this occasion, but not all were signed-up members (*Grassroots*, July 1985).

The HDA set itself the following aims in its constitution:

- To seek the recognition of the God-given right of people to live with their families near their places of work.
- To campaign for the provision of family housing and special married quarters.

– To work for full residence and employment rights and an end to the present contract system.

– To work for the upgrading of facilities and amenities.

– To encourage and provide opportunities for adult education and cultural activities.

The task of organising previously unorganised people was not easy, and there was a long delay between formation of the HDA in 1983 and its official launching in 1985. Hostel dwellers had many questions for the founder members of the Association. What impact did the organisers think they would have on a system which had been in place for so long? How did they think they could effectively challenge the white power structure which had benefited from the exploitation of black labour? Why should hostel dwellers be expected to take the risks entailed in trusting the organisers and fellow residents? Why should one run the risk of arrest for 'meddling in politics' when there was so much to lose? Was it not better to bury oneself in the task of maintaining a job and providing for one's family? Had not previous attempts to organise black people been unsuccessful?

It took long, repeated discussions with individuals by founder members to convince a significant number of hostel dwellers that it was worth taking risks to organise themselves. The organiser of the HDA recalled how they used to go from 'door' to 'door' talking to people until late at night to convince them of the importance of this idea. He also indicated that sometimes 'it was like ploughing a field and planting good seed and the evil one coming afterwards to undo all the hard work'. The 'evil one', according to him and his colleagues, was represented by people connected with community councils, or town councils (local authorities in the townships) as they are now referred to, who perceived the formation of the HDA as a threat to their interests.

Among the early 'converts' were people who belonged to trade unions. The HDA was marketed to them as a trade union dealing with issues off the factory floor relating to living conditions. They could understand the logic of this, and had experienced the benefits of unity in action in the work-place. Among the many failures of the recruiting campaign is Mzo, a resident of New Flats.

Mzo, a man in his forties, has never been a member of any organisation. He claims that he has, however, been a keen observer of attempts by others to organise around a variety of issues, including trade unions. He recalls cases of failed efforts, betrayal of trust and self-interest of leaders in supporting his claim that organisations amongst abantu bethu *(our people) do not work. He perceives organisations as being more trouble than they are worth. He is unlikely to belong to any organisation in the future.*

Most hostel dwellers negatively disposed to organisational involvement cite the quality of leadership as the most serious weakness of organisations they know of. Most feel that leaders of community organisations are all the same, hiding their real intentions of feathering their own nests under the pretence of working for the common good.

Membership

Membership increased slowly from an initial Nyanga base to include growing numbers from Langa and Guguletu. In 1984 the drive for membership extended to Lwandle in Somerset West and Umfuleni in Kuils River. By 1987 hostels in the Brackenfell area near Paarl were also included in the structures of the HDA. The pattern of growth in membership differed from area to area, but seems to have been inversely related to the quality of accommodation available to hostel dwellers. There seems to be a lower proportion of people from better-off areas such as Special Quarters and Old Flats in Langa in the ranks of the HDA. The participation rate of those living in employer-built hostels is also low.

Several reasons are advanced by the HDA for this pattern. They claim that people in better-off accommodation do not feel the pinch of dehumanisation to the same extent as the rest of the hostel dwellers. Most of these people have lived in Cape Town for a long time, and this seems to have enabled them to devise their own strategies for survival independent of organisations, making it less worthwhile for them to take the risks inherent in organisational allegiances. There is also a stronger presence of community council representatives in the Old Flats in particular, who actively worked against the HDA, which they saw as a competitor in constituency politics. There are some additional factors related to the low level of membership in some hostels. The occupants of the Old Flats and Special Quarters, given their relatively long periods of residence in Cape Town and connections with other social networks, are much more sophisticated than newly arrived hostel dwellers. They are also more cynical of claims of solutions to problems they see as intractable, and thus require more in-depth canvassing than was offered by the HDA operatives.

Some residents of Special Quarters have expressed irritation with what they perceive as childish boasting by some HDA officials about access to unlimited funds and good political connections. There is also a measure of impatience bordering on arrogance on the part of some officials of the HDA in their dealings with hostel dwellers perceived by them to be uncooperative. A specific example of this occurred when a watchman at the entrance of an employer hostel would not let my research team into the premises. This refusal was understandable given his brief, but the HDA official showed little tolerance for such hesitancy. His parting words to the watchman were,

'You are your own oppressor', to which the watchman retorted, 'I won't risk my job for someone I don't even know.' While the frustration of the HDA official is understandable, one cannot expect people to respond to requests such as these without proper prior consultation. Finally, a significant proportion of the hostel residents I spoke to had never heard of or been approached by the HDA.

The HDA executive's claim to a membership of 10 000 in 1988 is difficult to verify directly, as inadequate records were kept by both the regional office and the branches, and existing records were lost in fires which destroyed their Nyanga and Langa offices in 1988 and 1989. It would seem, however, that this estimate is not unrealistic (Ramphele, 1991:360).

The HDA started as a 'men's hostel association' and retained this exclusive male membership up to the 1986 annual conference. The presence of women in the hostels was unacknowledged even by hostel dwellers themselves; they were seen as 'illegitimate', and thus not taken seriously into consideration. It was also a matter of custom that men worked together to solve problems without due reference to women. One executive member put it bluntly: 'We are still fighting to live with our women legitimately, they cannot be involved in that fight.' Furthermore, it was argued by male residents that having women in the HDA would complicate men-to-men relationships because of jealousy and other factors. 'How would one explain to a man why his wife was kept busy in a meeting until late at night?' was a typical question. There were also practical problems relating to the need for women to prepare meals in the evenings when most meetings took place.

It became increasingly difficult, however, for the HDA to retain the loyalty of its membership in the face of opportunities for family housing opening up in Khayelitsha after 1985. The influence women exerted on their men in the 'privacy' of their conversations as couples was a significant factor in this declining loyalty. The organiser of the HDA argued for the opening up of membership to women thus: 'If a car does not have women as passengers, it runs the risk of being stuck – women have their own way of putting a spanner in the works.' This was an acknowledgement of the power of women to influence processes from which they are formally excluded.

The HDA structure

The HDA has a regional structure, comprising hostels in the Western Cape, which in turn have local branches. These have executive committees elected on a 'door to door' basis. Each 'door' elects a representative, who in some cases is the same person elected as an *isibonda*. Separate women's committees exist in various areas and are subordinate to the men's committees, which are part of the main HDA structure. Delegates are elected from various local branches to the regional conference *(inkonfa)*, which sits once a year, although emergency conferences can be requested when the need arises. The regional executive is elected at the annual conference, and consists of a chairman, vice-chairman, secretary, assistant secretary, organiser and publicity secretary, treasurer and four additional members. The first executive was elected at the launching conference. With one or two exceptions, all members of that first executive have been re-elected to the same positions to date (see Thomas, 1987). All members of this executive are male, with the exception of two women who were elected as additional members in 1989.

Policy and administrative functions are the prerogative of the regional executive, which operates under a mandate from the annual and emergency regional membership conferences. The HDA also employs staff to carry out its various activities. The publicity secretary–organiser heads the staff of the HDA and acts as its chief executive officer. A clerical staff member assists the chief executive officer with his duties. An assistant organiser has been employed since 1988, and he is also the vice-chairman of the HDA.

Projects of the HDA

In pursuance of its goals as set out in the constitution, the HDA has undertaken several projects, which are funded by various agencies such as the Australian, British and Canadian embassies, international trade union groups, church organisations locally and abroad, and some American philanthropic foundations.

The health project

Hostel dwellers are acutely aware of the relationship between their living conditions and their health status, and are conscious that existing health services are not responding to their needs. In some cases individuals claim that they are discriminated against at the Day Hospitals in the townships, because they are seen as 'outsiders' by the urban-based health workers.

These factors motivated the HDA to work for the establishment of an alternative health service appropriate to the needs of their constituency. The original idea was to have a mobile clinic, run by a doctor, servicing all the areas where they had members. The insistence on a doctor was partly motivated by wanting 'the best' for themselves, given their perception of always being treated as inferior beings. Hostel dwellers wanted to demonstrate to their detractors that they could also have 'their own doctor'. There was a lack of confidence that a mobile clinic run by a nursing-sister could be an effective alternative to existing services. Attempts by the organiser to enlist the support of 'progressive medical doctors' to run this scheme were unsuccessful.

The final product, a mobile clinic run by a nursing-sister assisted by community health workers selected by hostel dwellers from among themselves, was accepted under protest. Finally, people were convinced that they should at least try out the proposed model. They were also encouraged by the example of the SACLA[1] Clinic community health project in New Crossroads and Khayelitsha. Criteria for selection for the role of community health worker were availability for voluntary work, literacy and an ability to work with people and to deal sympathetically with those in need. Training for community workers was undertaken using various existing resource groups. The Health Care Trust ran an unsuccessful course. The major problem was language, as the trainer could not speak Xhosa, nor could the participants understand English sufficiently to follow the course. Subsequent training with the help of the Red Cross was more successful.

The community workers were expected to devote two to three hours a day doing 'door to door' calls, assessing needs and advising individuals to adopt better health-promoting life-styles. The question of promoting cleanliness and improving the general appearance of hostels was also seen as a necessary adjunct to any health-promotion exercise. In this regard the problem of bedridden people was raised as a major one for people sharing limited physical space. It was suggested that such people should be identified and be referred to the geriatric services for consideration for old-age home facilities such as those in Langa or Nyanga.

The mobile clinic was launched in September 1986. A panel van was converted into a reasonable mobile consulting room and dispensing facility. The clinic moved from area to area for each day of the week to cover Langa, Guguletu, Nyanga, Umfuleni and Lwandle, serving a population of approximately 75 000 people. Most of the activities centred around treatment of minor ailments, referrals to existing services for those needing further attention, home visits by the nursing-sister to follow up problems identified by community health workers, and health education for those attending the clinic. The last-mentioned mainly concerned immunisation of under-fives, the need for family planning and promotion of a healthier life-style within the limitations of hostel life.

The service was discontinued in 1988 in Umfuleni and Lwandle, following the institution of adequate clinic services in these areas by the relevant local authorities. The referral system was expanded during 1988 to include other Day Hospitals and doctors. The evaluation of the service by hostel dwellers ranged from very positive to negative. Benefits derived were listed as greater access to existing services, greater confidence by hostel dwellers in campaigning for services, greater understanding of disease causation and prevention, and higher motivation for cleaner environments in some areas. Complaints against the service related mainly to the lack of a doctor

1. The South African Christian Leadership Association (SACLA) was started as a Christian response to the problems of young people who wanted to serve their country in ways other than national military service. Dr Ivan Toms was the leading figure in this venture. SACLA runs a comprehensive community health project in New Crossroads and Khayelitsha,,which acts as part of the primary health care service on the Cape Flats.

and inadequate curative services, particularly the limited prescription of injections, which many callers associated with more effective treatment. There were also complaints about the attitude of the staff, who tended to be seen as outsiders who did not understand their patients' particular problems. The nursing-sister reported various problems, such as the poor quality of care provided by the community health workers (whose numbers and enthusiasm declined due to poor initial selection and inadequate pay) and confusion over the scope of the services provided.

The low attendance figures and the complaints against the quality of care offered by the mobile clinic were seen by the nursing-sister as a sign of rejection. She felt that there were two main reasons for this: the service was seen as being too expensive for the benefits it offered, and the diminishing attendance figures indicated that the need for the service no longer existed. Some patients told her that they preferred to go to private general practitioners in the city areas. Attractions of general practitioners included readily available injections, the idea of being seen by a real doctor, and the opportunity to shop in town. A significant number of the women in the hostels come to Cape Town from their rural bases for what they perceive as superior health-care services in the urban setting, and using a clinic similar to their local rural services would not make sense to them. Furthermore, illness episodes provide legitimisation for a city trip for some women whose husbands would not be amenable to financing a window-shopping exercise. A final decision was taken at a regional executive committee meeting on 8 February 1990 to close down this project and concentrate on others that were more successful.

The child-care project

This was started in September 1988 to provide emotional and intellectual stimulation for children in the hostels. It also provided an opportunity for giving them one wholesome meal per day (high-protein soup, bread with peanut butter, and milk). The project was initiated with the support of the mobile clinic staff, but supported by outside agencies such as Operation Hunger, which provided food, and individual church groups, which donated old toys, mattresses and some cash. The staff consists of community pre-school motivators assisted by unpaid female volunteer child-minders in the various areas. Child-minders run play-groups for children ranging from 2 to 10 years. Parents are requested to pay a fee of R5 per month as a contribution to running costs, but no child is supposed to be turned away if unable to pay. Child-minders get some irregular 'thank you' money out of these contributions.

There are many problems with the existing child-care project. The lack of proper facilities, for example, becomes unbearable in the rainy season when outdoor play is impossible and the limitations of physical space become acute. It is difficult for women to volunteer to be child-minders without regular payment. It seems that most of these women 'volunteer' for as long as they have no alternative job options, but leave as soon as they get jobs. This makes continuity and training difficult.

There is at present no senior trained person who has a vision and could guide the project meaningfully and solicit more support for it. The qualities required for such a position are not readily available in the hostels, given limited intellectual and psychological space. This becomes problematic in view of the muted resistance by hostel dwellers to outsiders being employed in such jobs. The ideal of community participation at this level is difficult to realise.

It is also difficult to secure active participation of parents in meetings relating to the project, and in contributing regularly to its upkeep. Many parents see educare as 'child's play' and do not understand why they should involve themselves in such a trivial matter. After all, children's play has never been the concern of parents, particularly fathers, and it has always been a free activity. Why should they pay for the privilege of their children playing with others? The lack of exposure to pre-school educational services and the benefits they offer lies at the heart of this attitude. The limited horizons of parents and the failure of those in authority to provide creative facilities for those living in impoverished environments have implications for the further constraints on the development of poor children's intellectual space.

The advice office project

The provision of advice relating to a wide range of issues became one of the important draw-cards of the HDA. Individuals call during office hours at the HDA offices in Langa with queries concerning unemployment benefits, compensation payments, unfair dismissals, pension fund payments, sick benefits and so on. People seem to be broadly satisfied with the quality of service, and many have been able to resolve problems they had found daunting.

Mr Somo had been unemployed for three months and was entitled to benefits, which he had applied for. After six months of not hearing from the UIF[1] *office and struggling to make ends meet, he approached the HDA office. He was at that stage not a member, but his problem was attended to. A couple of phone calls to the UIF offices uncovered the reason for the inordinate delay. The cheques had been posted months before, but had got 'lost' in the postal system. He was issued with a new cheque by the UIF office covering all his benefits, while investigations proceeded. Finally, it was discovered that a post office employee in the township had been fraudulently cashing cheques from both UIF and some pension funds to line his own pockets. The employee was arrested. The grateful worker has since become a member of the HDA.*

1. The Unemployment Insurance Fund is a government-supported scheme to provide insurance against unemployment, sickness and maternity leave needs for workers. Employees and employers make monthly contributions to the fund.

Many hostel dwellers have had similar gratifying experiences, although not all problems are satisfactorily resolved. It seems that the important function of the advice office has been to provide a sympathetic ear for people in distress, who often do not have anyone to turn to or any idea of how to deal with bureaucracy.

Towards the end of 1989 the advice office began to deal with an increasing number of complaints relating to employers threatening to close down hostels under their jurisdiction. The reason advanced by employers was that their obligation to provide accommodation for their workers had fallen away with the abolition of influx control. The HDA's strategy has been to remind employers of their moral obligation to ensure a smooth transition from hostel accommodation to individual housing. It has been impressed upon them that they cannot simply walk away from the problem after years of benefiting from the labour of hostel dwellers. Negotiations are in progress in this regard.

The upgrading project

In pursuance of the aim of the HDA to fight for the rights of hostel dwellers to live with their families, the Western Cape Hostel Upgrading Trust (or the Trust) was formed in 1987. Its main purpose was to investigate, plan and undertake all activities aimed at the conversion of hostels into family housing. Members of the board of trustees include architects, lawyers, urban planners, community members from the hostels, and one township resident. Members are expected to make specific contributions towards the project, related to their fields of expertise. Community members represent wider interests to ensure some community participation at all levels. The Trust utilised the services of the Urban Planning Research Unit (UPRU) at the University of Cape Town and the Urban Foundation to help with negotiations with the local authorities for land and transfer of title to the hostels to the Trust.

These negotiations were bogged down in 1985 and 1986 by the irreconcilable positions of the HDA and the Western Cape Administration Board. The bone of contention was the inclusion of community councillors in deliberations. The HDA saw it as politically suicidal for it to be seen by township residents to be negotiating with these discredited officials. The Western Cape Administration Board, on the other hand, saw this as an opportunity to urge the legitimacy of community councillors on hostel dwellers, whom they perceived as desperate enough about land acquisition to compromise. It was an interesting case of material versus political survival and an example of the dilemma faced by poor people in being pressurised to negotiate with authorities perceived by political activists as illegitimate, in order to gain access to what they are entitled to as citizens.

In the political climate of the mid-1980s no self-respecting community organisation would have dared to enter into deals with the hated community council system, for fear of incurring the wrath of political activists. Yet the reality of the control over allocation of land by these community councillors could not be denied. The authorities were hoping to squeeze the limited physical, intellectual and socio-economic space of hostel dwellers to make a breakthrough in legitimising their own system. To their credit, the HDA held firm. In the changed political climate of the early 1990s negotiations have become easier and the authorities less insistent on enforcing the authority of community councillors. Political space has opened up and the problem has become less acute.

The Trust set itself the task of effecting conversion of hostels into family units for the benefit of all hostel dwellers, regardless of HDA membership. It has also undertaken to find cheap finance for this to ensure benefit to all members of this population. The Trust made some progress during the course of 1988 and 1989, securing two council-built hostels for a pilot project. The pilot scheme will be used to test some of the important elements of the upgrading project, such as the question of community participation and the issue of affordability of units. A delicate balance will have to be found between public and private space, given limited land availability in the townships and the need to improve the dismal conditions. Techniques to enhance the quality of communal space will be experimented with to get the maximum benefit out of the limited resources available. The Trust hopes that this pilot scheme marks the beginning of the process of phasing out at least the physical aspects of the dehumanising hostel system.

At first little progress was achieved due to lack of commitment from government and the private sector to finance the upgrading process. In June 1992, however, the authorities made R11 million available for the upgrading of hostels in the Western Cape, so it is to be hoped that the situation will soon be improved. The extent to which the legacy of limited space will be undone by this upgrading process remains to be seen. Will the removal of the 'scaffolding'[1] of apartheid lead to a change in the shape of social relations? Existing land allocated to townships is in great demand and the potential for conflict is real. The opening up of political space alone will not be sufficient to redress the inequalities of the past. A more integrated process of transformation is required.

Political activities of the HDA

The HDA has established close contacts with local civic, trade union and 'progressive' political organisations over the years. It has also adopted the rhetoric associated with popular mass-based political groupings in South Africa, and is an affiliate of COSATU.

This political positioning has important implications for the HDA. It gives it a certain credibility as an organisation, which is vital both for fund-raising purposes and for the legitimacy of claims for its

1. Wilson and Ramphele ask the same question in relation to the wider South African poverty problem: Will the abolition of material poverty undo the spiritual and moral deprivation of the past (Wilson & Ramphele, 1989:310)?

constituency in an environment of scarce resources. It has undercut any attempt by the government security forces to use hostel dwellers as vigilantes against local township activists, as has allegedly been the case elsewhere in the country, especially in the PWV area over the last few years. It has also enabled the HDA to ensure that its claims to redress the legacy of the past will not be lightly dismissed or ignored by a future government.

A final point of interest with regard to the HDA's political position is the rhetoric of a commitment to a non-racial and democratic South Africa. Symbols of the HDA are important statements of its political stance, and it has flags for major meetings and campaigns. The main feature of these flags is the depiction of the separation of families, with a bus in which the man sits and waves to his sad wife carrying a baby on her back. The bottom of the flag proclaims 'Away with Apartheid!' Other symbols are T-shirts with slogans such as 'Unite Families, Away with Apartheid'. Posters, newspaper cuttings and other media are used extensively in the HDA offices to declare the organisation's political stance on a number of issues.

A critical appraisal of the HDA

An evaluation of the performance of an organisation such as the HDA has to be done within the framework of its own set goals as well as in relation to similar organisations operating in similar circumstances. The first condition is not difficult to meet, but the second is problematic, as there are no comparable hostel dwellers' associations. Hostel dwellers in other areas, particularly on the mines, are increasingly using their trade unions to take on housing as an area of focus.[1]

General appraisal

The HDA has done remarkably well, given the constraints under which it has operated. The attainment of the goals it set for itself, namely the right to family life, the end of the contract system and acceptance of the right of hostel dwellers to permanent urban residential rights, cannot however be directly attributed to the efforts of the HDA. These victories are the result of a complex process involving local, national and international campaigns. The HDA effort was a small but important part in this process. The right to family life is no more in dispute. The 1986 repeal of the pass laws and the relaxation of influx control have had a positive impact on the self-image and feeling of belonging of hostel dwellers.

The issues of upgrading hostels into family units and the provision of recreational facilities are being addressed by the Trust. Not much can be done to enhance the cultural and leisure activities of hostel dwellers without a significant change to the quantity and quality of physical space available to them. Lack of basic amenities hinders hostel dwellers from changing their life-style into a

1. COSATU has a housing committee which co-ordinates issues arising out of workers' concerns in this area and includes them in negotiations with management.

healthier and more creative one. They seem to have grown tired of improvising. The creativity and ingenuity found among hostel dwellers in Langa during the 1960s (Wilson & Mafeje, 1973) seems to have run out of steam. Most of their energy seems to be focused on survival. There are, however, various intangible aspects to the HDA, which bear closer examination. These relate to its public image both inside and outside the hostels, the level of community participation and its leadership style.

Public image

A carefully orchestrated publicity campaign dating back to the launching of the HDA has ensured a reasonable public image in the Western Cape and to some extent nationally. Evidence of this publicity effort is contained in a thick file of press cuttings at the HDA offices. A video depicting conditions of life in the hostels was also made in 1989 and has been successfully used to create awareness of the problems facing hostel dwellers. This has increased support for the upgrading project even among conservative employers and local authority officials. The publicity secretary and organiser has also become a well-known figure nationally. He is acknowledged by township residents, squatter communities and hostel dwellers as a person of considerable skills in the political arena.[1] Hostel dwellers are now generally acknowledged as part of the wider township community.

Community participation

The level of participation by ordinary hostel dwellers in the activities of the HDA is characterised by several features. First, the participation level varies from area to area, being highest in Guguletu and lowest in Nyanga. This variation mirrors the strength of local leadership and its capacity to represent the HDA as an attractive organisation. Nyanga is interesting in this respect, considering its role as the cradle of the HDA. One might have expected higher participation rates, but there seems to be strong hostility to the HDA in some quarters, directed mainly at certain personalities within the regional executive. The HDA organisers blame the poor support they have on the quality of local leadership, which they perceive as being tied to the community council system. Ordinary hostel dwellers allege that conflicts between these competing elements are personality problems related to the quest for power.

Second, participation varies with the nature of activities undertaken. Leadership training workshops, which were run on a monthly basis between May 1986 and June 1987, were well attended and participation in discussions was reasonably good. The tendency for the regional executive members to dominate discussions was fairly successfully addressed in private meetings with the executive as well as in the context of the workshops. Attendance petered out towards

1. In July 1990, he was instrumental in bringing together the warring factions in Old Crossroads in an uneasy truce (*Cape Times*, 7 August 1990).

the end of that period. This may have been an indication that a point of saturation had been reached. Participants also expressed frustration at lack of progress with regard to the proposed upgrading programme. People demanded concrete results on the pressing issue of housing and would not accept that the process of upgrading could take years instead of months. This scepticism is an understandable response from people who had been made to wait for long periods with little experience of successful outcome. Participation at the level of public meetings is a complex issue to address. Even in sophisticated communities few individuals actively participate in public debates. The constraints on uneducated people, lacking in self-confidence and not used to the art of rhetoric, cannot be underestimated. It is thus not surprising that a few individuals tend to dominate such discussions.

It is interesting to note, however, that the self-confidence of some groups of hostel dwellers increased over time as a result of their exposure to public debate. For example, women used to participate freely in the women's committee meetings from their inception in 1986, but never ventured to speak in general meetings. This situation changed at the 1989 annual regional conference. The women adopted a strategy of supporting each female speaker with appropriate songs, thus expressing their unhappiness with their subordinate position in regard to decision making within the HDA. The women generated a measure of support through this strategy, and they were promised that their concerns would be addressed. Their show of strength and solidarity resulted in the election of two women to the regional executive as additional members at the end of the conference.

It would seem that limited access to situations where one can practise the art of rhetoric has implications for community participation. The custom of excluding the young and women from public debates denies them the opportunity to develop the confidence to challenge the status quo. The power of collective action by those feeling excluded and the ingenuity of the less powerful are also demonstrated by the action of the women.

The lack of organisational experience of most HDA members is a major barrier to participation. They have no models with which to compare the HDA. Fear of the unknown is also a factor: many individuals experience this in relation to asking uncomfortable questions at meetings, because of the unpredictability of responses to such questioning. Meetings also take up considerable time. Constraints on individuals who have to devote most of their available time to survival should also not be underestimated.

Leadership style

The leadership of the HDA is made up of the regional executive, local committee members and women's committee representatives. It is a hierarchical structure dominated by the regional executive.

The general secretary, with the highest educational qualification in the executive committee (Standard 8), handles most of their correspondence as well as advising on administrative processes within the HDA office. This expertise is gained from his job as a store clerk. The two full-time executives have brought trade-union organisational expertise into the HDA. The leadership represents an interesting convergence of various strengths, expertise and potential.

The weakest link in the HDA chain is the administrative side of the organisational structure. Records are not properly kept, expenditure control is inadequate, vehicles of the HDA are not adequately monitored to control petrol and maintenance costs, and so on. The only redeeming feature is the practice of having annual audited financial statements. Of interest, however, is the unwillingness of the executive to address this weakness through training. Several attempts at this have failed, which may mean that it is not seen as a priority in a situation of so many competing claims on time. This weakness is acknowledged even within the regional executive. The low level of formal education is used as an excuse by HDA executive members for their incompetence in the field of administration. For example, one does not need to be educated to know the value of keeping a log-book for vehicles driven by different drivers. This is particularly surprising given the experience of some of them as drivers in the private sector, where they were keeping log-books as a matter of course.

The seating arrangement in meetings of the HDA symbolises the value attached to hierarchy. All regional executive members sit in front of the audience. Where there is a platform, chairs are arranged on it around a table for this purpose. The physical separation from the public and the elevation of the executive onto a platform make an important statement about the relationship between the members and the leadership. HDA members do not consider it a problem. 'Leaders are important and must be given the respect due to them,' one said.

The HDA is not alone in adherence to hierarchy. South Africa is generally a society characterised by hierarchical relationships. Hostel dwellers' structures reflect the wider environment which constitutes the national political space. The annual re-election of the same leaders is also an interesting phenomenon. The election procedure at the annual conference is a swift affair. At an appropriate point on the agenda, a member of the local area committee proposes 'a return of the whole table'. ('The table' referred to here is a metaphor derived from the table around which all the leaders are normally seated.) This is quickly seconded and agreed to 'unanimously', completing the election process in less than three minutes. It is not surprising that the executive has been re-elected every year without fail. Even sophisticated members of society find it difficult to challenge practices which constrain democratic processes, so for people unfamiliar with the etiquette of meetings, questioning a chairperson conducting an election in which that person has a material interest would be most difficult.

The views of members on the wisdom of not rotating leadership positions are interesting. From the ordinary membership side, there seems to be a strong body of opinion that supports continuity. The reasons advanced are that the HDA has come this far because of the dedication of the existing leaders, and that no risks should be taken trying out unknown quantities. There is a perception that the future is going to be tough, and one needs strong leaders to safeguard the interests of hostel dwellers. There are those who would consider a change in leadership, provided that a phasing-in process with a mixture of old and new members to minimise the risks attached to inexperience was implemented. Some members feel strongly that leadership has become 'a thing belonging to some individuals' and that such a situation is not good in the long term.

The views of the executive members also differ. One stated that they had started this process and would like to see the upgrading project through before handing over to a new group. Others have expressed doubt about the capacity of other people within the hostels to run the HDA successfully, although all recognise the need for practical hands-on experience in developing leadership skills.

Two cases will be cited here to show some of the problems of indispensable leaders.

Thandi was a clerical assistant with the HDA between 1985 and 1987. She worked hard and her previous experience in trade union and community organisations enabled her to work well with people. She was also reasonably educated (attempted Standard 10) and had a good facility with English and general office routine. She was also active in her community in Khayelitsha where she had started a play-group.

She committed the 'error' of appearing in the local newspapers as a community worker asking for donations in kind to support the play-group. Potential donors were to contact her at her work number, the HDA office. A storm broke out in the HDA office. The chief executive officer charged that this was sabotage of the HDA's own fundraising efforts and a sign of insubordination, because only he had the authority to issue any statement related to the HDA. It was also recalled that Thandi had shown increasing stubbornness at work over the previous weeks and this was seen as part of the same pattern.

The regional executive agreed to call an emergency conference at which Thandi was publicly tried for insubordination. Only two people in the whole audience of over two hundred questioned the procedure, but were ruled out of order. Thandi was fired on the spot.

At issue in this case are two concerns. Was there sufficient justification for the HDA to feel threatened by Thandi's fundraising efforts? Were the procedures adopted to deal with the perceived threat to HDA interests appropriate? It is possible that the HDA executive felt genuinely threatened. After all, township people have always been perceived by hostel dwellers as acting against their interests. Thandi may have touched a raw nerve. It would be wrong, however, to imply that everyone in that emergency conference agreed with the conduct of the disciplinary process and the summary justice, but their silence was taken as consent. They may not have participated in the social drama that was played out in that conference, but they were nevertheless part of it.

A second case relates to a community health worker, Nomsa.[1]

Nomsa was an experienced community health worker, who started the HDA mobile clinic before they could employ a qualified nursing-sister. She had been involved in starting a nutritional clinic in Old Crossroads in 1976, which has now been expanded to include Khayelitsha and benefits many children. She was one of the founding women of that squatter community.

She had had bitter experiences in Crossroads which alerted her to the capacity of community leaders to dominate organisations. Her insistence on proper democratic procedures within the HDA generally, and in staff relations in particular, soon put her at loggerheads with the chief executive officer. She was one of the two people referred to above who defended the right of Thandi to a proper hearing. This did not go down well with those bent on summary justice.

The final straw was an argument she had with the aforementioned officer, in which she likened him to the oppressive community leader in Old Crossroads. This was the ultimate insult for a leader seeing himself as progressive. She was, however, quick enough to resign and deny the HDA the opportunity to fire her.

Of particular interest here is the tendency of a few individuals to dominate community organisations and the acquiescence of other members of the organisation in such a process. Several executive members of the HDA have indicated their acute awareness of this as a weakness, but seem to feel that they have no choice but to let the chief executive officer have his way. The main reason advanced for this 'lack of choice' is that there is too much to lose in the event of conflict with him. He is perceived as the only person within the hostel community with the political ability to engage the hostile world on their behalf, as well as being seen as a gifted orator and organiser. He is thus indispensable.

Conclusion

The right to family life and to seek jobs without the problems of the contract system and influx control regulations, which motivated the formation of the HDA, is now entrenched, thanks to the opening up of political, economic and ideological space in the wider South

1. See pp. 82–3 and Ramphele, 1989:413 for life history details.

Africa. The HDA seems to have had considerable success in serving its members with regard to advice offices and other social services, despite its limitations. This success relates mainly to creating avenues for expressing the frustrations of people with little or no access to the state bureaucracy.

The health project was a success in so far as it increased hostel dwellers' access to existing services. It failed as an alternative service for a number of good reasons, which should alert enthusiastic community workers to the complexities of development work. Hostel dwellers wanted accessible services of an equivalent standard to those available to other sections of the community. Attempts to institute what they regarded as a second-rate service were bound to fail.

Provision of family housing has proved to be more problematic. The legacy of exclusion from resource allocation in Cape Town seems to be a millstone around the neck of hostel dwellers. The dual impact of escalating housing costs and the diminishing availability of land is considerable. Past subjection to physical space constraints is likely to lead to ongoing battles for space. Conflicts with the rest of the township community over land, a scarce resource, will be difficult to contain.

The most difficult area seems to be that of democratic practice and community participation within the HDA. Key constraints to community participation seem to revolve around time and the fear of risking the displeasure of other members of the community. The trade-union background of some of the officials and the affiliation of the HDA to COSATU do not seem to have a sufficiently positive impact on the creation of a more democratic culture within the HDA. Undemocratic practices seem to be related to the quality of leadership available in the hostels. The perception by hostel dwellers that they have little choice but to continue with existing leaders entrenches the notion of indispensability of some individuals and negates attempts at accountability. The feeling of powerlessness to challenge undemocratic practices here becomes a self-fulfilling prophecy.

International experience with transition from authoritarian rule indicates that it is a difficult process. O'Donnell and Schmitter identify three phases in such a process: liberalisation, democratisation and socialisation. The liberalisation phase is defined as that period during which political space is opened up, releasing the steam of political frustration. Previously voiceless people are allowed to air their views. The democratisation phase is marked by increasing participation in decision-making processes. Socialisation is an ongoing phase in which people develop and internalise a culture of democracy (O'Donnell & Schmitter, 1986:6–14). South Africa as a whole is still in the liberalisation phase. It is thus unreasonable to expect the HDA to have progressed ahead of other sectors of the South African society. Despite national political space constraints, one still needs to pose the questions: At what point do individuals assume responsibility as active agents of history? Is acquiescence inevitable in the context of such serious space constraints? Can an outsider intervene meaningfully in the face of the politics of space as played out in the hostels? These are some of the questions I will be addressing in the next chapter.

hebeen

Dancing, shebeen

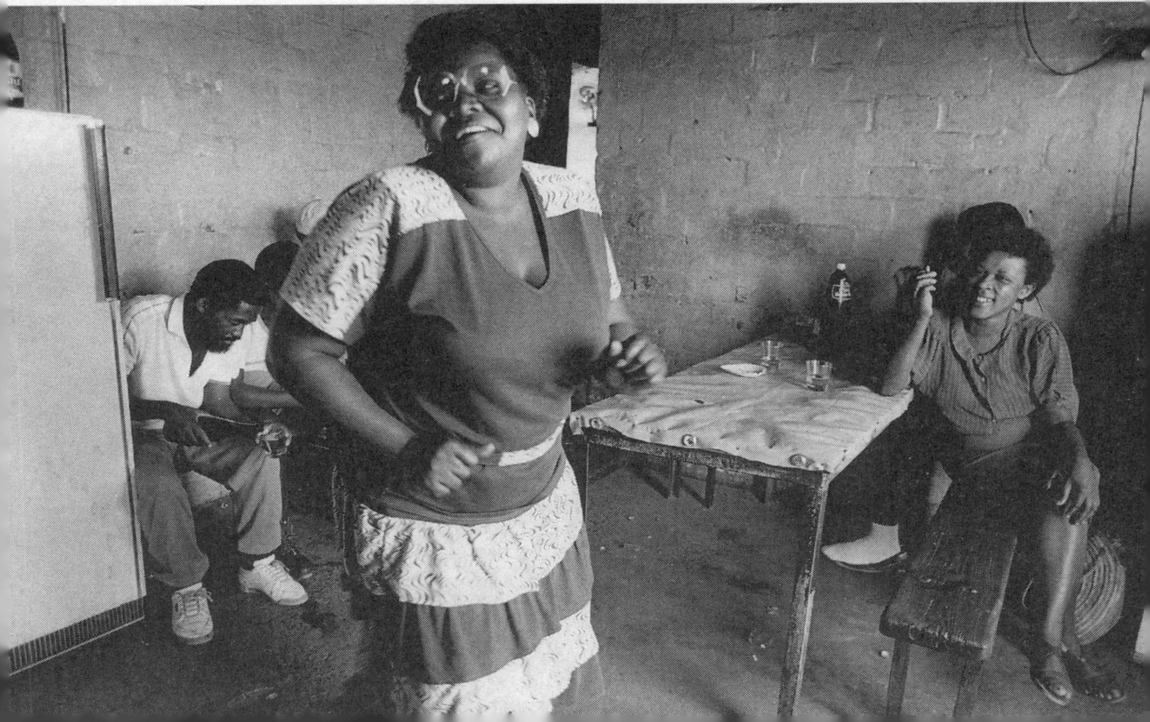

Funeral for young hostel dweller killed in fight over girlfrien

Young man returns from initiation into manhoo

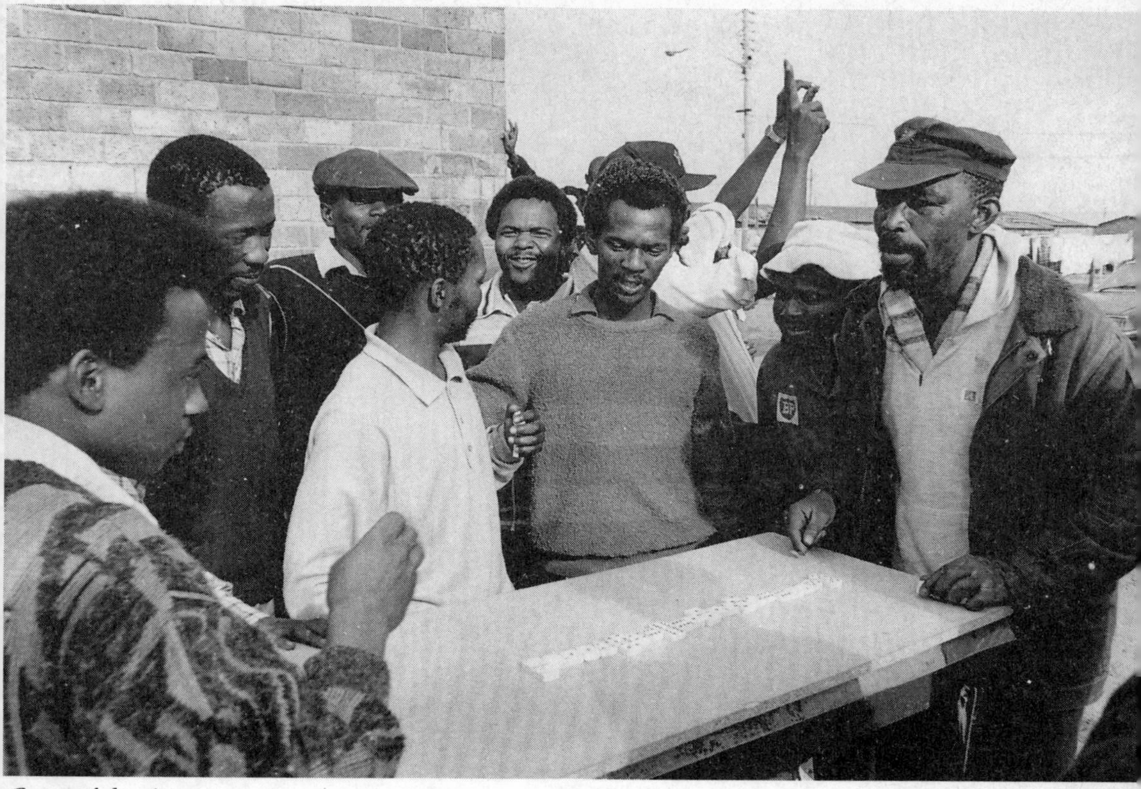

Game of dominoes

Bus terminus, beginning of Easter Weekend

Bus company advertisement stating stops in Transkei

Last farewells – Sunday taxi to Transkei

8 Empowerment and the Politics of Space

> *The methods of coping open to poorer city people are often, though not always, tied up with the availability of middle class or intellectual groups able to appeal to their experiential perceptions* (Bozzoli, 1987:33).

Introduction

In this chapter I will explore the concept of empowerment and its appropriateness as an intervention strategy in the context of hostels in the Western Cape. I will test theories on empowerment against my personal experience as a participant observer and an agent of empowerment in these hostels, and will evaluate the impact of empowerment on the politics of space, as well as the limitations of this process.

The concept of empowerment

Empowerment is used in this book to denote a process aimed at shifting the perceptions of subordinate people, enabling them to assume greater control over their own lives. There is considerable controversy around the validity of the concept of empowerment. Some people argue that it is a fashionable term coined by those bent on patronising subordinate people such as women, workers or rural folk. These critics contend that people have power in themselves and do not need outsiders to come and 'empower' them. This argument echoes the point made by Nyerere that people cannot be developed, but have to develop themselves (Nyerere, 1986). Empowerment has also been discredited by its fashionable use in international parlance. Criticisms that were levelled at development strategies spearheaded predominantly by the West and directed at poor countries are now being applied to the concept of empowerment. It is seen as a disguise for continuing the same global political games that have underdeveloped the poor in the Third World (see *WIP*, 1989, No.59:32–5; Ferguson, 1990).

Rejection of a patronising approach and recognition of the importance of global politics in social interaction and power relationships are at the very heart of the definition of power as espoused in the introductory chapter of this book. This definition ascribes agency to individuals in any social setting by recognising that power is the use of resources of whatever kind to secure outcomes (Giddens, 1981:348). Power is thus seen as action and refers to a range of interventions of which an agent is capable. Interventions in this context refer also to the decisions by individuals not to act, because such decisions in themselves constitute intervention in history.

Human beings, therefore, are by nature social agents, and interventions in history are products of their calculative approach within their situational constraints to secure desired outcomes. The goal of empowerment is to enable individuals and groups to widen the range of possible choices they entertain in the process of calculating risks attached to social acts that are directed at transformation of existing power relationships.

The process of empowerment

In the hostel context, this process entailed intervention by myself and others[1] in the lives of hostel dwellers, and attempts to enable them to assume greater control over their lives in spite of the constraints of space they live under. The Hostel Dwellers' Association requested my involvement in their struggle for recognition of their right to family life and dignified accommodation. I identified various perceptions that needed shifting in certain elements of the politics of space in which hostel dwellers are participants, at both the individual and community level. These elements include recognition and acceptance of space constraints in the broad context defined in Chapter 1; devising coping strategies to survive within these constraints; and incorporating and legitimising such coping strategies into one's life-style. The last-mentioned entails developing a culture which enables people to create meaning in their lives in spite of the dehumanising conditions of hostel life. Finally, communal strategies to challenge the legitimacy of space constraints imposed on hostel dwellers also constitute part of the politics of space. The HDA is the major player in the arena of communal politics. Its role in mediating between the needs and sensitivities of hostel dwellers and the demands of wider political groupings in the townships and nationally has to be evaluated against the reality of the politics of space (see Chapter 7).

Essential steps in the process of empowerment

Process of observation and monitoring. My entry into the hostels as a researcher–facilitator had a considerable impact on the social processes within them. This impact can be accounted for in several ways. First, the entrance of an outsider into any social setting alters that setting in a significant way, and in this case signified a certain recognition. The story of the woman child-minder interviewed by Cock and Edmund, 'Let me make history, please', illustrates this point. This child-minder was eager to tell her story to total strangers collecting oral history texts because she recognised it as her opportunity to be heard by other human beings (Cock & Edmund, 1987). She emerged to claim her place as a participant in the history that had so far not acknowledged her (see Wolf, 1982:23). The denial of full urban citizenship to hostel dwellers as represented by their living circumstances underlines the symbolic importance of my taking an interest in their lives. They needed to be respected as people to compensate for their treatment as labour units by employers and government agencies. The perceived lack of respect

1. The first agent of empowerment in this setting was Father David Russell in his capacity as chaplain of migrant workers (see Chapter 7).

and indifference to their rights by township residents were an added denigration.

Second, the process of asking hostel dwellers about their living conditions, coping mechanisms, choice of strategies and their possible implications is likely to set them thinking critically about their social actions. It is to be expected that when people are preoccupied with survival on a day-to-day basis, little or no time is devoted to abstract critical thinking. It could thus be argued that the research process itself created space for hostel dwellers to engage legitimately in the luxury of letting their minds contemplate their living conditions philosophically.

Third, expressing one's thoughts has the effect of forcing one to be more rational and logical than would be the case when one is merely day-dreaming. Social relations easily become habitual, leaving little room for critical evaluation. Having to articulate one's position on a number of social issues forces one to review that position in relation to the key elements of the rationale for whatever stance one has taken. Asking hostel dwellers, for example, to explain their domestic relationships, the impact of separation on their family politics, their participation in child-rearing and their relationship with township residents provided an opportunity for them to hear their own voices on various matters and to re-examine their views.

Fourth, the appearance of an outsider challenged many of the hitherto unquestioned social categorisations about gender roles at a number of levels. My position as a woman having to relate to men socially and professionally upset many 'traditional' male attitudes towards women. Men had either to treat me in the same way in which they treated the women in their lives, or to put me in a different category to justify my being treated differently. They opted for the latter and treated me as an honorary male.[1] As an 'honorary male' I had access to space normally set aside for men only. For example, meetings were held in the common rooms which at certain times were declared out of bounds for women; they became *ebuhlanti* (the cattle kraal), and I would be the only woman present. Another example was being served tea at the HDA offices by the male executive committee members on the HDA staff; hostel women visiting the office would be expected not only to make their own tea, but to serve the men as well. My honorary male status enabled male hostel dwellers to continue to function within a symbolic framework over which they retained control. They could thus talk about women as being childish and incapable of rational long-term planning without feeling that they were offending me personally. This retention of control over the symbolic sphere is an important element of power, which had to be renegotiated throughout our interaction.

My position as a medical doctor also presented opportunities for a shift in the perceptions of some hostel dwellers, enabling them to

1. The position of honorary male is a common one in many social settings suddenly confronted with the problem of women who do not fit in with expected roles. Such women are seen as 'matter out of place' (Rodgers, 1981:58). For example, Margaret Thatcher is treated largely, and to some extent projects herself, as an aberration from the norm applicable to other women (see Rodgers, 1981:50–71).

see doctors as people rather than demi-gods. My insistence on introducing myself and being addressed through my first name compelled hostel dwellers to evaluate their attitude and their deference to medical doctors. The infallibility of the medical profession, its system of explanation of diseases and its healing practices were to some extent demystified in my interactions with many hostel dwellers. The fact that I made mistakes and apologised for them allowed them to appreciate my vulnerability and, by extension, that of people in my position. The impact of this perception in the long term cannot be dismissed. The fact that the majority of hostel dwellers still believe in the superiority of medical doctors as people as well as healers should not be seen as a sign of total failure to change attitudes. It is partly a reflection of the attitudes to and the real power of the biomedical system in the wider society. The limited intellectual space hostel dwellers have access to makes them even more vulnerable to the acceptance of a subordinate position in relation to medical doctors. Changes which are occurring in other parts of the world with respect to the development of attitudes challenging the dominance of the medical profession are products of a long process of exposure to alternative information (Boston Women's Health Collective, 1985). It would be unreasonable to expect hostel dwellers to alter their perceptions radically in such a short period of time.

Finally, it could be argued that although the ideals of participatory research were not realised in this context, the research process was itself empowering for participants at all levels. Those involved in discussions at various stages, assisting in motivating others to participate, interpreting for interviewers during the surveys and collecting some of the data, were all better informed about the nature and purpose of research than they had been at the beginning of the process. The knowledge hostel dwellers gained in this exercise is likely to enable them to negotiate better deals with future researchers, and to take a greater interest in making their own observations about social processes around them. Research has to some extent been demystified for them by this experience. Evidence of gains hostel dwellers have made in this regard can be seen in their dealings with various parties to the hostel upgrading programme. They ask fairly detailed questions about various alternatives, as well as insisting on involvement in the planning and implementation of surveys undertaken as part of the process, at a level commensurate with their own capacities.

Issues raised in the process of empowerment

The discussion below will focus on some of the important issues which became subjects of intense debates in my interactions with various elements within the HDA. These issues have been singled out because of their centrality to the nature of power relations in the hostels, and also because they lend themselves to an exploration of the process of transformation within a limited time-frame.

The issue of gender. Reference has already been made to the progress of the HDA from a 'men's hostel association' to the open organisation it is today (see Chapter 7). Debates surrounding that change were important components of the process of empowerment. Both men and women in the hostels were aware of the contradictions inherent in the exclusion of women from membership, but both sides feared taking risks to change that situation.

What were the risks involved in opening membership of the HDA to women? First, such a step would entail recognition of women as permanent residents of hostels. This recognition had far-reaching implications for the men's attitude to the place of women as workers and as permanent residents of the urban areas. Many of our informants indicated their discomfort with the idea of women as hostel dwellers. Most of their objections were couched in terms which implied concern for the safety of women and children in such a corrupting environment and the potential of conflict involving jealous lovers and husbands (see Chapter 6).

It is, however, important to contextualise these concerns. Bozzoli's analysis of the impact of pre-capitalist social relations on the form capitalism and gender relations take in different settings is of relevance to our understanding of the legitimisation of present gender relations in the hostels (Bozzoli, 1983:139–71). Using ethnographic texts, she demonstrates that the capacity of African men to dominate their women and their peripheral role in essential domestic activities created opportunities for migrant labour to take root in South Africa in the form it has taken to date. The successful operation of migrant labour depended on the ability of African families to adjust to it, and survive over the years. Culture was, and still is, used as a resource by some African men in the hostels to justify the undesirability of women living in the urban areas. The successful adaptation of African women to the system of migrant labour ensured its perpetuation among this group of South Africans.

Walker emphasises the same theme, but points to the distortions which were introduced by colonialism in indigenous sex–gender systems as well as the reinforcement of such a system: 'the imperatives of capital flowed along the contours already suggested by the pre-capitalist structuring of gender relations' (Walker, 1990:27). Thus the distortions introduced by colonialism effected reinforcement as well as adaptations in sex–gender roles, which are proving difficult to transform.

There is tension between upholding the ideal of family life and coping with the dilemmas of space constraints. The appeal to 'tradition' to legitimise the exclusion of women from participation in HDA activities was an indication of deep-seated denial of their permanence in the hostels. Hostels are not ideal family accommodation, so the denial of the permanence of women and children in these limited spaces protected the men from facing a painful reality.

Second, the recognition of women as permanent hostel dwellers would threaten the legitimacy of traditional male authority structures (see Chapter 6). Such structures had been set up to serve men only, and continue to function as such. In pursuit of constituency politics, the HDA had incorporated the leadership of these structures within its own ranks and feared alienating some of the more conservative elements within them. The pragmatic considerations of the politics of space therefore delayed a change of policy for some time.

Third, hostel dwellers found the inclusion of women in the HDA threatening. It challenged their whole world view about the place of women. After all, some informants ventured, it is against Xhosa custom and tradition to have women entering public life; a woman's place is in the domestic sphere. The persistent use of metaphors relating to 'the kraal' *(ebuhlanti)* to refer to public meeting places is part of the attempt to create order in the disorderly limited space of hostels. The familiar modes of social organisation from the 'home base' are brought in as a resource to restore a measure of internal and external harmony. This strategy could also be seen as a desperate measure to symbolically protect 'men's spaces' from pollution by the intrusion of women, for at least part of the time (see Chapter 6; Rodgers, 1981:50–71).

In my interaction with hostel dwellers, fears relating to 'pollution of men's space' and the implications of women's membership of the HDA were addressed. Not only was it a question of providing hostel dwellers with reasons why such change was desirable, it was also important to provide opportunities for the exploration of different views on the subject in a non-threatening environment. The leadership training workshops referred to earlier provided space for such exploration. Most of the participants in the discussions had profound insights into the nature of gender relationships and the key elements which ensured perpetuation of existing relationships between men and women. Unwillingness to change is not a reflection of lack of 'gender consciousness' so much as a deliberate decision not to upset well-tested and established social structures. The fear of 'pollution' is acknowledged because it is seen as more legitimate than acknowledging the real fear of learning to relate to women in a different way.

The participation of women in these debates reflected their cooperation in perpetuating existing gender roles (see Ramphele, 1990a; Havel, 1985:31).[1] Most of the women accept being discriminated against as part of life. They have no vision of change in existing gender relationships. Some expressed the view that women deserve male domination, because of their 'weak nature' (see also

1. Havel explored the role of individuals in perpetuating the repressive system of socialist Czechoslovakia. He contended that the tendency of individuals to play along in the games of power makes it possible for such games to continue. They legitimise the lie that is being acted out (Havel, 1985:31).

Brittan & Maynard, 1984:219). The lack of knowledge of positive models of societies with egalitarian gender relations reinforces this belief. The widespread sexism in the labour movement, community organisations and the various formations of the liberation movement in South Africa reinforces the notion of unequal gender relations as being 'normal' or at best needing to be addressed 'after the struggle' (see Jaffee, 1987:70–92; Bozzoli, 1987; *WIP*, No. 61:30–3). Thus hostel dwellers' social relations are influenced by the national political and ideological–intellectual space in which they function. Conflict between the views of men and women in COSATU leadership on this matter came to the fore at their 1989 conference. A National Union of Mineworkers official appealed to workers not to fall prey to 'bourgeois morality' in their approach to sexism and sexual harassment within the union. Workers were urged to 'go back to their roots', reject bourgeois morality and develop working-class morality (*WIP*, No. 61:31). The nature of such 'working-class morality' was not clarified. Such statements fulfil what Havel terms 'the excusatory legitimacy and inner coherence provided by ideology as the pillar of a power structure' (Havel, 1985:31).

The labelling of concerns about sexism as 'bourgeois' is also a defensive stance by those feeling threatened by the challenges of examining their relationships with others. The appeal to 'working-class morality' is an attempt to isolate those persisting in the quest for transformation of gender relations as enemies of 'the working class'. In large measure such attempts have succeeded in most parts of Africa. African women often preface their discussions or statements about gender politics by distancing themselves from 'feminism' because it has become a dirty word in some circles. It is the objective of empowerment to expose the pillars of power hindering open discussion for what they are and enhance the ability of individuals to transform their interpersonal and social relationships.

Other women, although fully understanding and disagreeing with the sexist nature of their environment, have devised coping strategies which enable them to pay lip-service to male supremacy in order to advance their individual positions (see Chapter 6). Some of these individuals became an obstacle to change, because of their apathy in public discussions. They also did not want to take the risk of advocating changing relationships and abandoning the security of long-standing and tested survival strategies. For example, Sisi Buli (pp. 78–9) kept herself right out of these debates. She had developed a viable strategy which enhanced her position as a single head of a household, and did not want to risk the economic gains she had made. She made it clear to all that she was not prepared to 'waste time on things which were not going to work'. A few individual women were, however, only too pleased to have the space to express themselves on sexism within the hostels and their resentment at being excluded from the HDA. Similar tensions surfaced in the women's committees of the HDA. Some women saw these committees as opportunities for personal growth away from the public gaze of men, whereas others saw them as handmaidens of the HDA executive committee. There is value in women organising as women to build their own power base to enable them to participate effectively in the wider arena. The existence of trade unions is testimony to the need for subordinate groups to establish their own power bases. The challenge seems to lie in finding the right balance between operating as a separate group to pursue the group's interest and engaging the wider society and acting for the common good.

The experiences of women's committees in other community organisations do not provide positive models for transforming gender relationships. The casting of women as 'mothers' inhibits their capacity to challenge the fundamental assumptions of gender politics (see also Jaffee, 1987:73–103).[1] At the other extreme, the virulent anti-male rhetoric of some women's groups which label men as 'the enemy' does not contribute to healthier social relations and frightens off a lot of ordinary women.

The responses of men within the HDA to the gender debate have been varied. Some have accepted the inevitability of changing gender politics. This acceptance may be framed in defeatist terms such as the words of the FOSATU (Federation of South African Trade Unions) shop steward quoted by Jaffee: 'It is high time that we surrendered, brothers. This is the struggle and for the sake of the struggle we should be hand in hand with the women' (Jaffee, 1987:89). Other men avoid any discussion on this issue in the hope that no changes will occur. Finally, there are men who are openly hostile and attempt to prevent change. Sipho, a 50-year-old man, expressed himself strongly on the need to maintain existing gender roles: 'I have accepted being called an *isoka* (bachelor) even though it is a denigrating term, because I live in the hostels. I am not prepared to accept women meddling in matters pertaining to hostels. They do not belong here. My wife is at home and that is where she belongs.' Phumezo, a 60-year-old man, feels that the presence of women in the hostels has to be accepted. He is opposed to women being debarred from the front room: 'They should not be chased into the bedrooms like prisoners, because they have come to cook for us and look after our interests. They should have a say in how things are run here.'

The impact of these discussions on gender has been considerable. More and more women have been drawn into the structures of the HDA and some have developed confidence in themselves as change agents. A few have become unstoppable, and are bold in their insistence on involvement in decision-making processes. The creation of space to challenge the constraints of sexist ideology has liberated some women by allowing them to express what they may always have felt on gender issues. Part of the process of liberation is the

1. Jaffee presents an illuminating analysis of the position of women within the trade union movement. She addresses both the failure of women to break into the male-dominated hierarchies, in spite of their numerical significance, and the limitations of their being stereotyped as 'mothers' (Jaffee, 1987:86-91). This is a similar problem to that analysed by Sacks in relation to grassroots leadership in the USA, where women saw themselves as 'centre people' rather than leaders and spokespersons (Sacks, 1988:77–94).

knowledge that their anger and frustrations, which they have had to suppress for so long, are legitimate.

Some men have also been strengthened as individuals. They have been able to articulate their concerns and fears without losing face. They too know that it is legitimate to feel resentful about the demands of women for equality, given their own low self-image as poor black men at the bottom of the South African hierarchical system. The contradictions in their demands for equality and respectful treatment in the wider political system and their own role as oppressors of their womenfolk, both inside and outside the family, are now a matter of open debate. For example, at the regional council meeting where the decision to open membership of the HDA to women was taken, several speakers articulated the contradictions facing them. 'We cannot close our eyes to changing times,' one man said; 'there are going to be things happening in our midst which will chill our spines *(ezizaku senzela amasikizi)*, but one has to swallow deeply and press on. There is no time for attention to frills in a war *(a kukho ixhesha lo kuhombisa edabini)*. We are in a war, let us get on with it.'

My role as a facilitator was important in so far as I provided a forum for such discussions, additional information to contextualise the various viewpoints, and an ear for those wanting to discuss these issues privately. I also provided 'a model of deviance' which helped to demonstrate the possibility of a nonconformist life-style. In a society where gender stereotypes are as deeply entrenched as they are in South Africa in general, and among Africans in particular, to behave 'normally' entails being labelled a deviant from the norms of such a society. Under such circumstances, the presence of 'models of deviance' is essential to the process of opening up ideological and political space, and enabling people to contemplate crossing boundaries they previously thought uncrossable. Many more issues relating to transformation of gender politics remain to be addressed, but this has been a significant beginning.

The question of democracy. The HDA sees itself as part of the Mass Democratic Movement (MDM) by virtue of its affiliation to COSATU and open support for the ANC. It has thus committed itself towards working for a non-racial democratic society, and has embraced all the slogans and rhetoric of the MDM. The gap between that commitment and the practices within the organisation as outlined in Chapter 7 became contested territory during my research period.

The incorporation of the *izibonda* system of self-governance into the structures of the HDA (as outlined in Chapters 5 and 7) has a bearing on the question of democratic participation. The values attached to the 'traditional leadership' structures from which this system derives are at variance with those informing democratic leadership practices. Thus the fusion between the worst elements of the 'old' and the 'new' creates hybrids which inhibit transformation of power relationships. For example, the notion of replacement of old leadership with young and new people goes against the grain of lifelong leadership of headmen and chiefs, on whom some of the HDA leaders model themselves. In the view of some members, re-election to leadership positions was almost automatic, provided that one had not committed a gross error in the discharge of one's duties – the corollary being that failure to re-elect an official is taken as a vote of no confidence in that official. Thus this idiom of 'traditional leadership' has been incorporated into 'community leadership' without its ever being articulated as such.

There are interesting parallels between the 'traditional African' leadership style and models of leadership adopted by Marxist–Leninist regimes. The notion of a 'vanguard of the struggle' and the concept of the 'dictatorship of the working class' in Marxist parlance authenticate and entrench an oligarchy that rules over the majority in the name of the reified 'working class'. Questioning the legitimacy of the oligarchy or the autocrats who inevitably take over power becomes treasonable (Medvedev, 1971; Achebe, 1958, 1987). It may well be that the resemblance between the autocracy of Marxist–Leninist states and the African idiom of lifelong leadership lies behind the attraction people feel to one-party socialism in many African countries. There have been strong indications in the 1980s that South African trade unions and political and community organisations have also adopted this approach. The resuscitation of the Congress of Traditional Leaders of South Africa (CONTRALESA) does not augur well for democracy in the future South Africa. The political space in which the HDA functioned, therefore, did not provide alternative models for hostel dwellers to emulate.

Democracy also depends on the efforts and abilities of those being led to insist on a certain level of accountability and adherence of the leadership to an acceptable code of conduct. This process entails a level of participation by ordinary membership in the affairs of the organisation. My experience in the hostels suggests that there are real barriers to participation by ordinary people in decision-making processes relating to critical issues around their lives (see Chapter 7). These barriers reinforce the notion people have of being a 'victim of circumstances' rather than an active agent in the unfolding historical process. The 'victim image' is a valuable asset in the struggle for survival. It releases one from responsibility in social relations. Many of our informants repeatedly indicated that they perceived themselves as victims of both the wider political system and the power games played in community politics, including those of the HDA. When pressed to explain why they felt so powerless when they had the right to vote in community politics, they responded that their vote did not ultimately count as much as that of 'the powerful'.

There is widespread resignation to an authoritarian power structure. In a sense this becomes a self-fulfilling prophecy and leads to low levels of effective participation. Steele's analysis of the impact of the 'victim image' of African Americans has relevance for South Africa in general and hostel dwellers in particular (Steele, 1990). He notes that the values which are essential for active agency in history are in fact those perceived as negative in the struggle for survival.

> Oppression conditions people away from all the values and attitudes one needs in freedom – individual initiative, self-interested hard work, individual responsibility, delayed gratification, and so on. It is not that these values have never had a presence in black life, only that they were muted and destabilised by the negative conditioning of oppression (Steele, 1990:68).

Low levels of community participation also place heavy burdens on the leadership. Failure to secure speedy responses to critical questions due to poor attendance at public meetings leads to frustration on the part of leaders. Coping with such frustration may lead to independent action by leaders, who generally feel that they are acting in the best interests of the general membership. The road to autocracy from habits so developed is a short one. Limited resources within organisations such as the HDA also impose considerable burdens on those in leadership. Low levels of compensation for full-time officials and heavy workloads conspire to attract particular personality types to leadership positions – mainly those unable to compete in the open job market, or the dedicated, self-sacrificing characters. The consequences of employing incompetent community organisers are predictable, however, while the long-term impact of dedicated service upon the individuals concerned and the organisations they serve varies. In some cases it leads to the emergence of 'a culture of entitlement' among those involved. A culture of entitlement refers to the attitude of leaders that the people they lead owe them not only respect but unquestioning support for their decisions and actions.

An analysis of the historical evolution of dictators in Africa indicates that most of them started off as leaders of liberation movements (see for example, Hyden, 1983; Achebe, 1958, 1987; Ngugi, 1977). Thus to answer in part Soyinka's question about how political monsters such as Amin came into being, one has to examine the extent to which they were created by the acceptance by ordinary people of elements of 'the culture of entitlement' benefiting people who have made considerable sacrifices in the course of liberating their countries.

The top executive of the HDA is faced with similar challenges. In particular, the position of the chief executive with all the power concentrated in it has the makings of an autocracy. In my role as adviser, I questioned the wisdom of continuing with this concentration of power and the ritual of re-election of leadership, after the 1987 mid-year annual conference. My persistent questions irritated members of the executive, who indicated that they did not share my concerns. In desperation I decided to write a memorandum to the HDA setting out my misgivings. I was increasingly experiencing discomfort at the realisation that I was becoming an accomplice in the entrenchment of power in the hands of a few. The executive responded by way of a letter addressed to me. The strongest statement in this letter was reserved for my criticism of the powers of the chief executive officer:

> Regarding the question of a staff member being an executive, the executive felt that they will remain in an executive position forever, as long as they are not being excluded by the Council. In particular, the chief organiser who is holding the position of Information Director, is regarded by us as the Life President.[1]

Life presidencies symbolise the antithesis of democracy by any standard. My first reaction was to distance myself from the HDA and leave them to their own devices. They had after all the right to chart their own future, and at the same time I felt that they also needed to acknowledge my right not to be associated with an organisation espousing such an approach. I hesitated, however, because of the implications of such a step for the viability of the HDA as an organisation. My greatest concern in this regard was the impact my resignation would have on the upgrading programme which was to benefit so many people (see pp. 97–8). The leadership of the HDA was after all not to be equated with ordinary hostel dwellers.

I was confronted by the magnitude of the power vested in me to make or break the HDA's future as well as its programmes. This power derived from my position as a fundraiser and an unofficial public relations person for them. I could open or close doors. This power presented an awful dilemma for me. Should I follow my principles and jeopardise the chances of hostel dwellers implementing their proposed upgrading programme and thus moving out of the constraints of space that dehumanise them? Did I have the right to impose my own values on the HDA?[2] Or should I stand firm in the hope that they would review their stance and thus emerge a stronger and better organisation?

The search for an appropriate response was a long and painful one. In the end I had to distinguish between my role as an agent of empowerment and that of a provider of housing needs. The latter was the responsibility of local authorities, whereas the former entailed enabling hostel dwellers to take greater control over their lives. Life presidencies have never been found to contribute to the process of

1. Verbatim quote from a letter dated 18 November 1987 from the HDA to me.

2. Sacks faced a similar dilemma in her work with women at grassroots level, who deferred to men's leadership. As a feminist she found herself pressurising these women to change their approach, yet was uneasy about the imposition of her own views on them (Sacks, 1988:77–94).

empowerment. I also felt that my dissociation from the HDA on this point would be a stand for their own professed commitment to democracy. It would in essence be getting the HDA to live up to its own rhetoric, or else publicly acknowledge its departure from it. I thus decided to take the risk of a short-term break in the relationship I cherished so much in the hope of long-term gains. I therefore resigned as an adviser, fundraiser and general facilitator of the HDA.

The reaction of the executive was one of profound shock. They could not believe that I could respond so strongly to this issue. Some accused me of not caring enough about their plight. Others said that my response was typical of educated people *(izifundiswa)*, who do not understand the workings of ordinary people's organisations. The problem was that the little I understood about the workings of ordinary people's organisations did not inspire me with confidence in their capacity to act in the interest of 'the people' whose authority they invoked (Thornton & Ramphele, 1988:29–39). The experience of Old Crossroads was too vivid in my memory (Josette Cole, 1986). I did not want to end up saying that I had not known that I was party to the creation of a monster. My resignation led to a long process of renegotiation of the relationship between the HDA leadership and myself. It was a mutually beneficial experience. I learnt about the value of standing firm and the long-term benefits of applying the same standards to all people one deals with, instead of the short-term gains of paternalistic compromises.

The application of double standards in dealing with people perceived as victims has been found to lead to the further disadvantage of those on the receiving end of such paternalism (see Steele, 1990:146). The application of double standards is a statement to those so treated that one does not expect them to perform at the standard applicable to others. Such low expectations of people perpetuate inequalities by not challenging those labelled as disadvantaged to move beyond mediocrity. Gibbs's study of African American men also suggests that the low expectations Americans, including African American women, have of black men is partly responsible for the failure of most young black men to perform adequately at all levels in society. They have, in her own words, become an endangered species (Gibbs, 1988).

In my dealings with the HDA, I have tried at all times to avoid treating its members as victims. They have been victimised as a group, but to treat them individually as victims is to disempower them. My relationship with them was aimed at emphasising their agency in history. HDA executive members were reminded by this episode that they could not plead ignorance and poverty as an excuse for undemocratic practices. They may have been testing the limits of my tolerance of such behaviour. They could also have miscalculated and thought they could get away with their undemocratic practices on the strength of a mythical working-class or people's morality.

There is a larger issue flowing from this incident. How does one negotiate a mutually beneficial relationship in a situation of unequal power between an agent of empowerment and the people who are the focus of such a process? It seems to me important to acknowledge the existence of this inequality rather than to pretend to be 'part of the people'. One should direct the force of this disproportionate power towards removing constraints on subordinate people's ability to gain greater control over their own lives, rather than pandering to the whims of those in positions of power. Constraints to empowerment do include self-imposed ones. For example, it would seem that the letter written by the HDA leadership was aimed at showing support for the chief executive rather than demonstrating a fundamental commitment to the idea of a life presidency. This emerged during discussions with individual members of the executive, who felt that they had had to demonstrate their loyalty to the chief executive in the face of my criticisms. Loyalty in this case seems to be synonymous with an uncritical attitude. They were individually concerned about the dominating role played by the chief executive, but felt that they could not risk displeasing him through criticism and attempts to limit his power within the organisation. The perceived indispensability of officials within organisations such as the HDA is thus an important factor in hindering empowerment. People in the HDA feel trapped in having to retain the services of a gifted, energetic person at a cost to their own principles and long-term interests.

A second point that emerged in these discussions related to the practice of 'the double face'. This is the showing of deference and total loyalty towards persons perceived to have control over important resources, while cursing and criticising them in their absence. The classic example of this survival strategy is the exaggerated respect shown to white bosses by workers who denounce them when conversing amongst themselves. This serves to allow for risk-free venting of rage and frustration on the part of those perceiving themselves as powerless, but it does not facilitate transformation of such relationships. The HDA executive members, masters of this strategy in their work situations, were resorting to its use in these circumstances as well. The seriousness of the symbolism of such an approach and its long-term consequences deserves consideration. It seemed that the least one could do in such a situation was to name the game and get the HDA executive to deal with its consequences.

The major barriers to democratic practice have their roots in the limitations of the political space within which hostel dwellers find themselves. First, they are at the bottom rung of a hierarchical, undemocratic system in South Africa which has effectively excluded them from all major decision-making processes. 'People hovering on the edge of despair are always open to messianic myths' (Berger, 1974:38). Second, they are exposed to the workings of resistance organisations which are themselves not democratically run.[1] Resistance organisations have also been subject to the constraints of political space imposed by the dominant ideology of past South African governments and the repression by State security forces over the years. The opening up of political space signalled by the State President's speech on 2 February 1990 was an essential but not a sufficient condition for democratic transformation.

The political culture emerging from such a history is likely to reflect the impact of coping strategies which may have elements that undermine democratic practice. For example, leaders of organisations have had to protect their membership and ensure the survival of their organisations through various means including secrecy and centralised decision-making involving only trusted people. The element of risk attached to active involvement in organisations for change also undermined democracy, as the majority of ordinary people were not likely to risk their lives in such a situation. They were willing to reward those prepared to take such risks with loyalty and deference, even when they perceived the danger of abuse of power. Habits so developed die hard even when political space opens up. In March 1990, Van Zyl Slabbert reminded South Africans that forty years of apartheid rule have destroyed the 'normal' political infrastructure which has to make democratic policies viable (*Cape Times*, 21 March 1990). Democratic culture will need to be nurtured in South Africa; it cannot be taken for granted. 'Putting the last first' as advocated by Chambers may not always be feasible, given the tendency of people to minimise the risks attached to assuming responsibility in organisational structures (Chambers, 1983).[2] One should also not underestimate the inherent capacity of human beings to 'merge with the crowd' (Havel, 1985:38). Considering the anonymity of hostel life and the denial of the individuality and dignity of hostel dwellers, it takes little effort for them to merge with the crowd.

Criticism of the HDA has to be tempered with appreciation of the advances it has made in spite of the constraints upon it. Meaningful steps have been taken to improve the level of participation by all in the projects of the HDA. These have been particularly successful with respect to the upgrading project, where ordinary hostel dwellers are contributing to the planning and implementation of the scheme. Input of this nature helps prepare people to govern. It should be borne in mind, however, that South Africa is still in the liberalisation phase of transition to democratic governance at all levels. The road ahead is still long. New habits of mind will have to be developed to enable all to participate fully in decision making. What is vital is a firm commitment to learning to become more democratic.

Administration of the HDA. A combination of low levels of education, lack of experience in running an efficient organisation with

1. An analytic article by Harber discusses the same problems relating to the African National Congress and its inability to live up to its democratic rhetoric (*Weekly Mail*, 20–23 September 1990).

2. Chambers used this expression in his analysis of inequalities in power relations in rural areas in both Asia and Africa. He concluded that rural development strategies pursued by outsiders tend to perpetuate existing power relations, and saw this perpetuation as largely due to the failure to perceive 'invisible poor people' and to put them first instead of the 'traditional leaders' of such communities (Chambers, 1983).

clear procedures, and the paucity of positive models within the townships hampers the capacity of the HDA to develop an effective administrative machinery. The limited pool from which to recruit office personnel, and the scarcity of resources with which to reward them adequately, are added constraints. Because of its limited resource base, the HDA has had to function with low-grade administrative and clerical staff. The quality of office routine, accounting procedures and general level of responsible employment of assets reflect this weakness (see p. 102). My attempts and those of other interested parties to provide in-service training for the clerical staff were largely unsuccessful.

Part of the reason for this failure lies in the low priority accorded proper administrative procedures by the HDA executive. They perceived action 'out there' addressing the real issues of the day as most important, and therefore more deserving of an investment in time. I failed on many occasions to secure the release of the clerical assistant from the office to attend training courses. The relatively junior status of the clerical assistant, and perhaps her position as a woman and a young person, hindered her ability to effect even the limited procedures she was trained to implement. My attempts to intervene at an executive committee level were met with polite promises to improve their administrative performance, but with little follow-through. There was often a hint of impatience with my persistence in this regard by all members of the executive, with the exception of the general secretary, who had an appreciation of the importance of good administration from his work experience (see Chapter 7).

The marginalisation of administration is also widespread in the running of community and political organisations as well as trade unions.[1] It is partly a result of the unwillingness of donors to fund this aspect of community work. This unwillingness is based on the well-considered view that funding for development should benefit the end users and not be swallowed up by bureaucracy. What is neglected in this formulation, however, is the importance of investing in strengthening the administrative capacity of organisations for change as a legitimate and necessary condition for successful development. There is also evidence of greater tolerance by outsiders of incompetence on the part of community organisations, part of the double-standards morality, which perpetuates and legitimises such behaviour as 'the people's approach'.

The neglect of this aspect of development work has already resulted in charges of maladministration being levelled at some of the major recipients of funds in South Africa.[2] It is difficult to find a credible estimate of the level of inflow of funds into South Africa for development work, but it is likely to run into hundreds of millions of rands a year. The paucity of records of incoming donations is partly a result of the secrecy bred by years of repressive laws in-

1. See *Weekly Mail*, (21–27 September 1990).

2. For example, the Centre for Development Studies at the University of Western Cape (CDS) has had to contend with such allegations. As much as R2 million is said to be involved. The CDS promised to launch an investigation into the matter (*Cape Times*, 7 June 1990).

tended to discourage funding for resistance groups inside the country.

The support for resistance groups in South Africa has spawned a 'South Africa industry' on a world-wide scale. 'The South Africa industry' is well established internationally and is likely to continue to influence South African social relations. It has several features. First, politics is an entrepreneurial affair in the USA, with South Africa as a resource providing lobbyists and legislators with millions of dollars (Simon Barber, *Cape Times*, 13 March 1990). Second, funding for development work for the benefit of 'victims of apartheid' involves networks of professionals, some of whom have vested interests in the continuing conflict in South Africa. The casting of black South Africans as victims is central to the maintenance of this industry. The major problem with control of funds earmarked for development would seem to be related mainly to poor accounting and administrative procedures rather than to widespread wanton misuse of money. The continuing neglect of this area in development and transformation politics undermines the effectiveness of organisations and squanders scarce resources.

It is hardly surprising, therefore, that the HDA with its problems of limited space would also fall into the trap of poor administration. There are simply too few models of efficient administration for it to follow. To its credit, the HDA has annual audited statements. This at least ensures a measure of accountability. Optimal use of limited resources, which requires cost management and productivity evaluations, is unfortunately not covered in such reports.

The upgrading programme. An outline of the upgrading programme was sketched in Chapter 7. Its relevance in this section relates to the impact of increasing physical space on the transformation of power relationships. This impact will only be fully assessed once the programme has been completed. There are, however, process issues which have already arisen that warrant attention. First, the eradication of the system of migrant labour hostels is central to the process of empowerment in this environment. All the other processes of empowerment would be meaningless as independent projects if they were not seen as part of a whole, with upgrading of hostels as the key concern. Second, the importance of congruence between short- and long-term strategies for transformation of power relations should be kept in mind. Merely erecting family housing units to replace existing hostels will not necessarily change the nature of power relationships between those involved. Ideologies, practices and habits developed and legitimised through years of living under space constraints will not easily change when those constraints are removed. Such ideologies 'have become a façade behind which powerless people hide the low foundations of their obedience to authority' (Havel, 1985:28).

The development and promotion of 'the redemptive community', in which each individual is once more 'at home' with others, is one of the outcomes of living in an environment where the boundary between private and public space is non-existent (Berger, 1974:39). The quest for community in situations such as hostels has both 'progressive' and 'reactionary' elements. Community consciousness is essential; it enables those living in limited environments to create a measure of orderliness, and is an important survival strategy to limit the development of anomy.[1] The support one derives from such a community has its costs. Individuality is discouraged in the long term (see also Steele, 1990:68). The long-term consequences of a widespread 'redemptive community' ideology are likely to be detrimental to the development of creativity and freedom of choice for black people in South Africa. Both the benefits of a supportive community and the dangers of submerging individuality in collective consciousness need to be carefully considered in the case of hostel dwellers.

Foundations for change have to be laid in the present if the future is to be different. It was thus considered important by all concerned that barriers to full participation by hostel dwellers in the planning of the upgrading programme should be removed, so that they could experience a sense of control over this area of their lives. Workshops were held regularly to effect this.

Finally, if the upgraded housing scheme is to be successful as a living environment, it has to be owned by those people for whom it is intended. Their participation is crucial at all levels. For example, in the planning stage hostel dwellers have developed a sense of control over the process and acquired a knowledge base which will be useful in other situations. The emphasis by all participants on the importance of viable public spaces in the design of the proposed scheme should enhance the chances of these spaces being treated with respect by most users. Participation in fundraising has opened their eyes to the workings of big finance and the responsibilities of both donors and beneficiaries in developing a mutually acceptable package.

These efforts are the small beginning of an attempt to develop a meaningful process of involving poor people in designing, building and maintaining their own housing scheme, and lessons will be learnt from both its successes and failures.

Conclusion

Empowerment as documented in this chapter is a process of acknowledging the humanity of those people who have been systematically dehumanised, thereby enabling them to stand up and challenge the status quo. A large part of the effort in the case of hostels involves active measures to remove constraints in the form of red tape, for example the facilitation of access to health services.

1. This has been defined as a condition in which a person is deprived of stable, secure ties with other human beings, and in which one lacks the meaning that normally provides adequate direction in one's life (Berger, 1974:39).

Empowerment also critically examines the coping strategies used by disempowered people, and challenges those involved to recognise that some aspects of these strategies also contribute to a perpetuation of the status quo. Empowerment, while supportive of the efforts of poor people's struggles for survival, nevertheless focuses their attention on the power they have to move beyond survival towards transforming their social milieu. Self-imposed constraints, such as undemocratic procedures and leadership styles, need as much attention as that focused on constraints imposed by outside agents of power. The process of empowerment is premissed on the notion of the agency of human beings and their ability to perceive the relationship between the day-to-day choices they as individuals make and the final outcome of power relations in their society.

Debunking myths perpetuated by both the national South African political system and the local political leadership is an important part of the process of empowerment:

> Myth fosters total commitment, and people who are so committed tend to be blind to inconvenient facts, and indifferent to the human costs of their mythologically legitimated programmes. For this reason 'demythologisation' is both theoretically and politically important in the area of development. There is no alternative to having intellectual and political elites, but it makes sense to prefer theorists who have doubts, and policy-makers with scruples (Berger, 1974:46).

9 Conclusion

I have approached this study fully cognisant of my position as both a citizen and a native anthropologist, and of the real potential for conflict between the role of a citizen and native and that of an anthropologist. I have also enjoyed the privileges of being a native-citizen anthropologist. I have benefited immensely from the willingness of hostel dwellers to share their life experiences with me, and thus enable me to explore my own hitherto unarticulated fears, hopes and concerns. I have attempted to use my skills to expand the limited intellectual space hostel dwellers find themselves in, because it is in the field of intellectual space that there was the greatest interaction and perhaps greatest potential long-term returns.

The use of participatory research methods, despite their acknowledged limitations, enabled me to explore the problems posed by individual autonomy within the constraints of the social structure of hostels (see Heald, 1989). I have inadequately incorporated the psychological dimension of individual autonomy in my exploration of psychological space. Greater co-operation between the disciplines of psychology and anthropology is essential to the undertaking of a fuller exploration of this aspect of social science.

A focus of this study has been to demonstrate that both constraints of space and the transformative agency of human beings have a significant part in shaping the nature of the balance between replication or transformation of systems of power relations. Evidence presented in this book suggests that there is a constant tension between replication and transformation of social relations. This tension is generated by the complex processes involved in negotiating difficult choices which hostel dwellers have to make at all levels of social relations (see also Comaroff, 1985:6; Stimpson, 1988:157–8).

Hostel dwellers as social actors vacillate between acquiescence in the dominant oppressive order based on racial discrimination and the legacy of the migrant labour system, and resistance to that order. Transformation and replication are treated in this book as processes, not as events occurring at a point in history. Negotiation and renegotiation of social relations contain elements of both replication and transformation. Such processes constitute the politics of space in the context of hostels. The politics of space have both liberating and limiting features.

Liberating features of the politics of space

Individual hostel dwellers have ironically been enabled by limitations of space to move beyond some of the boundaries set by customary practice. Some men have become much more active parents in the bedhold than they might have been in a more spacious rural environment. Male hostel dwellers also cross taboo lines such as those relating to the place of men in childbirth and care of the newly delivered woman and new-born child. Men in the hostels are also forced by circumstances to do domestic chores traditionally regarded as women's work. Some men are employed in jobs traditionally associated with women, such as domestic service, because of the limited job prospects for people at their low educational level. Such men learn valuable skills such as cooking and general housekeeping. Mthembu for example proudly said: 'My wife knows that she cannot compete with me when it comes to cooking.'

Children living in hostels also find relief from endless domestic errands because of the limited private space for families (for details of the burdens children carry in poor households, see Reynolds, 1989; Wilson & Ramphele, 1987). The lack of physical and private domestic space thus allows children the space to enjoy childhood for a longer period than might be granted them in a normal household setting.

Limiting features of the politics of space

Constraining features of the politics of space are a dominant theme in this study. First, hostel dwellers have had to accept being defined as migrant workers in order to gain access to jobs in Cape Town. Their acceptance of the reality of living in single-sex hostels involves a choice between economic survival and the assertion of one's right to respect and dignity. Sipho's lament captures the pain of this Hobson's choice: 'I have accepted being called an *isoka* (bachelor) even though it is a denigrating term, because I live in the hostels' (see p. 114). The men whom Reynolds interviewed in Langa hostels were equally articulate about their plight: 'We are spilt just like water on the ground' (Reynolds, 1984:11). The repeal of influx control in 1986 has not erased this perception. Acceptance of denigration arising out of one's living circumstances constitutes a constant assault on one's self-image and sensibilities. Many of those interviewed in this study attested to the indignity of being members of 'bedholds' and being treated with disrespect by other people, including other Africans living in neighbouring townships. In his address to the Second Carnegie Inquiry into Poverty in South Africa, the President of the Carnegie Corporation of New York, Dr David Hamburg, made a comment of particular relevance:

> It is one thing to have a very low income but to be treated with respect by your compatriots; it is quite another matter to have a very low income and to be harshly depreciated by more powerful compatriots. . . . To speak of impoverishment in this sense is to speak of human degradation so profound as to undermine any reasonable and decent standard of human life (Hamburg, 1984:7).

South Africans may yet have to pay a high price for the long-term consequences of the profound human degradation visited on hostel dwellers over the years.

Second, in response to the reality of living under space constraints of the dimensions documented here, hostel dwellers have developed survival strategies which help them to create meaning and harmony in a disordered environment at both the individual and community levels. This study celebrates the ingenuity and resilience which spawn such survival strategies. People survive hardships because they have something to live for. Survivors have dreams, and hope for a better future sustains them.[1] Frankl, a survivor of the Nazi concentration camps, explains his own and other inmates' ability to survive the horrors of that period in Nietzsche's words: 'He who has a *why* to live for, can bear with almost any *how*' (Frankl, 1968:76). Hostel dwellers are sustained by the meaning they have found in their lives and are thus able to survive the indignities of their circumstances. The 'how' of that survival is the focus of this study.

But is there life beyond survival? What distinguishes survivors who realise their dreams from those who fail to do so? Evidence in this study suggests that the social costs of some survival strategies further limit the transformative agency of hostel dwellers and prevent them from realising their dreams. Of particular concern is the possibility of the transmission of accumulated social costs to future generations – the proverbial 'visiting of the sins of fathers on their children'. Kovaly, a survivor of the Second World War and of Hitler's concentration camps, reminds us: 'People who are ready to sacrifice their own well-being for some lofty goal are likely to extract a similar sacrifice from others who are not so willing' (Kovaly, 1988:75).

Many people in the hostels have sacrificed their dreams and personal well-being for the sake of the survival of their families and others close to them. Evidence presented here suggests that 'life beyond survival' remains elusive for most hostel dwellers and their families. A brief examination of examples of survival strategies with high social costs will illustrate this point.

Communal survival strategies

There are several communal survival strategies worthy of special mention in this regard. Development of a sense of community and strong networks of support is particularly important. Hostel dwellers have evolved an elaborate 'economy of affection' involving kin, 'home-people' *(amakhaya)* and friends, which protects many from falling off the edge of society. It is a warm and enriching system, although hostel dwellers do incur costs in the support they derive from this 'economy of affection'. Reciprocal obligations prove burdensome for some. Tensions between adult children and their parents are to some extent rooted in the different interpretations of the nature and extent of such obligations to one's kin (see also Reynolds, 1984). These tensions often lead to conflict within families, and sometimes to breakdown in relationships. Women, who constitute

1. I am indebted to Freda Paltiel, Senior Advisor, Status of Women, Health and Welfare of the Federal Government of Canada in Ottawa, for this expression (personal communication).

the majority of dependants, bear the brunt of such conflicts, which sometimes lead some over-stressed men to alcohol abuse and abandonment of all family links.

There is also guilt on the part of survivors of hardship within such a network of support: why did I survive when others have succumbed? Such guilt feelings reinforce a self-sacrificial sense in survivors, with serious consequences for the individual (see also Kovaly, 1988:73). Such people become vulnerable to unreasonable demands by those who are less fortunate. These demands may go beyond their means and force them into extraordinary actions. Nepotism, corruption and dishonesty at work may result from attempts to meet family demands in the face of limited means. It would seem that there is a need to re-establish a balance between support networks and development of individuals. Society has placed a heavy burden on family and other informal networks. Societal responsibilities in the field of child-care and care of the aged and sick have too often been shifted to impoverished families without any financial support by the State and other authorities. Women end up carrying the heaviest load in this regard, with no value being attached to their work. The quality of the human resource base has suffered and will continue to suffer from the impact of lack of space for individuals to develop their full potential.

Conformism is also a necessary part of creating harmony under such severe space constraints. The hierarchical dispute settlement structures provided by the *izibonda* system are central to the process of maintaining harmony. Hostel dwellers cannot afford the luxury of encouraging unbridled individuality. It has to be subordinated to the interest of group survival. In certain instances individual initiative is also thwarted. Under such circumstances mediocrity is likely to be rewarded and excellence discredited and penalised. Gordon's study of Namibian contract workers also provides evidence of this tendency – individuals have to be constantly on guard against being seen to be better off than their peers for fear of incurring their wrath (Gordon, 1977:101–46). The 'tall poppy syndrome' is a problem among insecure people – tall poppies are cut down to size to re-establish 'harmony'.

Another costly communal strategy is the emergence of a siege mentality which fortifies hostel dwellers against the hostile environment in which they find themselves. Township dwellers are in this sense defined as competitors for scarce resources. There is also a perception that township residents show little respect for hostel dwellers' humanity. The eviction of hostel dwellers from some Zones in Langa is often cited as an example. Under such circumstances the potential for violent conflict is great. This potential was translated into violence in vigilante action by hostel dwellers against township residents in the 1976–7 period in Cape Town.

The causes and nature of the violence which occurred on the Witwatersrand during the second half of 1990 and more recently in the Alexandra township, Boipatong and other areas in that region[1] have a certain resemblance to the violent confrontation referred to above in the Cape Town context in the 1970s. These incidents all bear witness to the danger of the siege mentality and its exploitation by those bent on divide-and-rule strategies. The forging of links between the HDA and the MDM during the 1980s has significantly reduced the potential for this form of violent conflict in the Cape Town area, and could serve as a model for others. One should not underestimate the depth of the wound of humiliation inflicted on generations of hostel dwellers. Respect for their human dignity is vital for healing the rifts of the past.

Intolerance of criticism from within and without, another feature of the 'siege mentality' within the HDA, has serious long-term consequences for the capacity of hostel dwellers to function in an open and more democratic society. Evidence of such intolerance was presented in Chapter 7. Personal and societal development is undermined by the lack of constructive criticism. The same could be said of many organisations of the oppressed which have increasingly grown intolerant of both internal and external criticism. Democracy cannot flourish where criticism is not tolerated.

Individual survival strategies

An examination of individual survival strategies of hostel dwellers also reveals some interesting features. Individual hostel dwellers exhibit variations in the nature of the strategies that each adopts in both time and space. These variations reflect the individuals' assessment of the affordability of the risks entailed in the choices they have to make. Three main types of response emerge: acquiescence; quiet, calculative operations; and vocal, militant operations. For example, Woyisa (p. 82), despite being a militant trade unionist and calculative operator who opted for single parenthood and defied a prescription by a traditional healer for *ukutwasa*, nonetheless chooses to acquiesce in her boyfriend's demands in the context of the bedhold. She perceives defying him as too risky – it could lead to her losing a vital urban accommodation base. Many other women both inside and outside hostels find themselves in a similar position of being unable to make free choices without compromising themselves in one way or another.

The outcomes of individual survival strategies also vary. Some people fall off the edge in spite of all their attempts to hold onto their dreams of a better future. Many of those finding themselves in the Langa and Nyanga old-age homes are examples of those who have fallen off. The majority of hostel dwellers cling to the margins of survival, balancing on a knife-edge. Some of those in this category manage reasonably, while others fare poorly. The use of alcohol and

1. See *Weekly Mail*, 21–27 March 1991; reports on the Goldstone Commission hearings, 1992.

drugs such as marijuana forms an important part of the armour of survival for individual hostel dwellers. Alcohol and marijuana act as a dark curtain that shuts out the blinding light of a humiliating life. The health and social costs of alcohol and drug abuse are, however, high.

Finally, there are a few individuals who seem to thrive in spite of their dismal circumstances. Some of them, such as Nomsa, have managed to transcend the limitations imposed by constraints of space and continue to pursue their dreams in the wider society (see pp. 82–3; 104). Some of the members of the HDA executive are also actively pursuing their personal dreams, as well as enabling other hostel dwellers to keep their hopes alive too. The capacity to take risks seems to distinguish these people from others. They keep pushing against the constraints of space they find themselves in instead of accepting them as given. They insist on roles as active agents of history.

It is noteworthy that some hostel dwellers have adjusted so well to limited space that they experience difficulty in functioning in more open space situations. For example, the need to maintain the 'brotherhood' established over the years has led occupants of a particular hostel block to debar women from staying overnight (see Chapter 6). Such behaviour suggests that some hostel dwellers may have become institutionalised and dependent on the support of the 'brotherhood' (Goffman, 1961), and this has obvious implications for hostel dwellers' capacity to function in a transformed society. It is therefore not surprising that some hostel dwellers on the Witwatersrand are said to be opposed to the conversion of hostels into private family units. They may have difficulty functioning in a different environment.

The adoption of the victim role, another survival strategy, deserves special consideration. First, it invokes a response from those around the victim. Responses elicited may include advocacy and the provision of material resources for the victim. The victim role is thus a resource in itself. A culture of entitlement emerges as a logical consequence of assuming that society is obliged to redress the inequities of the past. Hostel dwellers as a group have been victimised by dominant groups in South African society, and as such are entitled to redress. Society has to enable them to acquire reasonable accommodation, given the incalculable opportunity costs of not owning a home in the urban areas. Individual claims to entitlements, however, would be more problematic. The responsibility of society is to create opportunities for self-development, as well as to remove any obstacles in the path of self-actualisation, but the individual has to accept ultimate responsibility for successful performance. Failure to ensure individual responsibility could lead to a situation in which society would be seen as the agent for change, thereby disempowering the individual. Under such circumstances victims are denied and deny themselves agency in history.

Second, the victim status releases the person thus designated from responsibility for the condition he or she is in. Victims do not have to take responsibility for their own errors of omission and commission. Irresponsible behaviour, incompetence and general anti-social tendencies become legitimised as acceptable because of victim status. For example, the HDA leadership expected tolerance for poor administrative procedures and financial control from all the people they interacted with, simply because they are victims of a racist system. This is not to underestimate the problem of lack of skills and a culture of administrative competence, but the HDA's reluctance to take advantage of training opportunities indicated a lack of appreciation of the centrality of this function. Many black South African organisations, too, expect to be judged leniently on organisational competence. The adoption of double standards becomes a necessity in such a situation. Lower standards are justified when judging those defined as victims, who are thus denied the incentive for striving for excellence in whatever they do. The danger of mediocrity becoming the norm looms large under such circumstances.

Evidence from the USA suggests that the increasingly poor performance of African Americans on all major indicators is partly due to continued racism, but is also related to the low expectations others have of them (Gibbs, 1988; Steele, 1990). The deterioration in performance by blacks occurred not during the height of segregation, but after the civil rights victories of the 1960s. Steele suggests that some affirmative action programmes have been iniquitous to blacks. He asserts that some institutions patronise blacks through the use of double standards, and encourage them to fall back on a culture of entitlement, creating further long-term disadvantages for them (Steele, 1990:142). The challenge for transformation is thus to redress the inequities of the past without creating further obstacles to human development in its totality.

Empowerment in the context of limited space

This study documents how power relations within the hostels reflect those in the wider society. Power relations in South Africa consist of a pyramidal power structure with elderly men at the top, followed by younger men, with women and children at the bottom. The zero–sum notion of power also underpins social relations in most institutional settings of this society. There is differentiation among and between hostel dwellers, arising from these features of power relations. This creates tension between the need for hostel dwellers to co-operate in the interest of common survival and the reality of competition among them for space as a scarce resource.

My involvement in the hostels was part of an empowerment process. The focus of empowerment was on identifying, encouraging and supporting those survival strategies of hostel dwellers which would most probably lead to transformation of social relations at both the micro and macro levels. My involvement was also premissed on the fact that hostel dwellers cannot be expected to lift themselves up by their own metaphoric bootstraps, because many of them have none. In my role as a facilitator I have advocated, and continue to advocate on their behalf, that society meets its obligation to them and enables them to gain access to resources so long denied them. It remains their responsibility, however, to develop themselves, as Frankl reminds us: 'man [*sic*] is ultimately self-determining' (Frankl, 1968:132). This is the heart of the problem: 'freedom is stressful, difficult and frightening – a burden, according to Sartre, because of the responsibility it carries' (Steele, 1990:68). Patronising hostel dwellers does not seem to me an appropriate response to the fear of responsibility which they display, both collectively and individually.

It is my view that they have to accept responsibility for their interpersonal and community relations. Tolerance of undemocratic behaviour on the part of those in positions of leadership, for which individuals are not made accountable, cannot be justified. This is a real dilemma for hostel dwellers: the desire to be free from domination is set against the fear of taking risks. But without the willingness to risk loss, little or no transformative action would be possible. Comaroff is critical of black intellectuals who are seen as impatient with the strategies for survival among poor people which reinforce docility (Comaroff, 1985:261). She suggests that such impatience is born out of a failure to recognise the cumulative impact of humble human action on the long-term transformation of social orders. What Comaroff neglects to take into account, however, is the impact of long-established habits on the capacity of people not only to transform but to act as responsible active agents in a new social order. Nurturing docility in social relations has negative consequences for democracy in the long term. Barker's words are apt: '. . . those treated like boys, behave like boys, . . . those who, having no responsibilities laid upon them, owe none to any man [*sic*]' (Barker, 1970). Black intellectuals have to critically examine the impact of cultural relativism on their own communities. Visiting academics can 'afford' to theorise about the importance of cultural relativism, because at the end of their field-work they can go 'home' and lead normal lives where certain competencies are taken for granted. For a native scholar, criticism of negative elements of survival culture is inevitable. One cannot only celebrate survival, one would like to be part of a culture that also transcends and seeks to triumph over dominance in all forms.

The risks entailed in challenging dominance from wherever it comes cannot be underestimated. For example, risks attached to challenging sexism in interpersonal relations in any situation are considerable. In the hostels, space constraints place women in powerless positions relative to men. The risks of losing the only form of accommodation, and consequently access to a source of livelihood, are considerable. Gender relationships are also complicated by the contradictions of having a lover and competitor in the same person. Women in this situation neither command resources nor have men's recognition of their importance as persons, two factors which some analysts have found to be essential for women to effectively resist subordination (Stimpson, 1988:164). It is thus not surprising that some women have internalised oppression to the extent of saying that 'women need domination by men'. Transformation is inhibited by such attitudes.

Men also fear the implications of transforming gender relationships. The loss of privileges accruing to the dominant male status is only part of the problem. A more frightening aspect relates to the loss of the security provided by the 'brotherhood'. 'Deeper male conversion from sexism involves a willingness to enter into risks to himself. He has to recognise his own profound fear of loss of affirmation by the male group ego if he departs from male roles' (Ruether, 1983:191). Is it reasonable for hostel dwellers to take risks in gender relationships? There are no easy answers. It is, however, important to remember that one form of oppression becomes a paradigm for another (Brittan & Maynard, 1984). True democracy cannot develop without attention to gender politics.

Similar calculative choices are constantly being made in relation to other parameters of power relations. Failure to confront the fears people experience in making difficult choices, as well as the lack of positive models of social relations based on equity, accounts in part for the replication of unequal power relations among hostel dwellers and in the wider South African society. It is not going to be easy to overcome the legacy of space constraints:

> Shut up behind barbed wire, robbed of all rights including the right to live, we had stopped regarding freedom as something natural and self-evident. Gradually the idea of freedom as a birthright became blurred . . . [it] has to be earned and fought for, a privilege that is awarded like a medal. It is hardly possible for people to live for so many years as slaves in everyday contact with fascists and fascism without becoming somewhat twisted, without contracting a trace of that dry rot unwittingly and unwillingly (Kovaly, 1988:73).

South Africans have to acknowledge the legacy of apartheid, particularly the space constraints imposed on black people. It is not going to be easy for a people who have had to 'shrink' to fit the limited space they found themselves in, to stand up and walk tall. Habits developed over the years of oppression will die hard.

It is, however, the limitations of intellectual space that are likely to prove the most difficult to overcome. Critical awareness of oneself in history is essential for choices demanded moment by moment. In the absence of such critical awareness of one's own agency, it becomes more likely for one to flow with the stream and to become prey to ambitious politicians. Democratic systems function well if there is trust in such systems, as well as in the capacity of individual citizens to act as a restraint on political ambition acting against the common good. Such trust in 'the system' can only develop if the majority of people understand 'the system' and believe in their own capacity to exercise control over it and to influence its direction (see also Giddens, 1991, on modernity and trust in systems). The mass of uneducated people in South Africa have little prospect of developing such a trust and the self-confidence essential to becoming active agents of democracy in the short term. It is thus essential for those with more intellectual space to act in a manner which increases the capacity of ordinary people to expand their horizons beyond the limitations of their past and present. The emergence of an active civil society depends on critical awareness.

The transitional phase in which South Africa finds itself in the 1990s poses a challenge for all anthropologists and other intellectuals as citizens. Essential characteristics of this transitional phase are the opening up of political, ideological, economic, intellectual and psychological spaces, which will alter the nature of the politics of space at all levels of society. Anthropologists, given their capacity to study the particular in the context of general social relations, are well placed to examine, document and influence the formulation of future policies. As political authority shifts to those previously subordinated, so too will the advocacy role of anthropologists need to be refocused on hitherto neglected subsections such as women, children and those generally pushed to the corners of society. The oppressed, like all other human beings, have the capacity to become oppressors (Frankl, 1968:91). Critical scholarship is an essential part of the process of empowerment of those marginalised by society, to facilitate fundamental transformation of social relations.

Appendix: Methodology

Participatory research has gained popularity amongst a number of researchers both in South Africa and internationally (see, for example, Lund, 1982; Reason and Rowan, 1981). Different motivations are responsible for individual workers' change of direction, but all share a discomfort with the 'traditional' research paradigm's capacity to cope with the demand for creative approaches in a world of changing social relations. These motivations revolve to a greater or lesser extent around the issue of knowledge as power, and the need to address the question of the relationship of the researcher to the people who are the focus of study, in the context of complex power relations.

The ideal model of participatory research entails cooperative enquiry by researchers and their subjects. Several steps, which involve a two-way educational process at every level, have been identified. They include: joint identification of the problem to be studied; analysis of the best way of conducting the study; planning the actual work involved; acquiring resources for the study process; implementation; analysis and evaluation of the study; reporting of results; and incorporating the results in a future solution (Reason and Rowan, 1981).

Various scholars utilising this approach are beginning to acknowledge some of the constraints to effective participation in these collaborative efforts (Lund, 1982; Sacks in Bookman & Morgen, 1988), whereas for others, the romanticism that accompanies most novelties still obscures their analyses. Some of the major problems acknowledged are the lack of successful models, the impact of an all-pervasive authoritarian ethos and practice on most (if not all) social interactions, and the limited capacity of people to form 'new habits of mind' to break free from traditional hierarchical relationships (Orsy, 1987; Barnes, 1988).

Participatory research in the context of migrant labour hostels in the Western Cape

The request by the Western Cape Hostel Dwellers' Association (HDA) for my active involvement in their attempts to address some of the problems confronting them in this environment was motivated by a number of considerations. Firstly, they expressed a keenness for me to work with them in the field of health care, because of their concern about the impact of the hostel environment on the health status of the inhabitants. Secondly, they felt that as hostel dwellers, they faced additional barriers, which placed them at a disadvantage with respect to access to health care.

Methods employed

Various methods of data collection were utilised in my study in order to enhance both the width and the depth of the data base. It was also an inter-disciplinary exercise, drawing on the biomedical and anthropological approaches to and methods of research. Data gathering included the following:

In-depth open-ended interviews. Interviews were aimed at increasing the depth of the data base. Life histories were elicited using a question schedule as a guide. At the end of each interview, a medical examination was conducted to screen for common health problems, such as high blood pressure and glycosuria (sugar in urine). These interviews were conducted over a period of six weeks in October–November 1986.

All interviews were conducted in a caravan parked near the entrance to one of the hostels in Langa. Interviewees were taken from those available in the selected block, which consisted of 64 beds. This selection was arbitrary, and done on the recommendation of the HDA executive. It was seen as an ice-breaker for the entire project by both the HDA executive and myself.

The problem of bias introduced by this selection process was weighed up against the advantages of gaining the confidence of the hostel population and being seen to take their suggestions seriously. Plans were made to broaden the scope of these interviews to include people in other blocks in the same area as well as other areas, and thus address the issue of bias. Interviews in other blocks in the same area, as well as a few in other areas, revealed a lot of similarities in terms of the major issues being examined. These similarities reduced to a considerable extent the level of concern about the non-representativeness of the selected block.

There was an eagerness to participate by more people than could be dealt with. Nineteen men and nine women were interviewed between ten o'clock in the morning and four o'clock in the afternoon, over the six-week period. There were no weekend interviews generally, except in special cases where follow-up visits were arranged. The question of bias in favour of unemployed people was obviated by the fact that most labourers work shifts, which permit them to be home during the day.

I would arrive at about nine thirty in the mornings and sit around in the 'front room', where people would be having breakfast, and chat to people. Almost invariably, I would be offered a share in the breakfast and be drawn into conversations. This process would last until one of those around would indicate his or her readiness to participate. This period served as valuable participant observation time.

I also conducted interviews with three people in the selected block who had been initially reticent about participation. These also yielded interesting insights into the ambiguities and contradictions inherent in this social setting. The most important distinguishing feature of these interviewees was their unwillingness to express their opinions on conditions of life in the hostels. Among the reasons advanced for this unwillingness was that it was a waste of time. 'What is the use? Nothing will come of it,' one of them said. Another reason was fear of the consequences of their disclosures becoming public. Some of the questions raised were: Were the authorities not going to use the research data to penalise them further? What guarantees did they have that the interviews would be confidentially treated?

Group discussions. Group discussions were conducted in the same area in Langa where the above interviews were conducted but included other hostel blocks beyond the initial one. A total of fifteen group discussions were conducted, comprising five to ten people at a time during August 1987. These discussions involved both men and women as well as people of all age groups from 16 years upwards. The range of topics varied from health issues to concerns involving broad political problems, both in the Cape Peninsula and their rural bases in the Eastern Cape. Groups were never bigger than ten. A research assistant accompanied me on most of these visits.

'A day in the life of' interviews. These interviews were aimed at eliciting some details about how people in this setting organised their daily lives. These were conducted with all 28 interviewees in the caravan, all group interviewees as well as an additional ten individuals met at random around the hostels. When do their days start? How and what do they do to get ready for the new day? How and for how long do they commute if employed formally? What sort of work do they do? What about activities at the end of the day: when and how do they relax, prepare and eat supper, and finally retire to bed?

The demographic survey (Survey 1). Survey 1 was conducted between May and June 1987, using questionnaires. Hostels in the different areas of Langa were targeted to ensure coverage of the various types of accommodation available. Teams of interviewers comprising staff and students of the Department of Anthropology at UCT conducted this survey over two weekends. These teams augmented the efforts of the research team, which covered the same areas during the week, to minimise missing out on those not at home during the weekends. Some members of the HDA, predominantly executive members, gave their time freely to facilitate the demographic survey, which was undertaken during weekends.

The health survey (Survey 2). Survey 2 was conducted during November 1987, targeting a random sample of 10 per cent of all the beds in all the hostels in Langa, Guguletu and Nyanga. Women residents in the various areas acted as facilitators by motivating those randomly selected as part of the sample to come forward for interviews. Given the demands of this task, it was decided by the research team to pay those involved, but to leave the choice of suitable candidates to local HDA structures.

Survey 2 sought to define the health status of a representative sample of hostel dwellers and to document their choice of healers and health-care facilities for various ailments identified at the time. Participation in this survey was voluntary, and participants could choose the level of involvement. This latitude resulted in incomplete questionnaires in a few cases, or in people not undergoing all the procedures outlined. The response rate overall was 3 per cent (322 beds), compared with the targeted 10 per cent (1 200 beds). In this survey, 60 per cent of the bed sample volunteered for the health interview.

Some methodological problems. The in-depth interview stage presented no major problems, except for total exhaustion on my part from being overwhelmed by that environment. The squalor, noise, and constant and intense interactions with people on the edge of survival reminded me of Wikan's exasperation during her fieldwork in Cairo (Wikan, 1980). Like her, I soon realised that there is a limit to what one's psyche can take in such an intense setting.

The health survey was the most problematic aspect of the whole process. Part of the problem related to its technical nature, but there are other factors which contributed to the relatively poor response rate in this survey.[1] Firstly, the fact that facilitators were to be paid created intense competition amongst women in the various areas, all of whom sought to benefit from this windfall. Those not chosen were very bitter, and in one area where the local chairperson of the women's committee was overlooked, she used her influence to put a spanner in the works, resulting in a much lower response rate than had been expected. This factor demonstrates the 'power of powerlessness' that is embodied in the contradictory observation that 'women don't lead, but they do lead' (Bookman and Morgen, 1988:80)!

Secondly, many individuals were totally unaware of the purpose and nature of the survey, having not been involved in any of the preparatory processes outlined above. This reflects both on their own ability to be informed on events in their environment and on the organisational ability of the HDA. As in similar cases, the more that people get involved in events and processes around them, the more they are enabled to participate in matters that have a bearing on their lives (Ruchwager, 1987:136). Some of the people refused to get involved in spite of additional motivation by the research team, but many came forward. Other people who were also unaware of this project and were not included in the sample insisted on inclusion either out of fear of being left out of the upgrading pro-

1. The response rate from the total number of beds was very poor: only 3 per cent of those bedholds targeted came forward for the demographic survey. Of those who came forward 60 per cent volunteered for the health survey.

gramme or because they had some urgent health or social problem to present.

In some areas, notably Nyanga, where only 1 per cent of the total number of beds responded, there was open hostility to the research team, because of our association with the HDA. Residents blamed the poor organisational style of the HDA, as well as personality problems involving some of the members of the executive, for this hostility. There was also talk of an active campaign against the HDA being conducted by a local representative of the local town committee,[1] which involved threats of violence against the team, for its association with the HDA. This incident prompted our hasty withdrawal from the area. It also points to the risks inherent in working in highly-charged political environments, as well as the impact of the overall political milieu on the process, quality and outcome of participatory research.

In a section of Langa where hostility was anticipated, the research team distanced itself from the HDA and achieved a response rate of 83 per cent of the target beds in the sample, compared with an overall response rate of 17 per cent for Langa. This further indicates some of the trade-offs involved in a process of this nature and the need for flexibility in assessing the authenticity of the claim of representativeness of community organisations.

1. Town committees were introduced in 1988 to act as local authority structures in African townships and to represent residents of these areas in the Regional Services Councils.

Bibliography

Abercrombie, N. and Turner, B. 1982. The dominant ideology thesis. In A. Giddens and D. Held *Classes, Power And Conflict*. University of California Press, Berkeley.

Achebe, C. 1958. *Things Fall Apart*. Zimbabwe Educational Books, Harare.

Achebe, C. 1987. *Anthills of the Savannah*. William Heinemann Ltd, London.

Amadiume, I. 1990. *Male Daughters, Female Husbands – Gender and Sex in an African Society*. Zed Books, London.

Anonymous. 1989. (a) Roads to Cosatu congress. *Work in Progress*, No. 59.

Anonymous. 1989. (b) Challenging sexual exploitation. *Work in Progress*, No. 61.

Ardener, S. 1981. *Women and Space: Ground Rules and Cultural Maps*. Croom Helm, London.

Arnold, M. 1978. *The Testimony of Steve Biko*. Panther Granada Publishing Ltd, London.

Bachelard, G. 1969. *The Poetics of Space*. Beacon Press, Boston.

Barker, A. 1970. Community of the careless. *South African Outlook*, April, Vol. 100: 54–5.

Barnes, B. 1988. *The Nature of Power*. University of Illinois Press, Chicago and Urbana.

Benatar, S.R. 1986. Medicine and health care in South Africa. *New England Journal of Medicine*, 315:527–32.

Berger, P.L. 1974. *Pyramids of Sacrifice – Political Ethics and Social Change*. Basic Books, New York.

Bertelsmann, R. 1987. International feminism and the women's movement in South Africa. *South African Outlook*, June, Vol.117 (139):62–6.

Biko, S. 1986. The definition of Black Consciousness. SASO leadership training paper. In A. Stubbs (ed.) *Steve Biko – I Write What I Like*. Harper & Row, San Francisco.

Biko, S. 1986. Fear – an important determinant in South African politics. In A. Stubbs (ed.) *Steve Biko – I Write What I Like*. Harper & Row, San Francisco.

Bookman, A. and Morgen, S. 1988. *Women and the Politics of Empowerment*. Temple University Press, Philadelphia.

Boonzaier, E. 1988. 'Race' and the race paradigm. In E. Boonzaier and J.S. Sharp (eds) *South African Keywords*. David Philip, Cape Town.

Boonzaier, E.B. and Sharp, J.S. (eds) 1988. *South African Keywords*. David Philip, Cape Town.

Boston Women's Health Collective. 1984. *The New Our Bodies Ourselves*. Simon & Schuster, New York.

Bourdieu, I. 1977. *Outline of a Theory in Practice*. Cambridge University Press, Cambridge.

Bozzoli, B. 1983. Marxism, feminism and southern African studies. *Journal of Southern African Studies*, 9 (2):139–71.

Bozzoli, B. (ed.) 1987. *Class, Community and Conflict – South African Perspectives*. Ravan Press, Johannesburg.

Bradford, H. 1988. Formulating resettlement: a review of the surplus people. *Social Dynamics*, 14 (1):67–74.

Bradshaw, H. *et al.* 1987. *Review of South African Mortality*. Technical report, Medical Research Council.

Brittan, A. and Maynard, M. 1984. *Sexism, Racism and Oppression*. Basil Blackwell, Oxford.

Bührmann, M.V. 1985. *Living in Two Worlds*. Human & Rousseau, Cape Town.

Bundy, C. 1972. The emergence and decline of a South African peasantry. *African Affairs*, 71 (285):369–88.

Bundy, C. 1988. *The Rise and Fall of the South African Peasantry*. David Philip, Cape Town.

Burman, S.B. 1988. Defining children. In E.B. Boonzaier and J.S. Sharp (eds) *South African Keywords*. David Philip, Cape Town.

Burman, S.B. and Barry, J. 1984. *Divorce and Deprivation in South Africa*. Carnegie Conference Paper No. 87, Saldru, University of Cape Town.

Burman, S.B. and Reynolds, P. (eds) 1986. *Growing Up in a Divided Society – The Context of Childhood in South Africa*. Ravan Press, Johannesburg.

Burton, C. 1985. *Subordination, Feminism and Social Theory*. George Allen & Unwin, London.

Cabral, A. 1973. *Return to the Source: Selected Speeches*. Monthly Review Press, New York.

Chambers, R. 1983. *Rural Development: Putting the Last First*. Longman, London.

Cheater, A. 1987. The anthropologist as citizen: the diffracted self? In A. Jackson (ed.) *Anthropology at Home*. Tavistock, London.

Cheetham, R.W.S. and Griffiths, J.A. 1982. The traditional healer/diviner as psychotherapist. *South African Medical Journal*, 62:957–8.

Chinemana, F. 1988. Liberated health in Zimbabwe? The experience of women 1981–1983. Unpublished paper presented at the third workshop on Poverty, Health and the State in southern Africa (CHISA), Columbia University, New York.

Claassens, A. 1980. Riekert and Wiehahn: unions and migrants. Social Science (Hons) thesis (unpublished), University of Witwatersrand, Johannesburg.

Clifford, J. 1988. *The Predicament of Culture: Twentieth Century Ethnography, Literature, and Art*. Harvard University Press, Cambridge, MA.

Cock, J. and Edmund, E. 1987. Let me make history, please. In B. Bozzoli (ed.) *Class, Community and Conflict – South African Perspectives*. Ravan Press, Johannesburg.

Cole, J. 1986. *All American Women – Lines that Divide, Ties that Bind*. The Free Press, New York.

Cole, Josette 1987. *Crossroads – The Politics of Reform and Repression 1976–1986*. Ravan Press, Johannesburg.

Comaroff, J. 1985. *Body of Power, Spirit of Resistance*. University of Chicago Press, Chicago.

Connell, R.W. 1982. A critique of Althusserian approach to class. In A. Giddens and D. Held *Classes, Power and Conflict*. University of California Press, Berkeley.

Cornell, J. 1984. *Workshop Health Services and Employment in Manufacturing Industry in Greater Cape Town*. Carnegie Conference Paper No. 289, Saldru, University of Cape Town.

De Beer, C. 1984. *The South African Disease – Apartheid, Health and Health Services*. South African Research Service (SARS), Johannesburg.

De Gruchy, J.W. 1987. Religion and healing in our crisis context: towards a theology of medicine. Unpublished paper, Department of Religious Studies, University of Cape Town.

Devereux, S. 1983. Nyanga squatter diary July 1981–December 1982. In D. Horner (ed.) *Labour Preference, Influx Control and Squatters: Cape Town Entering the 1980s*. Saldru Working Paper No. 50.

Dewar, D. 1984. *Urban Poverty and City Development: Some Perspectives and Guidelines*. Carnegie Conference Paper No. 163, Saldru, University of Cape Town.

Downing, T.E. and Kushner, G. (eds) 1988. *Human Rights and Anthropology*. Cultural Survival Inc., Berkeley, Los Angeles.

Dubos, R. 1977. Determinants of health and disease. In D. Landy (ed.) *Culture, Disease and Healing: Studies in Medical Anthropology*. Macmillan Publishing Company, New York.

Dumitriu, P. 1964. *Incognito*. Collins, London.

Elias, C. 1984. *A Housing Study: Legislation and Control of Supply of Urban African Accommodation*. Carnegie Conference Paper No. 157, Saldru, University of Cape Town.

Elliott-Binns, C.P. 1973. An analysis of medicine. *Journal of the Royal College of General Practitioners*, 23:255–64.

Engelhardt, H.T. 1975. The concepts of health and disease. In H.T. Engelhardt and S.F. Spiker (eds) *Evaluation of Explanation in the Biomedical Sciences*. Reidel Publishing, Dordrecht.

England, F. 1987. Symbolic warfare: the battle for ownership of symbols in the Anglican community. MA thesis (unpublished), University of Cape Town.

England, F. and Paterson, T. 1989. *Bounty in Bondage – The Anglican Church in South Africa*. Ravan Press, Johannesburg.

Fanon, F. 1966. *The Wretched of the Earth*. Grove Press, New York.

Ferguson, J. 1990. *The Anti-Politics Machine*. David Philip, Cape Town.

Finlayson, R. 1985. Xhosa women's language of respect: *isihlonipho sabafazi*. Africa Seminar unpublished paper, Centre for African Studies, University of Cape Town.

Frankel, S.J. 1981. The Huli response to illness. D.Phil. thesis (unpublished), University of Cambridge.

Frankenberg, R. and Leeson, J. 1976. Disease, illness and sickness: social aspects of the choice of healer in a Lusaka suburb. In J.B. Loudon (ed.) *Social Anthropology and Medicine*. Academic Press, London.

Frankl, V.E. 1968. *Man's Search for Meaning: An Introduction to Logotherapy*. Hodder & Stoughton, London.

Freud, S. 1973. *Introductory Lectures on Psychoanalysis*. Freud Library Vol. 1. Penguin, Harmondsworth.

Friedan, B. 1963. *The Feminine Mystique*. Norton, London.

Gaitskell, D. 1979. 'Christian compounds for girls': church hostels for African women in Johannesburg, 1907–1970. *Journal of Southern African Studies*, 6 (1).

Garnsey, E. 1982. Women's work and theories of class stratification. In A. Giddens and D. Held *Classes, Power and Conflict*. University of Califòrnia Press, Berkeley.

Gatley, S. 1989. Community attitudes to alcohol and drug abuse in the Port Elizabeth townships. *Urbanisation and Health Newsletter*, Medical Research Council.

Geertz, C. 1988. *Works and Lives: The Anthropologist as Author*. Polity Press, Cambridge.

Gerhart, G. 1978. *Black Power in South Africa. The Evolution of an Ideology*. University of California Press, Berkeley.

Gibbs, J.T. 1988. *Young, Black, and Male in America – An Endangered Species*. Auburn House, Dover, MA.

Giddens, A. 1977. *Studies in Social and Political Theory*. Hutchinson, New York.

Giddens, A. 1981. *A Contemporary Critique of Historical Materialism*. Macmillan, London.

Giddens, A. 1982. *Profiles and Critiques in Social Theory*. Macmillan, London.

Giddens, A. 1983. *The Nation-State and Violence*. Hutchinson, New York.

Giddens, A. 1984. *The Constitution of Society*. Polity Press, Cambridge.

Giddens, A. 1990. *The Consequences of Modernity*. Polity Press, Cambridge.

Giddens, A. and Held, D. 1982. *Classes, Power and Conflict*. University of California Press, Berkeley.

Gilligan, C. and Murphy, J.M. 1979. Development from adolescence to adulthood: the philosopher and the dilemma of the fact. In D. Kuhn, (ed.) *Intellectual Development Beyond Childhood. New Directions for Child Development*. Jossey-Bass, San Francisco.

Gluckman, M. 1955. *Politics, Law and Ritual in Tribal Society*. Blackwell, Oxford.

Goffman, E. 1961. *Asylums – Essays on the Social Situation of Mental Patients and Other Inmates*. Anchor Books, New York.

Gorbachev, M. 1987. *Perestroika, New Thinking for Our Country and the World*. Collins, London.

Gordon, R. 1977. *Mines, Masters and Migrants – Life in a Namibian Compound*. Ravan Press, Johannesburg.

Gordon, R. 1989. White man's burden. *Journal for Historical Sociology*, 2 (1):41–65.

Hamburg, D. 1984. *Address from the President of the Carnegie Corporation of New York*. Carnegie Conference Paper No. 309, Saldru, University of Cape Town.

Hammond-Tooke, W.D. 1962. *Bhaca Society*. Oxford University Press, Cape Town.

Hammond-Tooke, W.D. 1975. *Command or Consensus*. David Philip, Cape Town.

Hartmann, H. 1982. Capitalism, patriarchy, and job segregation by sex. In A. Giddens and D. Held *Classes, Power and Conflict*. University of California Press, Berkeley.

Hassan, I. 1985. The culture of postmodernism. *Theory, Culture and Society*, 2 (3):119–29.

Havel, V. 1985. *The Power of the Powerless*. Hutchinson, London.

Hayden, D. 1984. *Redesigning the American Dream*. W.W. Norton, New York.

Heald, S. 1989. *Controlling Anger – The Sociology of Gisu Violence*. Manchester University Press, Manchester.

Heap, M. 1989. Health and disease in south-eastern Lesotho: a social anthropological perspective of two villages. *Communications*, No. 16, Centre for African Studies, University of Cape Town.

Heap, M. and Ramphele, M. 1991. The quest for wholeness: health care strategies amongst residents of council-built hostels in Cape Town. *Social Science and Medicine*, 32 (2):117–26.

Heilbrun, C.G. 1988. *Writing a Woman's Life*. Women's Press, New York.

Hemsworth, B.N. 1983. Biological changes due to topical application of skin lightening compounds. *Journal for the Society of Cosmetic Chemists*, 24:727–33.

Heron, J. 1981. Philosophical basis for a new paradigm. In P. Reason and J. Rowan (eds) *Human Inquiry: A Sourcebook of New Paradigm Research*. John Wiley & Sons, London.

Hirschon, R. 1970. Society, culture and spatial organization: an Athens community. *Ekistics*, 178:187–96.

Hirschon, R. 1978. Open body/closed space: the transformation of female sexuality. In S. Ardener *Defining Females: The Nature of Women in Society*. Croom Helm, London.

Hirschon, R. 1981. Essential objects and the sacred: interior and exterior space in an urban Greek locality. In S. Ardener *Women and Space: Ground Rules and Cultural Maps*. Croom Helm, London.

Hirschon, R. and Gold, J. 1982. Territoriality and the home environment in a Greek urban community. *Anthropological Quarterly*, 55 (2):63–73.

Hodge, N. (ed.) 1987. *Killing a Man's Pride and Other Short Stories*. Ravan Press, Johannesburg.

Horner, D. (ed.) 1983. *Influx Control in the Cape Peninsula*. Saldru Working Paper No. 50, University of Cape Town.

Human Awareness Programme, 1984. *State Pension Scheme and Private Pension Funds – How They Affect Black People*. Carnegie Conference Paper No. 138, Saldru, University of Cape Town.

Hunter, M. 1936. *Reaction to Conquest*. Oxford University Press, Oxford.

Hyden, G. 1983. *No Short-Cuts to Progress*. University of California Press, Berkeley and Los Angeles.

Isasi-Diaz, A.M. 1988. A Hispanic garden in a foreign land. In L.M. Russell *et al.* (eds), *Inheriting Our Mothers' Gardens*. Westminster Press, Philadelphia.

Jaffee, G. 1987. Women in the trade unions and the community. *South African Review*, No. 4, Ravan Press, Johannesburg.

Janzen, J.M. 1978. *The Quest for Therapy: Medical Pluralism in Lower Zaire*. University of California Press, Los Angeles.

Janzen, J.M. 1979. Pluralistic legitimation of therapy systems in contemporary Zaire. In J.A.A. Ayoade *et al.* (eds), *African Therapeutic Systems*. Crossroads Press, London.

Janzen, J.M. 1980. *Health: The Universal Human Aspiration*. Development Monograph Series, Akron.

Janzen, J.M. 1981. The need for taxonomy of health in study of African therapeutics. *Social Science and Medicine*, 15b:185–95.

Jones, S. 1990. Assaulting childhood: an ethnographic study of children in a Western Cape migrant hostel complex. M.A. thesis (unpublished), University of Cape Town.

Kapferer, B. 1988. Anthropologist as hero. Three exponents of post-modernist anthropology. *Critique of Anthropology* (review article), 8 (2):77–104.

Keesing, R.M. 1981. *Cultural Anthropology: A Contemporary Perspective*. Holt, Rinehart & Winston, New York.

Kennedy, I. 1980. The Reith Lectures Nos 1–6, Unmasking Medicine. *The Listener*.

Kentridge, M. 1986. *Housing in South Africa: From Political Privilege to Basic Right*. Post Carnegie Conference Series No.14, Saldru, University of Cape Town.

Kirsch, R. 1979. Health needs in southern Africa. In G. Westcott and F. Wilson (eds) *Economics of Health Care in South Africa*. Ravan Press, Johannesburg.

Kleinman, A. 1978. Concepts and a model for the comparison of medical systems as cultural systems. *Social Science and Medicine* 12b: 85–93.

Kleinman, A. 1980. *Patients and Healers in the Context of Culture*. University of California Press, Berkeley.

Kleinman, A. 1987. Anthropology and psychiatry: the role of culture in cross-cultural research on illness. *British Journal of Psychiatry*, 151:447–54.

Koestler, A. 1964. *The Act of Creation*. Pan Books, London.

Kovaly, H. M. 1988. *Prague Farewell.* Victor Gollancz, London.

Kriel, J. R. 1989. Patient dissatisfaction and the philosophical assumptions underlying modern medicine. *South African Family Practice*, July, Vol.10, No.7.

Lamont, A.M. 1987. Guidelines for the Accommodation of Single Persons in Black Residential Areas. UNISA research report.

Lee, S. G. 1969. Spirit possession among the Zulu. In J. Beattie and J. Middleton, *Spirit, Mediumship and Society in Africa.* Routledge & Kegan Paul, London.

Levett, A. 1989. The discourse of childhood. *Psychology in Society*, 12:19–32.

Lewis, D. 1989. Intellectuals, the working class and politics. *Transformation: Critical Perspectives on Southern Africa*, 10:64–9.

Liddell, C. *et al.* 1989. Activity and social behavior in a crowded South African township nursery: a follow-up study on the effects of crowding at home. *Merrill-Palmer Quarterly*, 35 (2):209–26, Wayne State University Press, Detroit.

Liddell, C. *et al.* 1991. Historical perspectives on childhood in South Africa. *International Journal of Behavioral Development*, 13:10–27.

Lipton, M. 1986. *Capitalism and Apartheid: South Africa 1910–1986.* Wildwood House, London.

Lock, M. and Scheper-Hughes, N. 1990. A critical-interpretative approach in medical anthropology: rituals and routines of discipline and dissent. *Theoretical Perspectives*, 47–72.

Lockwood, D. 1982. Sources of variation in working-class images of society. In A. Giddens and D. Held *Classes, Power and Conflict.* University of California Press, Berkeley.

Lonsdale, J. 1988. *South Africa in Question.* African Studies Centre, Cambridge.

Lund, F. 1982. *Community Self Survey in Lamontville.* Centre for Applied Social Sciences, University of Natal, Durban.

Mann, M. 1982. The social cohesion of liberal democracy. In A. Giddens and D. Held *Classes, Power and Conflict.* University of California Press, Berkeley.

Matshoba, M. 1987. Killing a man's pride. In N. Hodge (ed.) *Killing a Man's Pride and Other Short Stories.* Ravan Press, Johannesburg.

Mayer, P. 1963. *Townsmen or Tribesmen.* Oxford University Press, Cape Town.

Medvedev, R. 1971. *Let History Judge.* Alfred A. Knopf, New York.

Mfenyana, K. 1988. Attitudes of rural African patients towards the use of drugs as prescribed by doctors. *Family Practice*, 4:137–47.

Mills, J. 1988. The differing agendas of participants in the Boschfontein project: the issue of accountability. Unpublished conference paper, Association of Sociologists of Southern Africa, University of Durban-Westville.

Mills, G. 1989. Space and power in South Africa: the township as a mechanism of control. *Ekistics, 334 and 335:65–74.*

Mitchell, J.C. 1969. On quantification in social anthropology. In A.L. Epstein (ed.) *The Craft of Social Anthropology.* Tavistock Publications, London.

Mitchell, D. 1985. Health and medicine in South Africa now and forty years on: a personal view. *South African Medical Journal*, 81:113–19.

Moore, L.H. 1986. *Space, Text and Gender – An Anthropological Study of the Marakwet of Kenya.* Cambridge University Press, Cambridge.

Morley, D. 1983. *Practising Health for All.* Medical Publications, Oxford.

Murray, C. 1975. Sex, smoking and the shades: a Sotho symbolic idiom. In M.G. Whisson and M.E. West *Religion and Social Change in Southern Africa.* David Philip, Cape Town.

Murray, C. 1981. *Families Divided.* Ravan Press, Johannesburg.

Nattrass, N. and Ardington, E. (eds) 1990. *The Political Economy of South Africa.* Oxford University Press, Cape Town.

Ndaba, N. 1984. *Nutritional Status of Adults in Willowmore.* Carnegie Conference Paper No. 209, Saldru, University of Cape Town.

Ngubane, H. 1975. The place of spirit possession in Zulu cosmology. In M.G. Whisson and M.E. West *Religion and Social Change in Southern Africa.* David Philip, Cape Town.

Ngubane, H. 1977. *Body and Mind in Zulu Medicine.* Academic Press, London.

Ngugi, W. 1977. *Petals of Blood*. Heinemann, London.

Nicholson, J. 1984. *The Pension Crisis in KwaZulu*. Carnegie Conference Paper No. 143, Saldru, University of Cape Town.

Nyerere, J. 1986. *The Hunger Foundation Report*.

Obbo, C. 1981. *African Women: Their Struggle for Economic Independence*. Ravan Press, Johannesburg.

O'Brien, M. 1981. *The Politics of Reproduction*. Routledge & Kegan Paul, London.

O'Donnell, G. and Schmitter, P.C. 1986. *Transitions from Authoritarian Rule*. The Johns Hopkins University Press, Baltimore.

Olivier, L. 1987. The physical and psychological problems of the black, white, Indian and coloured peoples of South Africa. Unpublished paper read at the Fifth Psychiatric Congress, Cape Town.

Orsy, L. 1987. New era of participation in church life. Unpublished conference paper, National Pastoral Planning and the Catholic Parish and Diocesan Council Network.

Pejic, M. 1988. Street children of Brazil. *Critique of Anthropology*, 8(1):65–76.

Perlman, J.E. 1979. *The Myth of Marginality – Urban Poverty and Politics in Rio de Janeiro*. University of California Press, Berkeley.

Peskin, M. and Spiegel, A.D. 1976. Urban hostels in the Johannesburg area. In P. Mayer (ed.) *Migrant Labour. Some Perspectives from Anthropology*. Rhodes University, Grahamstown.

Pinnock, D. 1984. *Breaking the Web: Economic Consequences of the Destruction of Extended Families by Group Areas Relocation in Cape Town*. Carnegie Conference Paper No. 258, Saldru, University of Cape Town.

Platsky, L. and Walker, C. 1985. *The Surplus People*. Ravan Press, Johannesburg.

Ramphele, M. 1986. *Zimbabwe – The Lessons for Us*. Saldru Working Paper No. 65, University of Cape Town.

Ramphele, M. 1989. (a) The dynamics of gender politics in the hostels of Cape Town. *Journal of Southern African Studies*, 15 (3):393–414.

Ramphele, M. 1989. (b) Space and the definition of childhood. Unpublished conference paper, Victoria Falls.

Ramphele, M. 1990. (a) Participatory research, myths and realities. *Social Dynamics*, 16 (2):1–15.

Ramphele, M. 1990. (b) Do women help to perpetuate sexism? A bird's eye view from South Africa. *Africa Today*, 37 (1):7–17.

Ramphele, M. 1991. The politics of space: life in the migrant labour hostels of the Western Cape. Ph.D. thesis (unpublished), University of Cape Town.

Ramphele, M. and Ramalepe, R. 1984. *Rural Health Care – The Tears and Joy*. Carnegie Conference Paper No. 204, Saldru, University of Cape Town.

Ramphele, M. and Meiring, P. 1986. Some problems of elderly Africans in the townships of Cape Town in 1985. Unpublished paper.

Ramphele, M. and Boonzaier, E. 1988. The position of African women: race and gender in South Africa. In E. Boonzaier and J. Sharp (eds) *South African Keywords*. David Philip, Cape Town.

Reason, P. and Rowan, J. 1981. *Human Inquiry: A Sourcebook of New Paradigm Research*. John Wiley & Sons, London.

Reck, G.G. 1988. Introduction: fiction's niche in anthropology. *Anthropology and Humanism Quarterly*, 13 (3):79.

Reynolds, P. 1984. *Men Without Children*. Carnegie Conference Paper No. 5, Saldru, University of Cape Town.

Reynolds, P. 1989. *Childhood in Crossroads*. David Philip, Cape Town.

Rodgers, S. 1981. Women's spaces in a men's house: the British House of Commons. In S. Ardener *Women and Space: Ground Rules and Social Maps*. Croom Helm, London.

Ruchwager, G. 1987. *People in Power: Forging a Grassroots Democracy in Nicaragua*. Bergin & Garvey, Massachusetts.

Ruether, R. 1983. *Sexism and God-Talk. Toward a Feminist Theology*. Beacon Press, Boston.

Russell, D. 1984. Report to Cape Town Diocese of the Anglican Church.

Russell, L.M. *et al.* (eds) 1988. *Inheriting Our Mothers' Gardens*. Westminster Press, Philadelphia.

Ryan, A. 1969. *The Philosophy of the Social Sciences*. New College, Oxford.

Sacks, K.B. 1988. Gender and grassroots leadership. In A. Bookman and S. Morgan (eds) *Women and the Politics of Empowerment*. Temple University Press, Philadelphia.

Sanders, D. 1985. *The Struggle for Health – Medicine and the Politics of Underdevelopment*. Macmillan, London.

Sarpong, P.B. 1985. The Ghanaian concept of disease. *Contact*, 84:2–10.

Saunders, C. 1988. Historians and apartheid. In J. Lonsdale (ed.) *South Africa in Question*. African Studies Centre, Cambridge University.

Savage, M. 1984. *Pass Laws and the Disorganisation and Reorganisation of the African Population in South Africa*. Carnegie Conference Paper No. 281, Saldru, University of Cape Town.

Scheper-Hughes, N. 1984. The Margaret Mead controversy: culture, biology and anthropological inquiry. *Human Organisation*, 43 (1):91.

Schirmer, J. 1988. The dilemma of cultural diversity and equivalency in universal human rights standards. In T.E. Downing and G. Kushner (eds) *Human Rights and Anthropology*. Cultural Survival Inc., Berkeley, Los Angeles.

Schumacher, E.F. 1973. *Small is Beautiful: Economics as if People Mattered*. Blond & Briggs, New York.

Seedat, Y.K. 1981. High blood pressure – the silent killer. *South African Medical Journal*, 59:173–6.

Segar, J. 1982. Food and health care in a betterment village. B.Soc.Sc. (Honours) thesis (unpublished), University of Cape Town.

Segar, J. 1988. Living in anonymity: conditions of life in the hostels of Cape Town. Unpublished paper.

Seleoane, M. 1985. *Nyanga East Men's Hostel: The Condition of Migrant Workers*. Saldru Working Paper No. 62, University of Cape Town.

Selvan, D. 1976. *Housing Conditions for Migrant Workers in Cape Town*. Saldru Working Paper No. 10, University of Cape Town.

Sharp, J.S. 1988. Two worlds in one country: First and Third World. In E.B. Boonzaier and J.S. Sharp (eds) *South African Keywords*. David Philip, Cape Town.

Sharp, J.S. and Spiegel, A.D. 1984. *Vulnerability to Impoverishment in South African Rural Areas: The Erosion of Kinship and Neighbourhood as Social Resources*. Carnegie Conference Paper No. 52, Saldru, University of Cape Town.

Sidel, R. 1986. *Women and Children Last: The Plight of Poor Women in Affluent America*. The Book Press, Brattleboro, Vermont.

Sigel, R. 1965. Assumptions about learning the political values. *Annals of the American Academy of Political and Social Science*, 361:1–9.

Simkins, C. 1988. *The Prisoners of Tradition and the Politics of Nation Building*. South African Institute of Race Relations, Johannesburg.

Simons, H.J. 1968. *African Women. Their Legal Status in South Africa*. Hurst, London.

Sivard, R.L. 1985. *Women – A World Survey*. World Priorities, New York.

Smith, D.E. 1975. An analysis of ideological structures and how women are excluded: considerations for academic women. *Review of Canadian Sociology and Anthropology*, 12 (4)Part 1.

Smuts, D. 1987. The other revolution. *Leadership SA*, 6 (5):60–3.

Soyinka, W. 1984. *A Play of the Giants*. Methuen, London.

Spiegel, A.D. 1979. Migrant labour remittances, rural differentiation and the development cycle in a Lesotho community. M.A. thesis, University of Cape Town.

Spiegel, A.D. 1988. Tradition. In E. Boonzaier and J.S. Sharp (eds) *South African Keywords*. David Philip, Cape Town.

Steele, S. 1990. *The Content of Our Character: A New Vision of Race in America*. St Martin's Press, New York.

Stimpson, C. R. 1988. *Where the Meanings Are*. Methuen, New York.

Strebel, P.M., Kuhn, L. and Yach, D. 1989. Smoking practices in the black township population of Cape Town. *South African Medical Journal*, 75:428–31.

Stubbs, A. (ed.) 1986. *Steve Biko – I Write What I Like*. Harper & Row, San Francisco.

Sutcliffe, M. 1988. A report and a visit to South Africa of members of the International Development Research Center, Ottawa, Canada. Unpublished paper presented at the University of Natal, Durban.

Taussig, M. 1987. *Shamanism, Colonialism, and the Wild Man: A Study in Terror and Healing*. University of Chicago Press, Chicago and London.

Temkin, O. 1973. Health and ideas. In *Dictionary of the History of Ideas*. Scribners, New York.

Terreblanche, S. and Nattrass, N. 1990. A periodization of the political economy of South Africa from 1990. In N. Nattrass and E. Ardington (eds) *Political Economy of South Africa*. Oxford University Press, Cape Town.

Thomas, E. 1987. Conflicts and their resolution in Guguletu migrant hostels: a study of the role of the Western Cape Hostel Dwellers' Association. Honours thesis (unpublished), University of Cape Town.

Thomas, E. 1989. Rotating credit associations in Cape Town. Unpublished paper presented to the Association of Anthropologists in Southern Africa's Annual Conference, University of the Western Cape, Bellville.

Thornton, R. 1980. *Space, Time and Culture Among the Iraqw of Tanzania*. Academic Press, New York.

Thornton, R. 1988. Culture. In E. Boonzaier and J.S. Sharp (eds) *South African Keywords*. David Philip, Cape Town.

Thornton, R. and Ramphele, M. 1988. The quest for community. In E. Boonzaier and J.S. Sharp (eds) *South African Keywords*. David Philip, Cape Town.

Tobin, J.J. 1989. Visual anthropology and multivocal ethnography: a dialogical approach to Japanese preschool class size. *Dialectical Anthropology*, 13:173–87.

Turnbull, C. 1974. *The Mountain People*. The Chaucer Press, Bungay, Suffolk.

Unger, R. 1975. *Knowledge and Politics*. The Free Press/Macmillan, New York.

Urdang, S. 1989. *And Still They Dance. Women, War, and the Struggle for Change in Mozambique*. Monthly Review Press, New York.

Van der Burgh, C. 1979. Smoking behaviour of white, black, coloured and Indian South Africans. *South African Medical Journal*, 55:975–8.

Van der Vliet, V. 1984. *Staying Single: A Strategy Against Poverty*. Carnegie Conference Paper No. 116, Saldru, University of Cape Town.

Van der Vliet, V. 1989. Traditional husbands, modern wives? Constructing marriages in a southern African township. Seminar paper, Department of Social Anthropology, University of Cape Town.

Van Gennep, A. 1960. *The Rites of Passage*. University of Chicago Press, Chicago.

Van Niekerk, A. 1988. Changing patterns of worker accommodation, Zebediela Citrus Estate, 1926–1953: the dynamics of external restraint and self-discipline. *Social Dynamics*, 14 (2):52–69.

Van Onselen, C. 1980. *Chibaro – African Mine Labour in Southern Rhodesia 1900–1933*. Ravan Press, Johannesburg.

Van Wezel, R. 1988. Reciprocity of results in Portugal. A photographic essay. *Critique of Anthropology*, 8 (2):63–70.

Walker, C. 1982. *Women and Resistance in South Africa*. Onyx Press, London.

Walker, C. (ed.) 1990. *Women and Gender in Southern Africa to 1945*. David Philip, Cape Town.

Walters, S.C. 1986. Education for democratic participation: an analysis of self-education strategies within community organisations in Cape Town in the 1980s. Ph.D. thesis (unpublished), University of Cape Town.

Ward, M. 1983. *Unmanageable Revolutionaries: Women and Irish Nationalism*. Pluto Press, London.

Weber, M. 1982. Selection from *Economy and Society*, Vols. 1 and 2 in A. Giddens and D. Held *Classes, Power and Conflict*. University of California Press, Berkeley.

West, M.E. 1975. *Bishops and Prophets in a Black City*. David Philip, Cape Town.

West, M.E. 1982. From pass courts to deportation: changing patterns of influx control in Cape Town. *African Affairs*, 81 (325).

West, M.E. 1985. Influx control: the 1983 statistics. Regional Topics Paper No. 85/2. South African Institute of Race Relations, Cape Town.

West, M.E. 1987. *Apartheid in a South African Town, 1968–1985*. Institute of International Studies, University of California, Berkeley.

West, M.E. 1988. Confusing categories: population groups, national states and citizenship. In E. Boonzaier, and J.S. Sharp (eds) *South African Keywords*. David Philip, Cape Town.

West, M.E. and Boonzaier, E.B. 1989. Population groups, politics and medical science. *South African Medical Journal*, 76:185–6.

West, M.E. and Moore, E. 1989. Undocumented workers in the United States and South Africa: a comparative study of changing control. *Human Organisation*, 48 (1):1–10.

Whisson, M.G. and West, M.E. 1975. *Religion and Social Change in South Africa*. David Philip, Cape Town.

Wikan, U. 1980. *Life Among the Poor in Cairo*. Tavistock, London.

Wilson, F. 1972. *Migrant Labour in South Africa*. Ravan Press, Johannesburg.

Wilson, F. and Ramphele, M. 1987. *Children on the Frontline*. UNICEF report, New York.

Wilson, F. and Ramphele, M. 1989. *Uprooting Poverty – The South African Challenge*. David Philip, Cape Town.

Wilson, M. 1971. *Religion and the Transformation of Society*. Cambridge University Press, Cambridge.

Wilson, M. and Mafeje, A. 1973. *Langa – A Study of Social Groups in an African Township*. Oxford University Press, Cape Town.

Wolf, E. 1982. *Europe and the People Without History*. University of California Press, Berkeley.

Wolpe, H. 1972. Capitalism and cheap labour power in South Africa. *Economy and Society*, 1(4):425–56.

Woolf, V. 1929. *A Room of One's Own*. London.

Women in Focus 1987. Editorial Comment. *Umtapo Focus*. Information and Research Unit of Umtapo Centre, Durban.

Wright, E.O. 1982. Class boundaries and contradictory class locations. In A. Giddens and D. Held *Classes, Power and Conflict*. University of California Press, Berkeley.

Yach, D. 1984. *The Impact of Smoking in Underdeveloped Countries*. Carnegie Conference Paper No. 181, Saldru, University of Cape Town.

Yach, D. 1986. (a) The impact of smoking in the developing countries with special reference to Africa. *International Journal for Health Services*, 16:279–92.

Yach, D. 1986. (b) *The Impact of Political Violence on Health and Health Services in Cape Town*. Medical Research Council report.

Yach, D. and Townshend, G.S. 1988. Smoking and health in South Africa. *South African Medical Journal*, 73:391–9.

Young, A. 1976. Some implications of medical beliefs and practices for social anthropology. *American Anthropologist*, 78:5–24.

Youngman, F. 1986. *Adult Education and Socialist Pedagogy*. Croom Helm, London.

Zola, I.K. 1978. Pathways to the doctor – from person to patient. In D. Tuckett and J. Kaufert (eds) *Basic Readings in Medical Sociology*. Tavistock, London.

1976–1990. *Survey of Race Relations* (annual). South African Institute of Race Relations, Johannesburg.

1985. *The Health of the Family: Some Key Issues*. World Health Organisation report, 38(3).

1985. Provincial Administration of the Cape of Good Hope, Department of Hospital Services. Report of the Director, Hospital Services.

1985–1989. Hostel Dwellers' Association annual reports.

1986. Annual Report of the Officer of Health of the Divisional Council of the Cape, Combined Health Control Scheme.

1986. City of Cape Town, Annual Report of the Medical Officer of Health.

1986. Republic of the Ciskei, Department of Health Annual Report.

1986. Transkei Government, Department of Health Annual Report.

1987. Department of Health and Population Development Annual Report.

1987. New directions in health care. *Critical Health*, No. 20. Health Information Centre Report.

1987–88. Health for Africa Conference Report.

Index

2240